AF477876

Pierre Courtade

John E. Flower

Berg French Studies
General Editor: John E. Flower

ISSN: 1354 - 3636

John E. Flower and Bernard C. Swift (eds), *François Mauriac: Visions and Reappraisals*
Michael Tilby (ed.), *Beyond the Nouveau Roman: Essays on the Contemporary French Novel*
Colin Nettlebeck, *Forever French: The French Exiles in the United States of America during the Second World War*
Bill Marshall, *Victor Serge: The Use of Dissent*
Allan Morris, *Collaboration and Resistance Reviews: Writers and the Mode Rétro in Post-Gaullist France*
Malcolm Cook, *Fictional France: Social Reality in the French Novel 1775 - 1800*
W. D. Halls, *Politics, Society and Christianity in Vichy France*
David H. Walker, *Outrage and Insight: Modern French Writers and the 'Fait Divers'*
H. R. Kedward and Nancy Wood, *The Liberation of France: Image and Event*
David L. Looseley, *The Politics of Fun: Cultural Policy and Debate in Contemporary France*

Pierre Courtade

The Making of a Party Scribe

John E. Flower

First Published in 1995 by
Berg Publishers Limited
Editorial Offices:
150 Cowley Road, Oxford, OX4 1JJ, UK
13590 Park Center Road, Herndon, VA 22071, USA

© J.E. Flower 1995

All rights reserved.
No part of this publication may be reproduced in any form
or by any means without the written permission of
Berg Publishers Limited.

Library of Congress Cataloging-in-Publication Data

A catalogue record for this book is available from the Library of Congress.

British Library Cataloguing in Publication Data

A catalogue record for this book is available from the British Library.

ISBN 1 85973 043 4

Printed in the United Kingdom by
WBC Bookbinders, Bridgend, Mid Glamorgan.

A Génia

'je ne suis pas un
homme qui décide
facilement'

(*La Place rouge*, 1961)

Contents

Introduction

In 1984 the Editions Bernard Grasset published *Un Dimanche inoubliable près des casernes* a novel by Jacques-Francis Rolland. Essayist, journalist, novelist and teacher, Rolland was active in the Resistance and became subsequently a militant member of the French Communist Party until he was expelled in 1956. In Roger Vailland's novel about the period of Nazi Occupation *Drôle de jeu* and its 'sequel' *Bon Pied Bon Oeil*, Rolland appears as Rodrigue, a character who, as the Cornellian resonance of his fictional name suggests, is a man of conviction and action, if also a little impetuous. Without being directly autobiographical, *Un Dimanche inoubliable près des casernes* draws heavily on Rolland's career and experiences. Its starting-point is the funeral of a PCF militant, Georges Granet, in the Père Lachaise cemetery in Paris, an occasion which brings together a group of men and women who have known him and shared his life, and who here find one another again for the first time after many years. From the beginning the tone is set by the official rhetoric of the party tribute, which presents Granet as the exemplary militant Communist. But it quickly becomes clear that the words are empty of true meaning and are merely part of a ritual which has little or no connection with reality.

In the course of Rolland's novel a number of critical issues facing the Party are addressed, from the Resistance, by way of the Party's anti-Americanism and the trials of Rajk and Kostov, through the discrediting of Stalin, to the events of May 1968. Most of these are filtered through the experiences of the protagonist, Pierre Mesleau du Die, who traces his career from his early anti-Nazi activities in the area around Grenoble to his involvement in the case of Pierre Hervé, who had dared challenge the Party's doctrinal position over art in his essay *La Révolution et les fétiches*, for which he was expelled in 1956. But while in many ways Rolland's portrait of Mesleau is autobiographical, it is consistently so at one remove. The novel is part confession and part *autocritique*, but is also shot through with cynicism and bitterness, and is not without some deliberate exaggeration. (Hence, perhaps, the phonemic echo of the narrator's name in '*mélo*drame', or even in *mélo du dit*.) While therefore it would be unwise, if not wrong, to look for any precise parallel between fact and fiction in the case of Rolland himself, so it would be in those of other characters as well.

Clearly, however, the historical personages are there, out of focus, blended or altered in age or function just enough to move the overall impression from the realm of straight recollection to that of imaginative reconstruction. Thus Robert de Bellève, who launches a new literary review, *La Grange*, in 1942, but uses it as a cover for resistance activity, has certain similarities with René Tavernier, whose review *Confluences* functioned in much the same way. Axel Ranger ('chevelure blanc-violet ondulée, ressemblait à une vieille dame coquette'),[1] who has been friendly with Gide, Malraux and Drieu la Rochelle, is self-evidently based on Aragon crossed with Roger Vailland. The fate of Ranger's play *Aérodrome*, disrupted by fascist sympathizers after a successful *première* and suspended by the police authorities on the grounds of concern for public safety, is clearly that of Vailland's play *Le Colonel Foster plaidera coupable* (1952). Or, in a rather different way, Zoltan Kollai, the Hungarian accused of harbouring and fostering sympathies for Tito, who gave himself up only to be tried, found guilty and tortured before being subsequently cleared, is a projection of Georges Szekeres. At the same time Rolland also lifts a galaxy of political and literary figures from real life and introduces them into his novel with little or no modification – Maurice Thorez, André Marty, Laurent Casanova ('le Jdanov français' (p. 244)), Jean-Paul Sartre, Roger Vailland, Claude Roy and, in particular, Pierre Courtade. But what of Georges Granet?

After a childhood spent in the north of Paris, Granet followed a classical education through to the *agrégation*, eventually becoming a history teacher in Grenoble. After the Liberation he was a senior journalist for the Communist paper *L'Humanité*, having been invited to join the staff by Maurice Thorez. He specialized in foreign affairs, and spent the last years of his life as Soviet correspondent in Moscow (where he succeeded Pierre Courtade ...). He died in his sleep, aged 56. Even from these few details it is clear that, just as Axel Ranger is based essentially on Louis Aragon, so Granet is on Courtade. The factual points which Rolland has altered include, for example, his age at death (Courtade died aged 48 after a heart attack), his childhood and adolescence (Courtade spent them in Sceaux), and his academic progress and qualifications. Courtade had little success of this kind. He failed his *baccalauréat* on first taking it, and subsequently the entry examination for the Ecole Normale Supérieure on two occasions and the *agrégation*. He was never the editor of a literary review.

But it is not so much biographical facts which are important as Granet's ideological evolution. He is described at one moment by the narrator as 'prudent et calculateur' (p. 57); and at another as 'fervent, mais observateur plein de drôlerie; roseau pliant, exercé à l'esquive' (p. 157); a few pages later he is 'dérivant d'écueil en écueil, de tourbillon en tourbillon, malmené, meurtri, prêt à rompre, de nouveau emporté par le courant dont il ne pouvait s'arracher' (p. 185). For him, as for so many of his generation, Thorez and Stalin are *directeurs de conscience* (*politique*), arbiters and purveyors of unchallengeable judgements based on what was perceived to be an absolute ideological rectitude. And this is where *Un Dimanche inoubliable près des casernes* is important. While focusing in particular on Georges Granet, Rolland essentially chronicles the disintegration of this generation which has seen its genuine revolutionary hopes twisted, compromised and corrupted both at and from the highest levels down. Père Lachaise is indeed the ideal starting and closing point for this novel, a burial ground of frustrated ambitions and ideals. As in the closing paragraph the mourners move away and make their separate ways through the tombs, the narrator recalls a science fiction story which tells of a group of astronauts who, after the destruction of their ship, drift individually through space: 'Leurs scaphandres autonomes les préservent encore et ils communiquent par radio, mais ils s'éloignent inexorablement les uns des autres et l'usure rapide des piles affaiblit de plus leurs dernières paroles d'adieu, tandis qu'ils dérivent au coeur du gouffre infini, absolument noir qui va les engloutir.' (p. 311)

Rolland's image is apt. Embittered or disillusioned, that group of Party intellectuals – as opposed to the many fellow-travellers of the post-Liberation years – of which Courtade was one, gradually disintegrated. Had he lived longer there is no reason to suppose that Courtade would have been an exception. But whatever his disenchantment with official party policy or bureaucracy, his faith in revolutionary socialism as a political philosophy remained constant. This did not preclude moments of uncertainty, debate and even anguish, and the circumstances of his private life only made these more acute.

When René Andrieu remembered his former colleague in an article published in *L'Humanité* twenty-five years after his death, he described him as 'Un journaliste hors pair et l'un des écrivains les plus doués de sa génération. L'intelligence critique s'alliait chez lui à l'élégance souveraine du style. Ce mousquetaire de la plume était une fine lame.'[2] But apart from this almost obligatory tribute to a man who had been the principal foreign correspondent of France's Communist daily paper for well over a decade, the anniversary passed virtually unnoticed. To some degree at least the silence was not surprising. Whatever changes occurred in his private, personal opinions, Courtade remained to the end of his life a declared enthusiastic admirer of all things Soviet, including first Stalin and then Khrushchev. He did not, for example, express in public any disapproval of the Soviet invasion of Hungary in 1956, and refused to add his name to those of Sartre, Simone de Beauvoir, Vercors, Claude Roy, Claude Morgan and his close friend Roger Vailland and others who denounced the use of force in an open letter published in *France Observateur*. Many of those close to Courtade at the time maintained subsequently that in private he voiced considerable disquiet and that, had he lived long enough to witness the events in Prague twenty-two years later, his attitude would have been quite different.

A contrast of this kind between a public and a private persona was not particularly unusual amongst intellectuals of the Left during the two decades following the Liberation, of course. The demands of Party discipline or even the pull of deep sympathy would be challenged, and in some cases completely eroded, by a liberal humanitarianism, or simply by common sense. This is not to say that it was not possible to sustain a belief in the fundamental values of revolutionary socialism; rather that there was an increasing awareness of their having been misinterpreted, misapplied and eventually distorted. For a whole generation a first moment of truth came, again in 1956, with the Khrushchev report and revelations about Stalinist atrocities, which in many ways marked the beginning of a series of events and crises that would lead to the collapse of Communism that the late twentieth century has witnessed. But this was not a matter of political and intellectual history alone. For many, the discrediting of Stalin was a psychological blow of some force. As Claude Roy amongst others has observed, in his essays *Moi* and *Nous*,[3] this was the equivalent not just of the death of an inspirational political leader, but of a father figure as well. A generation that had accepted or had closed its eyes to persecution, trials, false evidence, lies and dominating self-interest had now either to acknowledge its error or somehow to preserve its faith. The degree to which this was achieved varied considerably, but the seeds of doubt had been sown.

In Courtade's case those who knew him intimately declare that in spite of everything that happened he managed to cling to his faith in the ultimate victory of revolutionary socialism. And however naive it may appear with hindsight, the optimism at the end of his last novel, *La Place rouge*, would seem to echo this quite accurately. But at the same time these people will acknowledge that Courtade's faith was neither blind nor painfree; and there are others who go further, claiming that it was a public façade only. Andrieu once again found the right words: 'Il lui semblait porter en lui [...] une insupportable contradiction [...] C'était un optimiste historique, très perméable à l'inquiétude, déchiré souvent mais fidèle.'

For a more immediate evaluation of Courtade, without the benefit of hindsight, we should turn to the obituary notices and commemorative articles of the summer of 1963. The official tone and position are found in the tomb-side oration delivered by Etienne Fajon on 17 May and reproduced in *L'Humanité* a day later: 'Il a servi le Parti jusqu'à son dernier souffle à travers les tempêtes, sans réserve et sans défaillance. Nous lui devons ce témoignage puisque d'autres, qui ne lui pardonnent pas sa droiture, voudraient dresser de lui, maintenant qu'il est mort, le portrait déformé d'un homme assailli par les questions et par le doute.'

Not surprisingly a similar tone is found right across the Communist press. On the very day of his death (15 May) a notice in *Libération* reads: 'Il sacrifia [...] sans hésitation toutes les chances d'une brillante réussite matérielle pour se consacrer entièrement à la défense désintéressée des idées qu'il avait adoptées en pleine conscience, et auxquelles il resta fidèle jusqu'au bout.'

But gradually a more personal note could be heard; not all were willing to hide the real Pierre Courtade behind the façade of official rhetoric. Hélène Parmelin, writing in *Les Lettres Françaises* the following day, remarked on his fundamental melancholy; Armand Lanoux in the same paper spoke of a man who sought to conceal 'ses scrupules, ses troubles et ses doutes par un humour incisif très souvent dirigé contre lui-même'; Aragon in *L'Humanité* referred to 'une insupportable contradiction', a point also made by Vailland. Courtade was, his friend claimed, 'un des hommes qui incarnaient le plus vivement les contradictions de notre temps [et il] est mort en riant de lui-même.'[4] And Pierre Hervé, whose early friendship with Courtade would eventually be broken, went so far as to suggest that the contradiction which others saw as natural was in fact cultivated: 'Il était volontiers tourmenté; il jouait avec virtuosité de l'ennui et de l'amertume; il se faisait hésitant.'[5]

The longest and most thorough tribute to Courtade in the Communist press appeared as the leading article by André Gisselbrecht in the June issue of *La Nouvelle Critique*, for long the most theoretical and rigid of the Party's publications. Despite a token 'Pierre Courtade était pour nous une sorte de modèle', Gisselbrecht concentrates on Courtade as an intellectual and imaginative writer rather than as an exemplary representative of Party orthodoxy. He refers to the autobiographical nature of much of his fiction and to its 'grands thèmes tout simples de la vie intérieure' – the passing of time, love, happiness and death; but it is difficult not to feel that behind this and behind appreciative remarks about Courtade's perceptive assessments of human nature there lies a covert criticism. A distinct reserve can also be sensed when Gisselbrecht describes Courtade's ability to depict those not sharing a socialist view of life as though it were a positive feature of his works: 'Courtade n'a jamais été assez loin de l'Autre – l'adversaire, ou l'inconscient, ou l'apolitique – pour ne pas être capable à chaque instant de se mettre à sa place.'

In a review like *La Nouvelle Critique*, even in 1963, it is difficult to estimate the extent to which an evaluation of Courtade and his work has to be tempered by the standard Party line. Elsewhere, reviewers were less inhibited about pointing to an inherent tension and even contradiction in Courtade between faith and doubt. Françoise Giroud wrote in *L'Express* (16 May) for example: 'Pierre Courtade est le symbole même des contradictions déchirantes qu'un communiste français de sa génération a eu à assumer pour tenter de demeurer d'accord avec lui-même et avec son Parti.' In a magazine hostile to Communism and the PCF this was not enough, however. Regretting that Courtade's activities as a militant journalist had caused him to neglect his 'dons éclatants de romancier', Giroud went on to attack him for his attitude over Tito and the Rajk and

Kostov trials: 'il a défendu et propagé le mensonge avec talent, avec acharnement, avec persévérance. Aveugle ou consentant? Peut-être les deux ensemble. Il était exclu qu'il acceptât d'en discuter sur le fond avec un non-communiste, avec quelqu'un qui n'était pas "de la famille".'

However hurtful such words were to those close to Courtade, they were not without a degree of truth. Courtade was both player and victim in a tragedy that crushed many or left them permanently scarred, and his death at a relatively young age heightened his particular dilemma. Edgar Morin, himself a one-time PCF militant who would subsequently have harsher things to say about him, wrote in *Arts* on 22 August 1963 that Courtade had been 'exemplaire parce qu'il fut un des esprits les plus fortement ravagés.' He went on 'nul n'a vraiment reconnu cet homme, ce destin extraordinaire', and later in his memoirs, *Le vif du sujet*, wrote: 'C'était un personnage tragique, un héros de notre temps au sens lermontovien, une grande intelligence qui s'est fait – laissé? – rabougrir, ratatiner. [...] Quel homme aurait-il pu être? Il a subi le destin. Il a été ravagé par la tragi-épopée de notre génération qui s'est vue? crue? acculée à l'alternative fascisme – communisme.'[6] In the light of comments such as these we can see that Courtade's case is both individual and typical. This book is an attempt to explore it, and to assess the contribution he made to the intellectual and literary climate of that generation in mid twentieth-century France to which Morin refers, and of which many representatives gathered at the graveside of Pierre Granet.

To trace and collect the material by Courtade himself for such a project has not always been straightforward and it must be certain that a large number of manuscripts – especially letters and drafts of articles – have still to come to light. In the collections of the Bibliothèque marxiste in Paris, for example, the boxes and shelves full of unsifted memoirs, diaries and correspondence bequeathed by significant PCF members will inevitably yield material by, about or addressed to Courtade. But gross understaffing will ensure that these archives will not be catalogued for several years at least. Private collections too – some of which have been opened to me – will also be a source of information. And what of the PCF itself? I have been assured that there is no specific dossier on Courtade in the Party's archives; and yet it was policy to compile and to keep records on important members, especially those who sat on the main committees. It seems not unreasonable to suppose as well that police holdings (currently inaccessible), and those relating to certain Resistance networks and still largely unsearched, will contain yet more. And as access to archives in the former Soviet Union becomes easier, more than cuttings of the translations of Courtade's articles in *Pravda* may well emerge.

Of Courtade's major published works only *La Place rouge* (1961)[7] has remained more or less regularly available since his death. Although they sold reasonably well during his lifetime, none of his other works of fiction – three novels and two volumes of short stories – have enjoyed, or been given the opportunity to enjoy, greater success.[8] Courtade is not alone in this of course; other writers who allowed themselves to become monopolized by political ideologies have suffered a similar fate, whether on the Left or the Right. There is no doubt that Courtade's fiction has its weaknesses (though it also has strengths); but had he not sacrificed so much of his intellectual and creative energy to journalism and to peddling the Party line it seems not unreasonable to suppose – as indeed several of the obituary tributes claimed – that he would have established himself as a novelist and short-story writer of some merit. The journalism, and some of the essays which grew from it, cannot be ignored, of course. Courtade's talent in this field was widely recognized as being almost second to none, and if forty years later so much of what he wrote day in and day out in thousands of articles in the Communist press seems rebarbative and repetitive, its vigour and conviction are hard to deny. But, again as the obituaries remind us, behind the public man and the star of the Party's press existed another – anguished, uncertain, sensitive and perhaps ultimately alone. Some of the reasons for this can be attributed to his experiences, both public and private, from the mid-1940s; others, more fundamental, to his background, childhood and adolescence.

Despite the incompleteness or unavailability of some relevant material I have been assisted to no small degree as I have attempted to unravel this story by very many people. The staffs of *L'Humanité*, the Bibliothèque marxiste and, in particular, the Bibliothèque municipale de St Denis, who allowed me unstinted access to their collections of newspapers and provided me with conditions for working (including champagne†...) that I have not before enjoyed in any other public library in France. Of those who had known Courtade not all responded to inquiries or were willing to talk; but many did give generously of their time, delved into their private archives and were happy to be interviewed. I should like especially to thank: René Andrieu, André Carel, Pierre Corval, Pierre Daix, Pierre Grappin, the late Pierre and Annie Hervé, Maurice Kriegel-Valrimont, Svetlana and Max Léon, Jeannette et Jean-Jacques de Meyenbourg, Edgar Morin, Noël Morrier and the group of Courtade's former students whom I met in Nantua, the late Gaston Plissonnier, Jacques-Francis Rolland, Claude Roussel, Roger Tardy. Beyond these, however, my greatest debts are to Courtade's second partner Nicole Chatel, his daughter Sylvie and his sister Simone, all of whom have produced documents and anecdotes that have helped complete the picture. But it would have remained even less complete had it not been for the generosity and friendship of his widow Génia. I have known Génia Courtade for a long time. Once she became convinced of the potential interest and even value of this book I was given access to boxes of letters, notes and diaries, totally unsorted and buried deep in cupboards or thick with dust in the *chambre de bonne* at 37 Rue de Verneuil. Here we discovered the manuscript of a first unpublished novel (*Eric et Irène*), the anguished notebooks from Courtade's adolescence and tape recordings of some radio broadcasts. Inevitably there have been difficult moments. Not always has Génia either agreed with my readings or been willing to explore a particular angle any further than she thought necessary. The experience has also at times been a painful one for her, and like anyone working in this kind of field I have felt an intruder. I can do no more than offer my apologies, and hope that this modest attempt to look at the life and work of Pierre Courtade will not be the last.[9]

The section in Chapter 2 on *Elseneur* is a slightly modified version of my article in the *Journal of European Studies* (Vol. 23, 1993). I am grateful to my co-editors and publishers for allowing me to re-use it here. I should also like to express my warm appreciation to the British Academy for generous support at various stages in the course of research for this book; to the University of Exeter for granting study-leave; to Harry Guest and David Walker for their time and constructive observations; and to Daphne Morton and Phil Chambers for coping with what has not always been an easy manuscript.

NOTES

1. Rolland,*Un Dimanche inoubliable près des casernes*, Editions Bernard Grasset, Paris, 1994 p. 307. All further page references are included in the text. When the novel was published Rolland dedicated a copy to Génia Courtade: 'Je te dépose ce livre où l'imagination du romancier dispose librement des données du réel. Il n'y a donc pas de portraits véridiques, mais beaucoup de notre 'nous' collectifs.'

2. *L'Humanité*, 14 May 1988.

3. Gallimard, Paris, 1969 and 1972.

4. Roger, Vailland, *Les Lettres Françaises*, 16 May 1963.

5. *France Observateur*, 16 May 1963.

6. Seuil, Paris, 1969. See also Morin, *Autocritique*, Seuil, Paris 1970, pp. 126–8.

7. Details of Courtade's publications will be found in the Bibliography, pp. 239–240

8. A new edition of *Les Circonstances* is to be published in 1995 be Le Temps des Cérises, Paris.

9. The Archives Pierre Courtade will be housed at the Institut Mémoires de l'Edition contemporaine, (IMEC) 25, Rue de Lille, 75007 Paris.

– 1 –

The Formative Years

'ce n'est pas une destinée paisible que de vivre obscurément dans unpetit trou de province'
Letter to Jacqueline Dyard, 19 December 1932

Despite the fact that he spent virtually his entire life in or near Paris, Courtade's affection for the glorious countryside of his family's native Pyrenees and for the large village house, formerly the police station, at Bagnères de Bigorre remained constant. The Courtade family's origins in this remote region of France were relatively humble, at best lower middle-class. For two generations on his father's side there had been a tradition of working for the national postal services. His grandfather had delivered and collected letters in a number of villages in the area; his grandmother had supplemented her husband's income by making and mending clothes. Both are remembered with affection by Courtade's sister Simone and by his widow Génia. The former recalls her grandmother as an ugly, slightly formidable person ('un sacré caractère'), but as someone devoted to her grandchildren; Génia remembers the grandfather as an authoritarian figure, presiding over family meals at an immense table. On the maternal side Courtade's grandfather (who died only days after his grandson's birth in January 1915) was a policeman, and later the caretaker for the lawcourts in Bagnères de Bigorre. His wife, who had inherited some money from the sale of family property in the Basses-Pyrénées, did not work. She is remembered as a slight, rather pretty woman (confirmed by photographs), self-centred, and having a clear preference for Pierre of all her grandchildren. She did not die until 1943, 28 years after his birth.

Courtade's father (born in 1886) continued the tradition of working for the Post Office. He began his career with the railway distribution service, only to rise quite rapidly through the ranks to become director of the postal services for the

Courtade's parents with Marie, his father's sister (seated).

Hautes-Pyrénées, and, just before the war, found himself promoted to Paris, where he formed part of a team responsible for modernizing the capital's post offices. Louis Antoine Jean-Marie Courtade-Cabessanis was better educated than his own father. He attended the Collège de Bagnères de Bigorre, and subsequently the school of Notre Dame de Garaison in the Hautes-Pyrénées, which was run by Jesuits. But his education did not only benefit him professionally. It would also make him ambitious for his own son, and lead to considerable friction between them, especially during Courtade's teenage years. He would not die until 1959.

His wife, Jeanne Eugénie Labrayle Pabet, was four years younger. She was educated at the *école communale* at Bagnères, and subsequently at the local secondary school. She too was employed by the Post Office, where she met her future husband. She continued to work after their marriage, and in Paris was a telephone operator in the Rue des Archives. She retired just after the outbreak of the Second World War, and died in 1977. Unlike her husband, who appears to have been a thrusting, ambitious man (Génia recalls him as 'un monsieur très intelligent, très capable [...] un peu fruste') she is remembered as self-effacing, devoted to her family and gentle. Simone recalls: 'Nous n'aimions vraiment que notre mère.'[1] Photographs of her show an exceptionally pretty woman; and where she is photographed with her husband the couple appear self-assured, successful and distinctly *bourgeois* – an image which Courtade would spend much time deriding in later years.

Louis Courtade was mobilized in August 1914, and initially drafted into the postal services. By the following year he was transferred to the telecommunications unit, working through the nightmarish episode of the Chemin des Dames. Neither wounded nor decorated, he returned to Paris at the end of the war and to their flat at 3 Boulevard Arago, in the *13e arrondissement*. Meanwhile, on 3 January 1915, Jeanne had already produced their first child Pierre, returning to Bagnères for his birth. By the end of the month, however, she was back in Paris, where she awaited her husband's return; and they would then remain there until April 1926.

Courtade's early years appear to have been uneventful, though his mother regularly told the tale of how his cradle was rocked on one occasion by a bomb exploding nearby. A much loved son, he found himself with a baby sister Simone in 1921. His early schooling was at the local *école communale*, and holidays were mostly spent at Luz and Bagnères. Encouraged to write, his letters from the age of seven show considerable flair, and even a degree of precociousness. They deserve to be quoted at some length. Describing their train journey to the south-west in a letter to his father (8 July 1922), for example, we read:

> J'ai été longtemps dans le couloir. Je regardais les noms des villes sur les gares et le paysages le train sai arété en plaine foret parse que le chaufeur c'étais trompés de voies. A partir de lourde nous avons vus les montagnes et nous avons vus la basilique ou il y à des colonades de marbres et nous avons vus aussi l'église de pousac.[2]

A week later (16 July) we find an amusing observation of his grandmother's attempts to cope with a houseful of holiday guests: 'Mémé à louer à des gens qui sont nobles la bonne de ses gens s'appelle Ursule elle est de notre familles c'est la 2ième cousine à mémé, elle appelle sa patronne: Madame de la bourse plate parseque elle nais pas riche.'

With the benefit of hindsight it is tempting to foresee in these letters the Courtade of later years, with his gift for sharp and often ironic observation. Certainly there can be no doubt about the inherent quality of such writing from a seven-year-old, and during the following summers his letters are characterized by much the same style. In August 1923 the account of an excursion into the local mountains in search of raspberries is worth recording in full for its drama and evocation of atmosphere:

> Lundi je suis parti avec Pierre à la montagne. Je n'ai pas eu beau temps je n'ai put rien voir. Nous sommes partis le soir à 5 heures et nous sommes arrivér à la grange vers 8 heures, puis nous sommes partis au framboises. Pierre marchait le premier. Il arriva le premier à l'endroit ou sont les framboises moi je ne voulu pas le suivre car c'était dans des rochers et moi qui n'était pas habituer à marcher la dedans je risquais de glisser et de descendre sur les cailloux, il m'avait dit que quand les nuages n'étaient pas très forts on y voyait à 10 mètres et lui qui était au moins à 20 mètres de moi et les nuages qui arrivaient je risquais de ne plus le voir et de me perdre je lui criait Pierre! Pierre! mais j'avais beau crier lui se manquait de moi enfin à force de crier il est revenu et j'ai réussit à le faire rester, moi j'avais peur qu'il ne puisse retrouver son chemin dans les nuages, on partit, au bout de deux minutes il me fit

peur, il se jetta parterre et me dit qu'on n'est foutu, moi j'avais un peu peur car il me tardait d'arriver à la grange le plus vite possible enfin nous arrivames à la grange. Piere se jeta sur la paille moi je fit comme lui et nous attendimes sa soeur. Nous soupons, dehors il y avait un orage terrible, nous nous couchons. Le lendemain je n'est pas été au sommet je suis resté à la grange tout seul. Pierre est venu me prendre et nous sommes decendu à Luz.

A year later a brief description of a fishing trip is broken off in order to talk about 'un autre sujet suivant tes recommendations'. The change in pronoun is significant. The rest of the letter, which deals with bookshelves in his room in Paris, his 'instruments d'éléctricité et de physique', lessons (Latin and mathematics), his savings account and the weather is clearly addressed to his father. Already the parental roles are being classically attributed and, perhaps more significantly, the effect of the ambition for the son beginning to show. This continues. During the next three summers there are references to a violin (of which Simone has no recollection) and to painting. (Courtade would become quite seriously interested in painting during the last years of his life in particular, and many of his letters to Génia during the early years of their relationship and his private papers are scattered with small marginal drawings.)[3] After an amusing account early in July 1926 of how he had caught the local baker cheating her customers over the weight of one-kilo loaves he comments on a visit to Mont-St-Michel, and decribes his father rather mischievously 'avec une canne et l'appareil photo'. His wit seems not to have been appreciated, for in his next letter (26 July) he writes: 'J'ai reçu votre lettre à l'instant. Elle me donne un avant-goût des critiques, quand je serai écrivain. Je vais suivre les conseils de papa. Je vais également réduire la dose d'humour qui me paraît excessive et augmenter la dose de sentiments.' This was the reaction of an eleven-year-old!

No letters to his parents beyond the summer of 1926 remain, but one of the first (27 August) describes his having been taken ill with gastroenteritis. Examined by one of his uncles, Amédie Laffon, who later became Dean of the Medical Faculty at the University of Algiers and a notable specialist, he writes: 'il paraît que j'ai le coeur un peu faible en temps normal.' This is not the only reference to his health in these letters. In July 1926 a note from his mother to her husband assures him that '[Pierre] ne se fatigue pas'. On 30 July 1926 Pierrre makes a point of telling his parents how well he feels, but a week later (6 August) writes: 'Je ne fais pas d'excursion et je me repose bien. Je crois que j'ai eu, purement et simplement, la jaunisse.' But by the middle of September he is still receiving treatment: 'j'ai suivi à la lettre les conseils du médecin, je ne me suis pas fatigué et j'ai fait attention au régime' (13 September).

Earlier in the same year the family had acquired a new house in Sceaux in the southern outskirts of Paris, and had finally moved there in August. The move necessitated a change of school, and Courtade had to leave the prestigious Lycée Henri IV, where he had spent one year in the *sixième*, for the rival Lycée Lakanal in Sceaux, which would have a significant influence on his subsequent development. Changes of this kind would inevitably have been disturbing, and the concern for Courtade's health may have been no more than an expression of natural parental anxiety; but hints of a possibly fragile constitution (and an over-protective mother), coupled with a natural timidity, could be said to anticipate rather uncannily the pattern for much of his adult life.

The move to 14 Rue du Chemin de Fer, overlooking the Paris-Orléans railway line, was an important event for the Courtade family. The purchase of this semi-detached house was material recognition of their new social and professional status, and the family took advantage of a loan scheme set up by the government (the Loi Loucheur) to move out of central Paris and an apartment which was now too small. But Sceaux did not conform neatly to any model of a new *petit bourgeois* community. It was a settling place for quite a few foreign families, including a number of Russian *émigrés* who gave it a slightly exotic atmosphere that Courtade would find quite different from the rather cautious, self-contained one of his immediate family. His parents were typical of the new Sceaux generation. They continued to work in Paris, commuting on the increasingly frequented suburban rail service, and spent most of their spare time decorating their house and cultivating the garden. Perhaps because of his rural background, but more probably for reasons of family economy, Louis Courtade decided to keep chickens and rabbits. By 1930 he had built a hen-house, and already covered much of the garden with concrete, in which, much to his neighbours' amusement, he scored Latin mottoes.

In later years Courtade would regularly recall the house and the social rituals of Sceaux, only to ridicule it all. In his first published novel, *Elseneur*, for example, the protagonist Karl writes in his diary:

> La maison et le jardin de banlieue fabriquaient une espèce d'homme abstrait, individu seul devant l'Etat. La solidarité des maisons ouvrières était brisée. Autorisé à exercer les ravages de la fantaisie individuelle sur quelques mètres carrés enclos de murs, le temps passé en déplacements, les heures consacrées à la lutte contre les fléaux naturels (rongeurs, fuites d'eau et de gaz, éboulements, gel, boue, pucerons, coccidose des lapins, pépie de poules, engorgement des fosses septiques, rouille) et à l'amélioration de l'habitat (travaux sur fil de fer, grillage, tessons de bouteille et utilisation des coquillages marins comme motifs ornementaux) était perdu dans le conversation et la lecture.[4]

And he would continue to produce similar passages in a kind of frustrated attempt at exorcism through to his last novel, *La Place rouge*. Such descriptions, and the fact that they occurred with such regularity, do, of course, reflect a fundamental psychological problem, from which Courtade liked to make a political point; but it was also one from which also he arguably never managed to free himself, and certainly not until his father's death in 1959. Claude Roy makes this point well in *Nous*,[5] and his interpretation is borne out by one of Courtade's school friends, Jean-Jacques de Meyenbourg. Courtade, the latter claims, 'souffrait du fait que ses parents étaient des prototypes de petits bourgeois'; and increasingly he made it his ambition to escape. The Meyenbourg family – Protestant, of Swiss extraction, with a hint of aristocracy and links with the world of entertainment – represented a world and values which at the impressionable age of thirteen or fourteen Courtade not surprisingly admired. Meyenbourg recalls: 'Pierre aimait venir chez nous car l'atmosphère y était joyeuse [...] Courtade avait avec mon père, qui était charmant, très causant, cultivé en diable, des conversations qu'il n'avait pas avec le sien. [...] Nous représentions pour lui quelque chose de plus ouvert que le monde des petits fonctionnaires dans lequel il vivait.'[6]

Of Courtade's first years in Sceaux there is little information. From what Jean-Jacques de Meyenbourg recalls (and in spite of what he himself may have suggested subsequently) he appears to have led a normal life for a boy of his age, enjoying a close, supportive family environment and acquitting himself well, if yet without distinction, at school. That his parents were ambitious for him there is no doubt. Travel was considered essential, and in July 1930 he was sent to England for a month as part of a group visit in order to improve his command of the language. This was the first time Courtade had been abroad and truly separated from his family. The prospect must have been daunting for all; but it seems to have given him a taste for travel which would remain with him for the rest of his life. He stayed with the Booth family at 49 Wolfington Road, West Norwood, a suburb about fifteen miles to the south of London. Already popular with the Victorians, it grew substantially in the early years of the century as a middle-class London overspill area with the installation of a railway link with the capital. It was in fact a kind of English Sceaux. Undulating and wooded, it was attractive. Wolfington Road, which has hardly changed, was typical. Curving up from the main road, it was lined with houses, most of which were substantial, single-fronted semi-detached dwellings built from pale grey brick and with small gardens back and front. Joseph and Maude Annie Booth had lived there for a decade. What Arthur Booth's trade and profession was is not recorded; but it would seem that in an economic depression the family found it necessary to boost its income by taking in lodgers. District records contain the names of several, and in 1930 Eveline Maude and Olive Edna Booth are also listed: presumably they were the household's daughters. Courtade records in one of his letters that the former met him at Victoria Station; but thereafter neither is mentioned. Nor indeed is one Manepunda Muthanua Cariapa, who is also on the electoral roll.

Courtade's first letter to his parents is full of precise, dramatic, colourful and sometimes gently ironic observations, both of his journey and of his first experience of English life:

Je vous écris dans une petite chambre fort jolie et fort propre, j'ai rangé toutes mes affaires et je suis chez moi. Par ma fenêtre à guillotine j'aperçois un paysage qui a quelque analogie avec Arcueil ... c'est Londres. Ce qu'il y a de plus envieux, de plus stupide, de plus lassant et de plus inesthéthique c'est que toutes les maisons sont rigoureusement semblables ... (je me suis interrompu pour aller breakfaster avec du thé, de la confiture, des tomates, du jambon frit et une espèce de croûte desséchée qu l'on trempe dans du lait sucré.) [...] Supposez des lotissements à perte de vue coupés de grands 'parks' où des enfants à casquette à tranches jouent au "cricket". Naturellement il bruine, et comme de juste on m'a assuré que c'est la première fois depuis un mois. Mais puisqu'on me l'assure c'est donc que je comprends l'anglais! parfaitement en trois ou quatre jours j'ai fait des progrès extraordinaires [...]

Mais il faut que je vous raconte mon voyage. Jusqu'à Dieppe nous avons regardé par la portière les collines vertes et fraîches, les bouquets d'arbres et les troupeaux de vaches et des établissements Gervais ... A Dieppe le train après s'être arrêté un instant à Dieppe-Ville, suit la jetée et les quais jusqu'au bateau. Cela m'a fait plaisir de revoir la mer, il y a longtemps que je n'avais respiré cet air mouillé et salé. Le bateau qui nous a transporté [*sic*] était un steamer anglais ... marins au nez pointu et aux yeux étonnés, ... ils fument des cigarettes d'orient et se balancent en marchant comme des chimpanzés. Le bateau est assez grand mais je n'en ai vu que l'arrière, les classes sont strictement séparées – "Second ... left. First class right". Un coup de sirène; on hisse le pavillon britannique et celui du "Royal Mail" [...] On part ... tangage, paquets de mers qui se brisent sur le pont, les misses poussent des cris les cigarettes s'éteignent ... les gentlemen se promènent en fumant la pipe, je suis très bien ... Les falaises de Dieppe disparaissent dans la brume, plus que deux misses sur le pont, les autres sont emportées dans les cabines, les "shipmen and attendants" circulent avec des gilets jaunes qu'ils offrent gracieusement, les pipes des gentlemen se sont éteintes ... la casquette d'un monsieur chauve est bien loin dans la mer ... une valise marche toute doucement vers les flots ... on l'arrête à temps. Les gentlemen regardent fixement le pavillon britannique qu'on vient de hisser pour saluer un bateau au large a "subject of his Majesty is not sea-sick". Je vois trouble. [...] J'ai le hoquet, il est quatre heures, nous apercevons les côtes anglaises, la sirène mugit, nous voyons vaguement les falaises crayeuses dans la brume, un camembert coupé au couteau et posé sur un papier vert. [...]

Les trains anglais sont merveilleux ... en troisième tout est rembourrée et astiqué [...] La campagne Anglaise est la continuation de la campagne Normande. Des collines où pousse une herbe très verte ... des cottages et des ladies en robe de soie et souliers vernis qui donnent du grain à des poules blanches bien propres. La campagne est découpée en carrés bien réguliers, non pas par des cultures comme chez nous, mais par des barrières en ciment armé.

The remaining letters from this first visit across the Channel are written in much the same vein. Despite what he finds to be the high prices charged for public services or entrance fees to museums and the London Zoo, the young Courtade was generally impressed by the low cost of living in England and the relative comfort of the average person. He approves strongly of the number of public swimming pools ('une pour deux mille habitants.   D'une propreté méticuleuse'), but is less complimentary about English food and eating habits: 'En résumé, les Anglais ne savent pas faire la cuisine. Ils font une mauvaise cuisine qui leur coute [*sic*] extrêmement cher, et mangent tout à la fois, comme des petits cochons, sur des nappes toujours blanches et des tables fleuries' (21 July). For a fifteen-year-old he also has some perceptive remarks to make about the architecture of Westminster Cathedral: 'C'est une immense église Byzantine, récemment construite, plus remarquable par la grandeur des formes et la hardiesse de l'architecture que par l'art proprement dit et la décoration, qui est à peu près nulle, habitude protestante qui persiste dans les églises catholiques Romaines' (21 July). On the difficulties of learning English he is also observant, finding that because of his nasal accent ('ma prononciation *nasale* que j'ai aussi en français' (21 August)) an American pronunciation is easier to imitate. This is neither particularly interesting or unusual in itself; but the condition also leads him to complain of certain breathing difficulties when he eats, and is another, albeit small, element in what will become almost an obsession for his health and fitness in subsequent years. In general, however, his letters suggest that his English experience was both enjoyed and successful. Friendship with another of Mrs Booth's students ('le Cambridgeman') helped, and Courtade would return to West Norwood for Christmas a year later, and spend the new year with this student in his home in Peterborough.

Amongst Courtade's correspondence and papers from this period are two newspaper cuttings. One is an advertisement for a book *Pour bien savoir l'anglais: odds and ends for the students of English* by F. J. Quanjer; the second is a poem by René Dutaur, a schoolboy from the Gironde, entitled *Espérance*. Sentimental and mildly sensual in tone, it expresses feelings which are going to be very much Courtade's own in the next few years:

On doit espérer!
Qu'importent les déceptions!
[...]
Qu'importent les misères, les échecs,
On doit lutter, Espérer.

Given his evident talent for writing Courtade not surprisingly turned his hand to poetry as well, and a dozen pieces written late in 1930 and during the first six months of 1931 remain. On what appears to be the earliest (dated 27 Août 1930) Courtade noted: 'I wrote this in London, just after having bought the Holy Bible, in which I discovered what is Real Poetry.' This poem, *Le Cantique des Cantiques*, has little, if anything, to recommend it, however. Written, like most of the subsequent ones, in uncertain alexandrines,[7] it attempts to capture a form of Old Testament resonance and grandeur in its appeal to an undefined but personalized love. The final stanza is enough to illustrate its tone:

> Vois! les Cèdres seront le dôme de ta chambre
> Qu'embaume le parfum voluptueux de l'ambre
> Et tu viendras vers moi qui tressaille et t'attend
> Quand l'Astre se mourra dans la mer d'Occident.

The other poems are hardly better, but they are the first attempts to give expression to adolescent unrest and sexual awakening. Echoes of Musset, Banville, Baudelaire and Verlaine ('O Pourquoi est-tu triste O mon âme et Pourquoi me troubles-tu?') are strong, and it is also clear that the language of the Bible – presumably not part of Courtade's experience in a family that was strongly anti-clerical – was quite genuinely a revelation. Two stanzas from *A mon Ame* illustrate these points:

> C'est vrai que je suis triste et que mon âme erre désespérée sur les
> > flots de l'ennui
> Pourquoi? C'est que le jour me damne
> Et que me damne encore bien plus la nuit
>
> Mais cependant je vois dans les brouillards du rêve
> D'idéales amours se figer dans ma fièvre
> Et des vierges en blanc et couronnées de fleur
> Valsent au son lointain des rhythmes de bonheur

One other feature should also be noted. On several occasions we find an allusion to academic achievement and to his father's continued concern for his son's success. In another untitled poem, dated from December 1930, in which Courtade attempts a light-hearted conversational style, the second stanza is revealing:

> D'abord la grippe et puis réveillon dans mon lit
> Au matin de Noël, mon père un gai papier me lit
> Là-dedans sont es-cribits mes hauts faits du trimestre
> Cris de douleur! Quand serai-je mon Mestre?

We might well deduce from this that the paternal ambition which was to be the cause of so much friction over the next few years was already beginning to manifest itself. In the immediate future, however, it could hardly have been better rewarded than by Courtade's success in early July 1931 at a speech-making competition ('Concours national d'éloquence') held at the Sorbonne in Paris. This led to his representing France at an international competition in the United States of America at Washington in October. The subject of his six-minute speech, both in Paris and in the final was 'La mission colonisatrice de la France'. Well-constructed, it reviews the history of French colonization, and acknowledges the responsibility that the French nation has exercised and the contributions it has made to education and to technical and medical improvements in its dependent countries. Not surprisingly, Courtade's position is traditionally conservative; but while his closing lines may be what his audience would have wished to hear, and are probably what he himself accepted at the time, they are hardly ones of which he would be proud a dozen years later:

> Nous avons su en cette matière éviter deux écueils redoutables: l'insuffisance d'un enseignement qui ne satisferait pas aux besoins de l'élite indigène, et la pousserait à aller chercher à l'étranger une culture que la nation protectrice ne saurait lui donner; et d'autre part, danger non moins redoutable, la formation de déclassés qu'un vernis de science joint à une insupportable présentation rangerait dans les rangs d'une opposition pseudo-intellectuelle. Mais tout cela ne suffirait pas à créer des relations d'amitié entre l'indigène et nous, si nous n'avions su nous l'attacher étroitement (et la grande Guerre nous a montré la valeur de cette affection!) par une politique intérieure où une série de modalités habiles permettent de concilier la loi et la coutûme; où l'homme de couleur est frère inférieur, mais un frère ...

In the event Courtade was runner-up, the prize going for the first time to a Dutch candidate, Henri Van Hoof. (Courtade was later to complain privately that there had been no native French speaker on the adjudicating panel.)

America is a country to which Courtade would frequently return in later years as a journalist, and indeed for which he would on occasions be temporarily denied a visa on account of his membership of the French Communist party. His impressions on this first visit, recorded in letters to his parents, are essentially of a country that is modern, wealthy and still developing, but one in which there is also a degree of brashness (ugliness even) and incompletion. He writes of New York:

> Du travail des sauvages, qui, parfois pris d'une irrésistible envie d'épater le public, font des choses laides mais absolument ahurissantes. Les rues sont mal pavées, sales, les clôtures nulles ou délabrées à côté de ça on rencontre soudain un building superbe en pierre de taille, de splendides magasins des travaux d'art comme le tunnel de Holborn. (16 October)

Widely and generously invited, the young contestants appear to have had an opportunity of experiencing American life in a variety of middle-class homes. Courtade was certainly impressed by a wealth and an ease of living which he could not help comparing with life in Sceaux:

> j'ai été passer la journée dans une famille américaine "moyenne" – ce qui correspond à notre situation en France, seulement ici, le ménage est fait par une négresse et un aspirateur, on mange au restaurant, pour faire le café on tourne un bouton et on attend, on grille le pain électriquement, on téléphone pour avoir des oeufs, la vaisselle est lavée dans une machine, la T.S.F. fournie par la maison – ce qui est du luxe en Europe est absolument normal ici. (26 October)

He was also overwhelmed by the general concern for young people, by a freedom within the educational system and by America's openness and youthful vitality in general. This was a country, he said, where, were he to become a teacher of French, he would return with pleasure. The comfortable, even wealthy, life-style clearly tempted him.

Courtade returned from his visit to family admiration and to some public acclaim with coverage of his exploits in a number of newspapers, including *Le Petit Parisien* and *Le Temps*. He was also required to report on his experience, and amongst his papers are notes, presumably towards a speech. One part of this deals specifically with family relationships in America: 'Rapports familiaux surprendraient européen par compréhension. Père et Fils et respects parents pour enfants. Sans pousser trop loin avons beaucoup à apprendre en ce sens de Amérique.' Courtade must have had his own situation in mind, and there is no doubt that tension in the family was growing as he approached the *baccalauréat*, the first major academic hurdle of his career.

During the last week of March 1932, just months before the examination took place, Courtade went abroad again, this time to Holland on a group visit organized by the Association Hollando-française. How and why this came about is not clear,[8] but it was important on two counts. First, also in the group was Jacqueline Dyard, with whom Courtade was to have his only significant romantic attachment before meeting Génia; second, because the short report he wrote of this visit bears all the features that Courtade would refine and which would become so characteristic of his best travel journalism in *Action* or *Humanité-Dimanche* – the evocation of atmosphere, the invitation to the reader to share the experience, the use of anecdote, the social and political observations. There should be no surprise that in the academic year 1931-2 Courtade was awarded first prize for 'Composition Française'.

Academically everything suggested that his future was assured, and already his parents (and his father in particular) had decided that he should set his sights on gaining entry to the prestigious Ecole Normale Supérieure and on the fiercely competitive *agrégation* examination. When therefore he learned in July that he had failed the mathematics papers in the *baccalauréat*, parental reaction was predictably stormy, and Courtade was forced to remain in Sceaux during the summer holidays revising for the repeat examinations. His father worked with him.

While there is no regular diary for this period, Courtade recorded his own feelings in one of his school exercise books:

Le 17 juillet 1932 j'ai appris mon échec au baccalauréat de philosophie. Quand je compare cette fin d'année scolaire toute de déceptions et d'amertume à la glorieuse période qui fut pour moi la fin de ma rhétorique une grande lassitude et un doute de moi-même profond et irréductible me viennent à l'esprit.

The emotional tension already hinted at in the previous year in some of his poems also surfaces again:

> Certes je regretterais quand même le temps où je fus sensible aux douleurs et aux joies humaines plus qu'aux idées et à la passion de l'ambition, mais du moins aurais-je la satisfaction d'une amélioration utile dans les facultés nécessaires à la réalisation du but qu'*on* a donné à ma vie [...] Père est orgueilleux pour moi, ambitieux pour moi. J'ai l'orgueil des triomphes passés et le mépris des gloires futures ...

The last lines seem to act as a trigger, and from this point the tone becomes increasingly angry and the writing less controlled, as though Courtade had finally allowed himself to express the feelings of bitterness and frustration he had been carrying within him:

> Alors! Alors! je suis un homme trop médiocre pour faire mon chemin dans les cadres actuels j'ai besoin de la vague pour être entraîné plus loin que ne me pousse ma volonté de succès. Et *l'on* m'a *trop changé* [pour?] que je puisse trouver mon bonheur dans les jouissances délicates d'une vie sans périls. Je veux vivre, je veux lutter, je veux vaincre parce que je crois qu'il y a quelque chose à faire pour démolir cette pourriture qui étouffe une triste humanité dans la faim et la fait crever sur des grabats. J'en ai assez de *vous* intellectuels délinquescents qui vont quintessenciant la souffrance terrible des pauvres.

The last page continues this outcry against the permitted state of the poor, and dismisses political programmes like 'Révision de valeurs' and 'Populisme' as empty and meaningless slogans in the face of true deprivation and suffering.

It is worth quoting at some length from these pages, because they contain in essence ideas, emotions and even obsessions which were to remain with Courtade in some cases for the rest of his life, colouring his imaginative and non-imaginative writing alike. The frustration at having been directed in his studies and the consequent self-doubt on his failure (and it would not be the last), the wariness of intellectualism and the angry tone could all be said to be typical of a seventeen-year-old boy in his position. At the same time the element of political concern – apparent as well to some degree in his comments about America and Holland – may have had some substance behind it.

When, a year earlier, *Le Quotidien* had announced that Courtade was going to America, he was described as 'un homme de gauche [et] secrétaire de jeunesses socialistes de Sceaux'. The local organization quickly denied any such formal responsibilities, but did recognize that as the son of a militant radical he could have left-wing sympathies. Pierre Hervé and Jean-Jacques de Meyenbourg too, while acknowledging Courtade's growing political awareness at this time, could not recall his having held any office. Yet by December 1932 a change appears to have occurred. In a letter to Jacqueline Dyard (3 December) he writes: 'I must be in Bourg-la-Reine at four o'clock for a socialist meeting of our Khâgne and, as I am secretary of the group, I can't miss it.'9 From England too, when he was visiting Norwood and Peterborough, another letter to Dyard suggests growing conviction: 'le vieux monde est pourri. Il faut que nous, avec notre jeunesse, avec notre sang, nous combattions *contre* lui, non pas *dans* lui, pour l'améliorer, mais pour le détruire, on ne construira pas ce que Jaurès appelait la cité future, en réparant les lézardes du vieux monde capitaliste, on la construira sur ses ruines.'

In any event, with success in his retaken examinations it was as though he would start afresh. Parental confidence was restored. It could be rationalized that failure in the *baccalauréat* had been one of those unforeseen and quite unpredictable setbacks that even the most gifted students have occasionally to bear. Fortunately the way was open once again for the parental dream to be realized – sure progress as planned to the Ecole Normale Supérieure and the *agrégation*, and beyond to a brilliant career. Certainly Courtade appears to have settled into the rarefied, intellectual atmosphere of the last tier of the Lakanal system. Pierre Hervé remembered him as bright but rather shy; Jean-Jacques de Meybourg has said he was brilliant.

Just as in later yeares Courtade would write satirically about social life in Sceaux, he looked back critically at this period, ridiculing the teaching of Jean Guéhenno, whose taste for abstraction and interminable debate he claims was unsuited to the real world around them. Yet from evidence at the time he appears to have immersed himself enthusiastically in his studies and allowed them to become part of his everyday life, and his diaries contain scattered quotations from and references to Montaigne, Vigny, Baudelaire, Rousseau, Seneca, Shelley, Lord Lytton and others. At the same time he continued to experiment with poetry, and for the first time tried his hand at some short fiction.

But what papers remain from the 1933–4 period tell as well a rather different story – that of an eighteen-year-old boy trying to come to terms, perhaps slightly later than most, with the emotional turmoil of adolescence. As we have already noted, Jacqueline Dyard, around whom Courtade's sexual anxieties were to crystallize, had already made an appearance in his life. But there were other girls too with whom he had uneasy relationships early in 1933. The first was Paulette, to whom in January he dedicates a sentimental, self-pityingly romantic prose poem, 'Aujourd'hui Ste Paule'

> mais ce qui est éternel ce qui a été vraiment unique dans ma vie c'est l'Amour que j'ai connu à cette époque, et le fou, que j'ai été, je ne peux plus aimer, c'est fini, je peux désirer, croire aimer, être tendre mais Aimer non!

The tone and style continue in much the same vein, producing over the following weeks mainly tortured, sometimes incomplete, sonnets accompanied by outbursts of mild sensuality:

> C'est ton corps qu'il me faut aux lignes pures
> Et tes seins devinés blancs et durs sous les plis
> Et ta gorge et ton cou qui (battent?) sous ma main [...] et cette
> odeur de chair neuve!
> Amour! Amour!
> Tes lèvres dont le goût doit être si fade, et si salé
> Avec un peu de sang
> Et le heurt de nos dents.

These lines are dated February 1933. Elsewhere fragments of poems refer to 'ce vieil amour', and by May Paulette has given way to Claire, and a relationship altogether more melodramatic and postured: 'Elle me parle du suicide, qu'elle a été tentée de prendre le revolver de son père' (2 May). In the long account of an afternoon visit Courtade describes and attempts to analyze his feelings. The result is immature. The pages are full once again of self-indulgence and uncertainty, and hints of sexuality are constantly suppressed; but there are interesting glimpses of self-awareness, as for example of his leaving: 'je m'en vais [...] dans le vestibule je l'embrasse, sur la joue, comme une soeur, comme une maman qu'elle me disait qu'elle voulait être, était-ce de la littérature ou un complexe (freudien). Je pense moins à elle en sortant.' The words reported may be hers, but the gloss applies equally well to him.

It is nothing unusual for an adolescent whose life had been as sheltered as Courtade's to want, if only subconsciously, to rediscover or recreate through his early amorous experiences the maternal love he had known from his earliest days. In this instance Courtade may have been aware of what he was writing; but increasingly elsewhere, especially at times of depression or anxiety, we find it expressed seemingly unconsciously. On 12 April, for example, we read:

> il n'y a de vrai que la souffrance. Cette envie de pleurer qui remonte de la poitrine et vous prend à la gorge et vous donne envie d'être humble, d'être petit enfant. La douleur qui est une délivrance, la douleur qui meurt d'elle-même, qui meurt de s'exprimer, qui finit de se livrer mais qui nous fait rêver de mains douces pour nous prendre la tête et de genoux pour reposer.

Elsewhere it becomes transposed into an image of peace and withdrawal:

> Ce soir seul dans ma chambre, sans nul bruit qu'un tic tac de réveil, ou quelques aboiements de chiens, le monde tout autour enfoncé dans la nuit, il est autour de moi un cercle de lumière ou je suis pour moi seul, à moi seul, près de moi.

And love, ideally, is pure: 'dormir ainsi à reposer dans une éternité de rêve, ses mains dans les miennes et sa tête légère aux cheveux clairsemés de soleil (des aurores dans une forêt d'automme) sur ma poitrine.'

At the same time we also find the aggressive (male) side of Courtade giving vent to feelings of frustration and anger at not

1934.

seeming to be able to be positive or constructive. The language and style are powerful; the target clear:

> Tout ce que j'avais pensé faire, tout ce que j'avais rêvé, tous mes espoirs! Fini, rien, je ne peux plus rien, je ne sais plus aimer, je ne sais plus écrire, je ne sais plus vouloir, et à 18 ans rien fait, rien *dit* – le talent est toujours précoce, pas de talent *moi*, sec, sec, le 'bizinette' est sec, le bizinette sera pion, pion, pion, à Roumarantin ou à Brives, c'est mieux, il se mariera après avoir demandé l'autorisation à son père, il deviendra méchant et insupportable. (3 March)

Five weeks later the same thoughts are expressed again: 'je n'avais pas de talent. Simplement une petite précosité d'enfant trop tôt dessalé et un peu perroquet (12 April).' And scrawled across another page early in May, in bold handwriting we read: 'Passé au conditionnel, voilà le temps pour raconter notre vie.'

As we have already noted, it appears likely that Courtade's first hesitant attempts at writing prose fiction date from those turbulent months of 1933 as well. Three pieces have survived, of which the first two are unfinished. The first describes the departure of an English friend, and develops into a brief reflection on life, death, and the need to sustain a positive attitude. The second appears to be an attempt to write an allegorical tale about a group of men journeying towards some form of (political?) truth and new awareness. The third and only complete piece (17 June), entitled 'Prince', begins as an address to an imagined exemplary figure, and develops into an attack on the conformist and materialistic nature of modern society and on the way in which individuals' imagination and capacity for action have been suppressed:

> C'est un spectacle navrant, que l'embourgeoisement du monde. Une quiétude fade s'est répandue parmi les hommes. La vie est décolorée. Les passions sont des passions de lucre et nous ne rêvons plus que de 'positions assurées' comme s'il y avait quelque chose de grand qui fût assuré! Quelques hommes, rares à la vérité, savent encore ce que veulent dire les mots 'dignité' et 'grandeur' mais la plupart s'épuisent dans la recherche du bonheur [...] Nous ne voyons plus autour de nous que 'circonstances économiques', comme si les idées n'étaient pas la sève et le sue du monde, comme s'il ne suffisait pas pour vaincre d'avoir l'âme chevillée et l'oeil qui voit loin, comme si la puissance du Verbe ne

faisait pas les Révolutions, comme si la contagion de l'exemple, n'incitait pas aux grandes actions.

Ainsi Prince, nous qui maintenant venons à l'âge de vingt ans et qui avons par nos pères entendu raconter la splendeur de ces années, nous sommes tels que démesurément désireux de vivre et aussi pleins de crainte qu'il est possible nous avons peur d'aimer, peur d'haïr, peur de prendre parti, et que ballottés de oui en non et de refus incertains en approbations indécises, nous ne savons pas ce que veut dire 'prendre parti'.[10]

Courtade's particular targets in this outburst are the right-wing Action Française movement, with its political message that has distorted the admiration for the classical heritage and capacity for rational thinking that characterize French culture, and the commercial world monopolized and controlled by the banks.

Arguably these few pages are, like the early poems, no more than the immature and stumbling first attempts at imaginative writing by a young man still trying to find his way. But taken together with the diary entries, random thoughts and reflections, they are beginning, in both content and tone, to anticipate significant features of Courtade's later work. Considerable time will have to pass before the social and political observations are developed into anything resembling a coherent position; but already certain preoccupations, motifs and even images can be said to have established themselves. The need for an authoritarian and respected male model is obvious; the loss of a male friend and the theme of the journey equally so. One stylistic detail in particular also stands out. In the first of these fragments of imaginative writing the narrator's sense of sadness at his friend's departure sweeps over him *'comme une mer*, un poids lourd sur la poitrine qui ne disparaîtra jamais'. In the second, as the men reflect on their situation 'il leur venait comme *des flots* tristes et gais des souvenirs'. In 'Prince' the young men are '*ballottés* de oui en non ...'. This recourse to water and in particular to the sea is to be found elsewhere. The sense of pleasure aroused in him by his affection for Paule overwhelms him 'comme une mer'; life in general bearing him along is 'la mer'. The image 'works' in two ways. On the one hand it is protective and embracing; on the other it invites inaction and threatens to stifle. Its appearance in this second sense in the first of the three fragments of fiction ('comme un poids lourd sur la poitrine ...') is one more echo both of his present moments of self-doubt and despair at his inability to act positively, and of his preoccupation with poor health. It is also uncannily resonant with anticipation. In the context of the first of these the phonemic echo of *mer* and *mère* is obviously significant; but the link between water and death was to be starkly and indelibly illustrated during the summer of 1933.

In mid July Courtade and a fellow pupil from Lakanal, René Jammes, spent much of their summer vacation on a youth camp at Tannenheim near Seeboden in southern Austria. With academic concern and their son's future career much in mind the principal reason for his parents' sending him was that he should improve his knowledge of German. It was also hoped that the experience would be a change from the life he had been leading at Sceaux during the previous year, with its family differences and tensions, and would be good for his general health. In his early letters Courtade dutifully refers to both. He talks of working with 'le professeur Korn' on the second part of Goethe's *Faust* and on Schopenhauer's philosophy, both of which suggest a competence in German far in advance of anything he had achieved at Lakanal. He also makes a point of commenting on the opportunities for swimming and boating, of benefiting from some fine weather and of having relaxed into the camp's general atmosphere: 'Je n'aurai même plus tous les jours deux ou trois drames de conscience d'ordre théorique' (14 July); 'je me sens plein de soleil [...] c'est ainsi que toute la journée je suis un homme de la nature' (21 July). Yet he had not managed to shrug off completely the kind of inner debate and anxiety that had been reflected in his diaries. On receipt of some newspapers from his father, including a copy of *Le Populaire*, Courtade's letter of thanks turns into an outburst on ideas and action, theory and practice, behind which the father–son tension can still be sensed:

> Ceux qui savent et ceux qui font représentent deux classes d'esprits, ce n'est que par de petites compromissions qui dramatisent et agitent inutilement la vie que l'on passe de l'une à l'autre. Je crois qu'il faut choisir comme dirait Guéhenno, cependant si l'on ne peut choisir, et l'on ne peut pas choisir la plupart du temps, il faut apprendre à mentir. (23 July)

Courtade here touches on the problem of theory and practice and on the need to adhere to a specific belief no matter what the circumstances, which in subsequent years would prove to be both his salvation and a cause for considerable anguish. In his present circumstances Hitler's policy of National Socialism provided him with an opportunity to illustrate the consequences of indecision – a characteristic that he would attribute directly to Guéhenno's teaching:

> ici, la connaissance même de la vie politique, l'expérience de l'Allemagne, celle de l'Autriche m'enseignent que c'est aussi le seul moyen pratique de sauver le socialisme. J'ai dans cet ordre absolument raison. Mais que je me mette un instant dans le domaine des actes, comme ma position devient plus complexe! [...] elle ne *colle* plus dans l'ordre des faits, dans l'action immédiate, dans la décision à prendre. Et voilà qu'ayant raison, j'ai tort. Alors je mens, et sachant où est le vrai, je l'écoute systématiquement, par un aveuglement, une volonté de ne pas savoir mais de faire. (Ibid.)

Early in August Courtade visited Vienna and Budapest. Not surprisingly his letters are filled more with details of buildings and scenery than with reflections on the political situation. Yet in Vienna he does show himself to be sensitive to the plight of a country whose president would be shot by the Nazis within a year, and whose people were going to suffer vicious repression: 'il y a sur cette ville une atmosphère de détresse et de tension extraordinaire.' Unfortunately there are no further records of how Courtade viewed National Socialism at this time; yet it is evident that, towards the end of his eighteenth year, his political awareness and the problem of translating conviction into action were beginning to define themselves.

Five days after writing this letter, the event that was going to mark him much more profoundly than any visit or political discussion occurred: René Jammes was drowned in a boating accident. Four students were caught in a violent and totally unexpected storm,[11] and, according to the account Courtade sent to his parents, Jammes panicked, caused the boat to capsize and died, probably of a heart attack. His body was never recovered.

Courtade (19 August) wrote first to his father ('annonce ça à maman avec précaution, qu'elle ne s'inquiète pas pour moi'). Although clearly in a state of shock, Courtade in this and subsequent letters gives the impression that Jammes was someone with whom he had already formed a strong friendship.

Jammes' death also prompted Courtade into more protestations of the need to be decisive and purposeful. A page from one exercise book has '*Vivre, Vivre*' scrawled across it, and in part of a postscript to the letter to his father he writes: 'Je comprends ce soir le sens de la vie, je sais ce que c'est je *veux*.'

The following day (20 August) a long letter ('Maintenant que je suis un peu plus calme') to both parents gave a detailed account of what had happened. In it Courtade also returned obsessively to the matter of his health and fitness and, not surprisingly, of the need to be resolute:

> Tannenheim est dans la désolation, mais déjà la vie reprend, ils ont été canoter aujourd'hui, et je songeais en voyant ces beaux corps bronzés au soleil, penchés sur les avérons, combien est lamentable notre éducation, combien il importe d'avoir des corps virils, solides, de belles machines et je revoyais mon pauvre Jammes s'en allant les mains dans les poches, un peu voûté, khâgneux toujours, khâgneux jusqu'au bout, car je *sais* ce que c'est que cette crise de folie, cette aberration qui l'a saisi, mais cela je ne peux pas vous le dire par lettre. [...] Si vous saviez quelle est ma douleur, mon désespoir et aussi ma *révolte* durant cette stupidité infinie.

A few pages later the now familiar motif reappears:

> Je sens que mon désespoir a changé en volonté, une volonté de mieux faire, de vivre plus pleinement. Le calme commence à se faire en moi, presque la 'lumière' qui revenait si souvent sous sa plume. Quand le drame est fini la Paix est déjà toute prête sans transition. Je me souviens de ce vers de Shelley justement qu'il avait commenté avec moi dans un de ses essais. "O Wind, when Autumn's there Can Spring be far behind." O Vent, quand l'Automne est là est-ce que le Printemps est loin?
>
> J'entrevois ce printemps, je travaillerai.
> J'entrerai à l'Ecole, comme nous nous étions juré d'y entrer ensemble.

Unfortunately his resolve would not be sustained, and not for the last time would actual achievement fall agonizingly short of ambition. We might also note that the original line from Shelley reads: 'if Winter comes, can Spring be far behind?'

Through the last days of August and early September Courtade had the difficult task of looking after Jammes' father, and his letters are a touching tribute to the man's simplicity and courage. He also makes the point of reassuring his parents about his own physical well-being by references to his swimming ('j'ai fait ce matin 700m à la nage (over-arm strong) sans arrêt!'). And quite separate from the whole matter of Jammes' death is an interesting reference to a conversation he had with a socialist deputy who had asked him to organize a conference for young socialists in Vienna in 1934. Possibly because of the political evolution of Austria during that year the project came to nothing; but it may point to a seriousness on Courtade's part in political matters, and also to the fact that he was perhaps more active in Sceaux than Hervé has suggested.

With the departure of Jammes' father on 4 September Courtade turned his mind to a journey – originally planned with René and another student friend – across northern Italy to Venice and beyond to Hungary. Yet Jammes' death still haunted him, and in the closing paragraph of his final letter from Seeboden he returned once more to his reflections on life and death, to the need to be positive and to the influence of Guéhenno's teaching:

> Je n'oublie pas, je réfléchis à cela tous les jours, c'est quelque chose d'étrange pour moi, au fond je n'avais aucune idée de ce que c'était que la mort. Mais non, je ne vais pas recommencer. Il faut que rien ne paraisse. Je me mettrais maintenant à parler, à écrire, à écrire ... [...] nous en parlerons ensemble, puisque le 'débat est ouvert'. C'est du Guéhenno, Ô khâgne! jusques [*sic*] où me poursuivras-tu. Cette manie de tant regarder et de tirer immédiatement de vastes conclusions générales!

Of his journey there is little record. A dozen pages describing the waiting room in Turin railway station on the night of 10–11 September, in which he experiments with different styles ('tragique grec', 'rabelaisien', 'policier') is all there is of any substance. Courtade returned to Sceaux by the middle of the month, determined to succeed in his final year at Lakanal. His resolve is recorded in his diary in the form of a pact with his dead friend and with a promise to be at Seeboden the following August to pay tribute to him:

Jammes pendant un an [...] à partir du 1er Octobre 1933 je ne m'appartiendrai plus, je travaillerai seulement, inlassablement, jusqu'à ce que mes yeux rougissent et que mon corps se brise. [...] je me suis engagé.

Je maintiendrai.

Neither the promise nor the resolution would be realized.

By the middle of October Courtade was well embarked on his programme of study leading to the entry examination for the Ecole Normale Supérieure. Events of the summer gradually faded, despite a memorial service held for René Jammes, on 11 October, at Palaiseau. His diary records this, as well as the account of the burial of a young boy Maurice Salze, the brother of a schoolfriend.[12] He also attempts a form of *résumé* of the past year. Much of this is entirely banal; but one remark in particular underlines a dimension to his character which would certainly be apparent over the next half-dozen years, and which, in a sense, would always be a source of potential conflict: 'Vie de l'esprit. Dans l'ordre politique, une haine qui se fait plus mure et plus systématique chaque jour de la Démocratie. Je la proclame maintenant' (22 October). This is further reflected in some undated pages later, in which Courtade sets out (in a way that was to become utterly characteristic) a 'plan of action'. Of fifteen hastily noted points, most deal with will-power and individualism:

1   De la douleur il ne doit sortir qu'une volonté.
2   Les muscles toujours tendus.
3   Les yeux peuvent seuls consenter à l'humanité.
4   Le poing tendu toujours.
5   Toujours vers l'avenir, oubli nécessaire et permanent du passé.
6   Ne pas s'accorder des amours de pacotille ou savoir ce qu'on fait.
7   Voir et expliquer toujours les défaillances de ma volonté.
8   Ne pas hésiter à se justifier temporairement même par le mensonge. Tout subordonner à l'action i.e. à la Vie.
9   Vivre. C'est avoir à chaque instant le sentiment du Définitif.
10   Il n'y a pas de choses sans importance.
11   [?] chaque jour à faire quelque chose qui m'est insupportable.
12   Etre pur – absolument.
13   Jamais impassible. Sauf cas de nécessité politique. Mais que cette impassibilité soit feinte.

14   Dans le domaine *artistique* de ma vie adopter les 13 attitudes
     exactement contraires.
15   Méditer et [?] *chaque* jour une heure.

The echoes of a kind of diluted Nietzscheanism are clear enough. But the insistence on health, physical fitness and self-control owe more to Courtade's evolution over the previous seven or eight years than – as far as we know – to any serious or systematic study of the German philosopher's work. The confrontation between private desires and the pressures to conform and satisfy parental ambition had been given further edge by the events in Seeboden.

Courtade's eighteenth year was to witness major changes in his sentimental life as well. His friendship with Jacqueline Dyard dated, as we know, at least from March 1932 and the visit to Holland. For the first year or so their friendship appears to have grown around a number of shared intellectual and political interests. In May 1933 Dyard wrote to him (in English) to arrange to meet at the Gare St Lazare: 'Perhaps if no bird hinders us by its song, we'll have a serious talk about socialism.' In a card from Seeboden (30 August) Courtade tells her of Jammes' death, and through that autumn and winter their relationship seems to have remained on the same emotionally neutral level as before. Letters discuss their academic work and are littered with references to Spinoza, Kant, Descartes, Pascal, Dostoievski, Molière and experimental psychology. On reading Guéhenno's *Conversion à l'humain* she comments (29 December): 'joie d'avoir trouvé, enfin, un intellectuel si humain, si bon, et pourtant si éveillé à toutes les idées, à toutes les inquiétudes [...] ce qui me plaît en lui, c'est qu'il *vit* le conflit entre la culture et le peuple, qu'il est sur la ligne – frontière "qui peut devenir ligne de bataille" dit-il.'

Already a month earlier (9 November) she had written about her pleasure in expressing 'des idées paradoxales, hérétiques, folles, bien souvent pour le plaisir d'effrayer les bourgeois qui m'écoutent avec stupeur', and it would appear from the letter in which she discusses Guéhenno that she had been a member of a young socialists' group for a year. The following January she announces that she has embarked on a systematic analysis of Marx's *Das Kapital.* As the political scene early in 1934 worsened, culminating in the mass demonstrations in February, her commitment grew, much, it would seem, to the concern of her family: 'Depuis jeudi dernier, je suis inscrite aux Etudiants socialistes, ou plus exactement au groups Rollin–Lamartine–Jules Ferry [...] mon père m'a défendu d'aller aux réunions. C'est dommage; je me sens un courage immense, parce qu'au fond, il s'agit de vie ou de mort' (7 February). In the same month she worked in the offices of *Le Populaire*, and within weeks posted tracts against the manufacture of arms (19 March). Early in May a letter reveals a seriousness about the political climate which, despite its naivety, went some way beyond anything Courtade had formulated:

Croyez-vous que Bergery, du Front Commun, soit un vrai chef? Les revues réactionnaires (*Revue hebdomadaire*) le désignent comme le Lénine français. Si ça pouvait être vrai! Les réactionnaires ont une peur terrible de nous. Il n'y a rien du plus réjouissant que la lecture de leurs journaux.

Mais tout le côté *politique* parlementaire de la lutte entre le pré-fascisme et le socialisme m'ennuie prodigieusement. C'est tellement vieux, tellement dix-neuvième siècle! Ne croyez-vous pas que les Francistes sont très dangereux. Leur programme, d'inspiration populaire, rappelle étrangement les appels d'Hitler aux Allemands désemparés. Ils sont vraiment redoutables parce qu'ils recrutent à droite et à gauche et qu'ils professent le mépris de tout ce qui est bourgeois et traditionaliste. (10 May)

From evidence such as this Jacqueline Dyard appears to have been a fairly self-assured young woman, more mature than Courtade and more committed in her political allegiance. But while she was clearly a sympathetic listener to his unending complaints, to his expressions of disgust with what he was finding himself studying at Lakanal and his frustration with Guéhenno's reluctance to draw firm conclusions, Dyard was not afraid to be critical.[13] In February 1934 Courtade wrote an article for *Le Cri des Jeunes*. Unfortunately this has not survived, but her response is informative:

Croyez-vous, Pierre, qu'en émaillant votre article de gros mots, vous serez 'peuple'? Mais ça se voit terriblement mon ami, que vous êtes un bourgeois qui veut *faire* peuple. Pardonnez-moi d'être sévère. Je crois que le peuple ne parle pas *exprès* l'argot. J'ai entendu des ouvriers parler; ils ne m'ont pas choquée. Tandis que vous! Cela vous est si peu naturel, que cela détourne étrangement. Et puis, ce n'est vraiment pas chic pour les ouvriers; c'est les considérer un peu comme indignes de votre style ordinaire. (22 February)

Courtade was not alone in experiencing this problem of course. Others older, important and even major figures of the French intellectual Left had already recognized the difficulty of writing *for* and *on behalf* of the working class. For Nizan, Aragon and the team of *Commune*, for example, it was of central concern in 1934–5, while Guéhenno explored it at length in terms of class allegiance and betrayal in *Caliban parle*. Arguably they never fully solved the problem, and while in subsequent years it was one that would not concern Courtade to any great extent, it was never fully acknowledged.[14]

Jacqueline Dyard's importance for Courtade, however, was more than that of someone with whom he could share his slowly emerging political ideas. The first hint of anything more than friendship occurred in a letter dated 25 February 1934 ('Mon ami, j'ai cru longtemps que je vous aimais. Je me suis trompée.'). Stutteringly a mutual affection began to emerge, and by the summer of that year their letters had a more intimate tone, and at long last the mode of address sporadically changed from *vous* to *tu*. Yet as her expressions became less inhibited, his replies were cautious and even fearful. The image of himself inside a glass cage from which he is neither able nor wishes to escape occurs on a number of occasions. On 6 May, for example, he referred to 'mes petites folies habituelles, d'étranges et soudaines "désaffections" qui me font souhaiter (et rêver) de vivre dans une forte cage de verre suspendue par un fil dans l'éther bleu.' Dyard took this as a form of aloofness ('votre indifférence cordiale' (10 May)), but it is difficult not to interpret it as the expression of a subconscious fear of sex and a deep reluctance – even inability – to wrench himself away from the protective shell of his home and of his mother's affection in particular. When, in August, she invited him to visit her in Ris-Orangis during her parents' absence Courtade prevaricated, hesitated and eventually ended their relationship. Even in love the pattern of ambition and expectation that collapses at the moment of possible realization continued.

By the same summer it is possible that Courtade had already met and found himself attracted to Eugenia Romoff, whom he would eventually marry. In a letter to his parents in March 1934 he mentioned 'une jeune fille qui n'est pas étudiante' and whom he has known for several months. Whether or not this is a reference to Génia is not particularly significant. Génia thinks she may have met Courtade occasionally early in 1934, but is certain she had not struck up any particular friendship with him. They were brought together formally by Jean-Jacques de Meyenbourg (who had also acted as a go-between in his relationship with Jaqueline Dyard). To supplement the family income, which depended substantially on a share of the royalties from the grandfather's estate, Madame de Meyenbourg took in paying guests. Amongst these were some Russian emigrés, who included Maroussia Romoff and her son Boris, suffering from mild tuberculosis, who were persuaded to move from the *13e arrondissement* in Paris to the cleaner, healthier suburb of Sceaux. The Romoffs had lived in the Boulevard de la Gare (today Boulevard Vincent Aurol) since 1912. Serge Romoff, who had been an eminent art critic in Russia, had left for France in 1905; his future wife left six years later, and they remet and settled in Paris. Romoff worked for the Imprimerie Union managed by two exiled Russians, Snejaroff and Chalit, whose premises were at Bourg-la-Reine and Sceaux. They were friendly with the de Meyenbourg family, and it was they who recommended that the Romoffs should move. Around the time of the 1925 Exhibition he had begun to renew links with a number of Soviet artists and critics in Paris, and decided in 1928 or 1929 to return to Moscow. There he became responsible for an organization Voks, set up to welcome and provide hospitality for visiting foreign artists. As the Soviet régime became increasingly intolerant, however, Romoff was accused of being too 'westernized' and too critical. He was imprisoned. Eventually, through the assistance of a woman friend who was close to the central régime, he was released, and escaped the worst of Stalin's purges.[15] Génia, accompanied by Courtade, visited him in August 1935. It was the last time she would see him alive, and he died there in 1939. According to de Meyenbourg they returned shocked by the conditions they had found there. Unfortunately no letters or diaries from this period remain, and the only hint we have of Courtade's reaction is through the account the Russian Jew Sacha Bernstein gives of his early life in the Soviet Union in *La Place rouge*.

In Sceaux the combination of the already different atmosphere of the de Meyenbourg household and the exoticism brought by people like the Romoffs, who only twenty years before had been resident in Russia, must have seemed quite extraordinary to Courtade, and a complete contrast to the more mundane family atmosphere in the Chemin de la Gare. More or less at the time Jacqueline Dyard was trying to persuade him to visit her, Courtade wrote to his parents on holiday in the Pyrenees: 'jeudi soir je vais boire de la vodka et manger des concombres au caviar avec des russes *rouges* authentiques' (1 August), and three days later: 'Nous avons fait une soirée russe-rouge chez de Meyenbourg. Vodka – tracteurs allégoriques sur les murs – papier rouge – et un portrait en pied de Staline.' Not surprisingly, such company was viewed with some misgiving by Courtade's parents. Even more so was Génia, who, from this evening on, became increasingly prominent in their son's life. Her family – foreign, exotic, part-Jewish and tainted with illness – hardly conformed to the model that they had in mind. Génia herself had relatively little formal education, and was earning her living making condensers in an electronics factory in Paris. Moreover, Madame Courtade, a kind and gentle woman by nature, was, according to Simone, ill at ease with anyone who belonged neither to the family nor to her immediate circle of friends.

Such a combination of circumstances boded ill for the beginning of a serious courtship. To contact and see one another was not easy, and de Meyenbourg once again acted as the link. A further problem was Courtade's own shyness (and fear?). Over a year after the party that had made such an impression on him, a jotting on a scrap of paper dated 5 November 1935 is revealing: 'vanité désordonnée, goût de l'épate, besoin de faire valoir au risque d'être ridicule, (manque de courage pour donner un rendez-vous à Génia).' Yet by the following year it was clear that the two would eventually marry and they did so, in a civil ceremony only, at the town hall of the *13e arrondissement*. Still unhappy about their son's choice, the Courtade parents refused to attend the wedding. As Génia recalls it, however, it was a happy occasion, attended by many friends and children. Jean-Jacques de Meyenbourg and Georges Altmann who also lived in Sceaux, were the witnesses. Within a week Courtade's parents had a change of heart, and organized a 'grand dîner' for the young couple. More importantly they provided them with a small but much-needed allowance.

The problems that Courtade had experienced with his parents over his relationship with Génia were not merely to do with their expectations and social class, however. Having shown promise and even brilliance at times at Lakanal he prepared, as had been planned, for entry to the Ecole Normale Supérieure in 1935, with every reason to assume he would be successful. In the event he failed, and the cycle of recriminations, anger and bitterness began all over again. Even more furious than he had been over his son's failure in the *baccalauréat*, Courtade's father arranged for him to change schools and repeat the year at Henri IV, the most prestigious and intellectually high-powered of the Paris *lycées*. But again it was to no avail. While on this occasion he passed the written examination, he failed the oral. Even so, all was not lost. Studies at Henri IV prepared students for a *licence* at the Sorbonne, and in the end Courtade had at least a qualification, even if it was not the one his parents (or indeed he) had hoped for. Moreover, the way was still open to him to envisage the possibility of a *diplôme d'études supérieures* and, in due course, the *agrégation*.

While according to de Meyenbourg Courtade was politically militant during these years, there is no evidence to suggest that his activities were any more than participation in a handful of minor demonstrations and the traditional annual paying of respects at the Mur des Fédérés in the Père Lachaise cemetry. (At one point in their correspondence Jacqueline Dyard refers to his 'vie de moine'.) Nor is there anything in his papers to suggest that he was in any way involved in the much more serious events of February 1934, when fascist and communist demonstrations created civil disorder of a kind unknown in Paris since the early years of the century. Nor again does he appear to have been engaged by the debates aroused by the Italian invasion of Ethiopia or the Spanish Civil War in 1936, or even, more surprisingly, by the emergence of Léon Blum's Popular Front government. No doubt such matters did prompt reaction; but there is no more trace of them in his notes and letters than there is of what his sister claims to have been his excitement and enthusiasm for Malraux's *La Condition humaine* when it was published in 1934. During this period 1934–6 Courtade seems essentially – though understandably – to have been preoccupied with his personal situation and circumstances. And in one of the few extant letters to Génia we find him reflecting, albeit with rather more maturity than before, in a strikingly familiar way:

> J'aime cette lutte, j'aime ces douleurs et ces conforts – non certes par un goût morbide de la difficulté, mais simplement parce que chaque jour

qui passe donne plus de sens à ma vie. Le seul sens que l'on puisse donner à ma vie: devenir un homme. S'il ne faut pas 9 mois pour faire un homme, mais plus – quarante ans – et peut-être est-ce la mort seulement qui nous assure que l'ouvrage est terminé, qu'on ne peut plus rien ajouter à cet enrichissement de la conscience par la douleur et par la joie. Que puis-je espérer d'autre, moi qui ne crois ni à la vie éternelle, ni aux consolations femelles de la sensibilité et des larmes? (5 April 1935)

The only event during these two years that clearly did provoke some reactions from Courtade was his visit to the Soviet Union with Génia later this same year. As we have seen, conditions there shocked them, and it was perhaps this experience of poverty and deprivation that prompted Courtade in November 1935 to draft a reply to an inquiry launched by *Vendredi*, a new left-wing weekly edited by Jean Guéhenno, on Henry de Montherlant's recently published *Service inutile*. This collection of articles and extracts from earlier works written during the previous decade and dealing with those topics readily associated with Montherlant – courage, vigour, aloofness, sensibility, misogyny, sport and morality – and written moreover by someone who never attempted to play down his aristocratic background, were not likely to meet with unqualified approval from a young man who, while he might secretly have envied a world of ease and privilege, was beginning to feel his way towards social and political values of a quite different kind. Whether or not Courtade sent this 'open letter' is not known, though if he did it was not published. But his response to *Service inutile* and especially to Montherlant's *avant-propos* is interesting. Looking back over the previous decade Montherlant writes at one point: 'J'ai vécu, je me suis fait plaisir, j'ai fait plaisir à ceux que j'aime, et aux autres beaucoup moins de mal qu'il ne m'était facile de leur en plaire.'[16] Such self-indulgence, and Montherlant's claim that he had stored away his worldly goods in order to go out and explore the world,[17] drew heavy if naive irony from Courtade – 'je lis très peu et difficilement parce que d'une manière générale j'ai l'impression au moins pour l'instant que tout ce qu'on écrit est parfaitement inutile.' But the attack Courtade mounts against what he considers to be Montherlant's refusal to acknowledge the existence of the poor and suppressed peoples of the world on whom the privileged society to which he belongs depends and is built is clearly sincere, and bears early signs of the anger expressed later in his articles about the negro population of America or the Algerians in *Action* and *L'Humanité*.[18]

That Courtade nonetheless continued to hanker – if only privately – after a life in which courage, will-power and the kind of spiritual and physical prowess[19] so favoured by Montherlant would be rewarded is unambiguously suggested by the incomplete drafts of two short stories written approximately a year later. Each in its own way presents a protagonist who feels the need to escape from a dull, mediocre existence to somewhere more exotic or challenging, where he may then prove himself. The first, a rambling piece entitled 'L'Homme – Dieu' has echoes not only of Montherlant but of Gide's *L'Immoraliste* and Malraux's *La Voie royale* as well. The manuscript is preceded by an outline.

> Dans un asile d'aliénés. Un homme fait à ses amis le récit d'un voyage qu'il a entrepris dans un pays imaginaire (l'Amérique du Sud). Dépouillé de tout progressivement, à travers des paysages splendides il parvient à une tribu de sauvages qui en font leur Dieu. Il accepte de se prêter à cette comédie, et dès lors il va vivre divisé contre lui-même tiraillé par des passions contradictoires – son désir d'être Dieu et [d'assurer?] la toute puissance, et sa passion pour un *usage* simple de la vie qui lui est donnée. A l'occasion d'une fête en se débarassant de ses vêtements hiératiques il veut prendre part comme tous ceux de la tribu aux danses sacrées qui sont des danses de joie, il découvre la fausseté du grand prêtre qui sous un feint libéralisme cache une âme ambitieuse et tout entière mue par la vanité. Il va tâcher d'échapper à l'empire du sorcier du village, pour cela le Dieu apprend un métier.

The second, much shorter, story concerns a young man who returns to a humdrum existence of suburban life in France ('cet immense poulailler clignotant où les gens ne viennent que pour dormir comme les brutes lasses') having spent five years in the colonies. Already physically weak, his condition is worsened by fever. He feels inferior not only physically but intellectually and politically as well, and in order to prove himself leaves to fight in the Spanish Civil War, where he is killed.

Beyond these two drafts there is no record of any fiction or poetry written during 1936. No doubt the prospect of marriage and the need to find some kind of employment caused Courtade enough concern. By the spring of the following year the small allowance from his parents, Génia's earnings and his own from some private English lessons enabled the young couple to rent two rooms in the Hôtel d'York in the Rue Thibaud in the *14ᵉ arrondissement*. And having been awarded his *licence* Courtade embarked on his *diplôme d'études supérieures*, for which the subject was the unlikely one of 'Thomas Carlyle and the Bible'. It was also suggested to him that he should spend a year in England as a French language assistant, and by the autumn of 1937 he found himself at King Edward VI School for Boys in Southampton.

From this year little remains. None of the correspondence with Génia has survived, and while she recalls going to visit Courtade once in London in November (there is a photograph of her there) she has no memory whatsoever of Southampton. Courtade returned to France at regular intervals; but from the handful of letters to his parents it is clear that he enjoyed his year in England and made the most of his opportunities. Academically an important consequence of attending a course on the history of English Literature between 1870 and 1920 at the local university was his decision to abandon his *diplôme* on Carlyle and to write one instead on Shaw and socialism.[20] From a letter of 12 March 1938 he appears to have worked at it regularly and to have made good progress, and it would eventually be successfully presented at the Sorbonne a year later.[21] There are hints too, confirmed by Génia, that he had definitely decided to make teaching his profession and, ideally, to secure a university post.

A few references to his colleagues at King Edward VI and to others lodging with Miss Sims in Wilton Avenue,[22] or brief descriptions of the local countryside and the sea, interspersed with inquiries about his family fill most of the letters. There are only very occasional references to the political scene – in France or in England – though Courtade does appear to have received on a regular basis *Vendredi, Marianne, Commune, Europe* and *Le Canard enchaîné*. In addition to his academic progress the most significant event of the year seems to have been his decision to stop smoking: 'd'une certaine manière je m'en trouve beaucoup mieux, financièrement d'abord, moralement (parce que c'est une chose très difficile et que je l'ai réussie) et physiologiquement parce que mes nerfs sont plus stables et que je respire mieux' (31 January 1938). Once again we have the two recurring preoccupations of will-power and health.

In the autumn of 1938 Courtade decided to study for the *agrégation* in English. He earned money giving private lessons;

Génia continued to work as a secretary for an electro-chemical company, and they lived in a small appartment in the Rue des Bluets in the *11ᵉ arrondissement*. The year was to prove difficult. Georges Altmann had found work as a journalist for Boris, Génia's brother, in Oran. While there his tuberculosis worsened. He returned to Paris, and in March entered the Clinique Rémy de Gourmont, where he would die two months later. By March too Génia's health had shown signs of deteriorating, and as a precautionary measure she was sent to a sanatorium in Assy in the Haute-Savoie, where she would stay until June. (Courtade, not surprisingly perhaps, had his own chest examined, and wrote triumphantly to Génia (28 March) that the specialist 'a déclaré que j'avais un thorax magnifique, il paraît qu'il est rare qu'il voit à Paris des poumons fonctionnant aussi bien, j'ai un coffre de coureur à pied!!'). Courtade appears to have been deeply marked by Boris's death, and it drew from him a long and emotional letter in which we have an extraordinary statement of a belief in life and a refusal of (and reprimand to Génia for) protracted and self-indulgent mourning:

> je ne peux plus supporter qu'on me parle de deuils. Tu peux m'écrire tout [ce] que tu *voudras sur Bichuika vivant*, mais *j'exige* que le mois d'avril soit aboli de ma vie [...] Je crois à la vie, à l'amitié, au souvenir, je crois au devoir viril de la tendresse, j'ai fait [...] tout ce que je pouvais faire dans sa maladie et dans sa mort, je lui ai rendu les devoirs d'un ami et d'un frère, j'ai souffert de sa mort la seule grande peine qui m'ait frappé depuis que j'ai une raison et un coeur pour m'émouvoir.

The same kind of directness would be expressed as well in his first novel *Eric et Irène*,[23] written in 1940–1, which, however, remained unpublished. On the positive side Courtade heard in March not only that his *diplôme* had been accepted but that he was advised to prepare himself for the *agrégation* that summer. In the event he failed, but only by one mark, and despite his disappointment it was a remarkably encouraging result given the little time he had had to prepare the examination and the fierceness of the competition: 'dans les 6 premiers non admissibles à l'Agreg [...] c'est à dire que je suis arrivé au concours 58ᵉ sur 280 environ [...]' (26 July).[24] Moreover Génia had been declared fit by the sanatorium, and when she returned

Military training in 1940.

to Paris they rented a flat in the Rue Oberkampf and Courtade began seriously to think of finding a teaching post for the following October, ideally either in the Paris area or in the Alps.

With the declaration of war on 3 September, however, their plans were instantly dashed. Génia moved with her mother to Thiers and Courtade went to live with his parents in Sceaux until he was drafted for military training at Laval on 16 September. Letters from Courtade during these few days are a mixture of irony, anger, bitterness and anguish, but with a repeated determination to be courageous and fight fascism. Declared unsuitable for the infantry on account of flat feet, Courtade followed a course of instruction to equip him to be part of the tank corps. Between September 1939 and July 1940 he was sent to over a dozen different military centres, including the Ecole spéciale militaire de St Cyr, before being demobilized from Pamiers. The letters which have survived from this period return time and again to the boredom of camp life, with its routine and petty administration, to bouts of ill-health and various attempts to obtain weekend leave. Only twice was he close to action. Early in June he was involved in the setting up of roadblocks against the threat of the German advance in Corbeil,[25] and a few days later he was under fire: 'Depuis 4 jours et 4 nuits je marche (à pied!) sur les routes, bombardé et mitraillé sans arrêt ou presque, je me suis tiré de tout [...] j'ai une chance extravagante [...]. Nous avons passé à travers les Panzer division à vélo!' Such experience was enough, according to Génia, for him to prove to himself that in spite of his raw fear he had the courage to see it through. And not for the last time would luck be with him; on a number of occasions during the next few years he would escape from situations that could easily have led to arrest, torture and execution.

With the armistice Courtade again sought a teaching post, and in September was appointed to the Collège de Nantua in the Ain. For many, indeed most, French citizens, the period following Pétain's signing was one of uncertainty, but also of hope that somehow the new government's policies would lead to regeneration and to the restoration of France as a significant force within Europe. History would prove otherwise, of course, and not all shared this opinion. Quite how Courtade reacted is difficult to judge, but one letter to Génia, 11 December 1940, expresses a determination which is not feigned:

> Je suis tout à fait prêt maintenant pour aller à la guerre. Tous les camarades qui sont restés avec moi après tous les filtrages auxquels nous avons été soumis sont les plus sains et les plus courageux – ce qu'il y avait de meilleur parmi nous ira au feu – les petits bourgeois lâches et les malades sont partis – si nous sommes tués ce qui restera fera un drôle de monde – et tous ceux qui partiront seront égaux et purs. Je les aime profondément. Il me tarde de voir les hommes.

Courtade's former pupils at Nantua also claim that at the daily obligatory celebration of Pétain and the Vichy government his disapproval was barely concealed, though it is likely that their recollection has been distorted by subsequent events. In any case, to indicate such feelings too openly was dangerous even in the *zone libre* and before the Resistance had begun to take shape.

In general terms Courtade's year at Nantua appears to have passed uneventfully. By the end of the year he had rented a flat at Cluses, where he and Génia would stay until the following autumn. The rest of the family had already moved from Sceaux in February 1940, and had eventually found their way to Thiers, where Courtade's father had been appointed head of the postal services and where they would stay until 1942, when he would be moved to Auch. Courtade is remembered by former pupils as having been a popular and conscientious teacher (there are several letters from grateful parents among his papers), if at times mildly eccentric, controversial and caustic. He is said to have worn a large cape-like coat ('je fais la classe en pardessus, je gèle de froid'), to have strode about the recreation area adopting Napoleonic poses, and to have covered the fifteen kilometres each day from Cluses on a bicycle with no saddle in order to maintain his fitness! In themselves such details are no more than anecdotic, but in view of some of the themes recurring in his papers and letters during the previous few years they are not entirely without significance. Some of the year's experience eventually found its way into 'Les Cheveux coupés en quatre', one of the short stories in *Les Circonstances*.

Courtade's other main, and significant, activity during this year was to write a first novel, *Eric et Irène*.[26] Originally to have been called *Le Mieux de la fin*, the title of the novel in its 'final' form refers to the two characters whose roles are critical in the life of the protagonist, Adam Barrault. As we might suspect, *Eric et Irène* is strongly autobiographical. Barrault is Courtade; Eric Weil and Irène Télin are based on Boris and Génia. Other characters have their models amongst Courtade's friends, and many of the episodes relate to quite specific moments in his life between 1935 and 1940. That Courtade was aware of the potentially limiting effect of this kind of writing is evident from a note dated January 1941: 'Il faut que ce roman sorte de l'autobiographie adolescente et pourtant continue à y puiser sa *réalité*. Pour cela il faut faire de certains personnages des *réalités* et non des fantômes qui viennent, prononcent quelques paroles qui disparaissent.'

The novel has four sections. The first begins with the description of an evening spent with friends at Irène's flat in Paris, and describes her relationship with Boris and Adam's own flirtation with Elisabeth, one of Irène's friends. It also deals with Adam's home in the Parisian suburbs, Boris's death and cremation, and his own work as a teacher at the Cours St Thomas, and closes with his decision to spend August at Lusigny in the Savoie, where he knows Irène has decided to go. This is the first occasion when he will have been on holiday without his parents. The second section, written in part as a diary, describes Lusigny and his meeting with Irène (who is accompanied by Elisabeth), and ends with their making love. The time they spend together and the threat of war and mobilization are described in the third section, and in the fourth Adam returns to Paris and is sent to a military camp. The experience is new and formative. He finds himself tested physically and mentally, and feels increasingly removed from his family. He rejoins Irène, talks vaguely of marriage – a proposition she rejects – and returns to the army and some minor military action. At the close of the novel Adam senses he is at last master of his own fate and on the threshold of a new life.

Weaknesses in *Eric et Irène* are plentiful. Adam's sister Cécile, based on Simone, has no significant role; the episode dealing with the Cours St Thomas is not properly integrated, though Courtade's idea of having the director M. Jacquinot as a projection of Adam aged fifty is interesting. Elisabeth (in whose portrayal is an echo of Jacqueline Dyard) makes little contribution other than provide an alterntive to Irène. There are flaws too in organization and tone. From the moment Adam arrives in Lusigny passages of self-analysis are increasingly ponderous, and Courtade's authorial voice breaks through on several occasions. One reflection as Adam contemplates the outbreak of war reads as though it has been transposed directly from Courtade's own diaries:

> il lui semblait qu'il était arrivé – et cela aussi avait sa source dans une habitude bien plus ancienne de diviser constamment sa vie en périodes avec pour chacune un programme de travail ou de tentatives diverses auxquelles avec une persistance digne d'un meilleur object, il attribuerait une signification biographique dans sa destinée.

Yet there are also positive qualities. Descriptions of suburban Paris, of an-early morning gathering of the bourgeois parishioners outside their local church, or of a Sunday lunch are marked, for all their autobiographical echo, by a descriptive verve, irony and social satire characteristic of Courtade at his best. One illustraton is the view Adam has from the train as he returns home having spent the night watching over Eric's body:

> A mesure que le train avançait le paysage se faisait moins aride, la verdure plus abondante et moins artificielle, il y eût même des apparences de champs et des bosquets – mais en même temps apparurent les demeures de la petite bourgeoisie, ce fut une succession de solides horreurs, de toits de tuiles mécaniques, de perrons de ciment, de verrières tarabiscotées, un dédale de grilles fraîchement peintes, de portails solonnels, de fenêtres étroites. Il vit des jardins où se nichaient des cigognes vernissées et des lapins en terre cuite, des bassins où mourraient des poissons rouges, et partout la couleur jaune, irritante de la meulière sortie de joints cimentés. C'était là qu'il avait grandi.

This, for the first time in Courtade's fiction, is a direct reference to the environment of his early years in Sceaux. Another, deleted, describes Adam's father's reservations about Eric's family – 'étrange, déracinée, sans patrie, sans réligion', which clearly reflect those of Courtade's parents about the Romoffs.[27]

Thematically *Eric et Irène* turns around Courtade's current obsessions, summed up by a marginal note with reference to Adam: 'le style de sa vie: la Velléité. Sa constitution spirituelle: Spectateur, jamais il ne s'engage.' And linked to this theme of indecisiveness is that of jealousy, an interesting projection of Courtade's subconscious reaction to Génia's relationship with her brother. In some notes for the opening section Courtade writes: 'Irène: elle a été incontestablement la maîtresse d'Erick [*sic*]. C'est elle qui projette dans la vie d'Adam – *le style de vie d'Erick* en même temps que son souvenir. C'est à cause de cela qu'en définitive il la fuit.' Throughout the novel Adam is tormented by the uncertainty of whether or not Irène and Eric have been lovers, but not only because of his relationship with Irène. A bond of friendship has also existed between him and Eric which has been so intense that on several occasions after the latter's death he feels himself possessed by his spirit. (In his notes Courtade comments of Adam at one point: 'il était Erick'.)[28] The principal cause of this is undoubtedly Courtade's genuine affection for Boris; but the memory of René Jammes may also have a part to play, especially when Adam becomes Irène's lover at Lusigny, situated by a lake.

But if the friendship between the two young men reflects fairly obviously Courtade's own uncertainties, the depiction of Irène does so even more. We are told nothing about her family background, but she is an independent young woman and Adam knows instinctively that any relationship with her will cause concern to his parents, and especially to his mother: 'Il pensait à sa mère qui redoutait qu'il ne tombe un jour entre les mains d'une mauvaise femme.' When Adam tells Irène of an afternoon he has spent with the art teacher, Mlle Lhomme, at the Cours St Thomas, she listens to him 'avec une tendresse maternelle qui provoquait en lui un abandon presque enfantin'. These two images of Irène – temptress and mother – persist. When he meets her by the lake in Lusigny ('le lieu le plus chaste du monde') she experiences for him 'un vague goût [...] pour une protection maternelle, indulgente et absolument désintéressée.' Adam reflects a few days later that 'elle aime tous les garçons d'une tendresse maternelle sage et attendrie.' Later, her letters to him during his military training are full of 'des paroles maternelles et indulgentes'.

None of this prevents their becoming lovers, but gradually the maternal side becomes dominant. 'A mesure que j'avance dans sa connaissance elle est moins désirable et plus nécessaire' remarks Adam at one point, and a few pages later: 'C'est au moment où je suis près d'elle que je suis le plus incapable de penser à mon désir.' And most revealing of all is his confession to her: 'Je voudrais être ton enfant [...]. Etre né de toi.' Of the two images of Irène, therefore, the maternal one initially prevails. As lover ('mauvaise femme') she must be rejected, replaced. Eric has already offered one alternative; military training will provide another: 'il était en avance de cinq minutes au rassemblement, impatient de marcher sur la route avec les autres sans avoir à se préoccuper de l'endroit où il allait.' On his return to camp after Christmas he imagines 'un ordre du corps et de l'âme presque monacal',[29] and finally 'il put accepter le souvenir d'Irène sans douleur et sans honte. Elle n'existait plus. Ni lui-même.'

But by now Irène as maternal figure has been rejected as well, and Adam, almost in spite of himself, turns back to his own mother, recognizing, as he leaves for his military training, that he wishes he will be more dear to her than her husband had been during the First World War: 'Il savait les déchirements de son père les derniers jours d'une permission, il voulait être "mieux" que lui, et que secrètement, elle le préfère.' Yet once he has returned to the army his attempts to contact his family are at best only half-hearted, and the novel closes with Adam convinced he can make the break with Irène and embark on a life of decisiveness and purpose. The last words are: '"Quand je songe à toutes ces bêtises d'où je viens, je peux dire que ça va mieux, ça va mieux [...]." Puis il se surprit à murmurer "le mieux de la fin".'

The tone of this ending is of course an all too familiar one, and even from this very brief account of the novel it will be apparent that much of it is obvious and naive. The principal personal elements – material, emotional and intellectual – are at best only thinly disguised, and while Courtade may well have been aware that by reworking them he might be able to avoid the autobiographical trap, he fails to do so. But even if, like other elements, it is transparent, the presentation of the central relationship between Eric, Irène and Adam is not without interest. Superficially it may well reflect the early signs of a restlessness within marriage that would come to a head in the mid 1950s. The transposition of Boris from brother to lover also reflects in a telling way Courtade's jealousy over Génia's reactions to her brother's death, which had surfaced in their correspondence. But it is in those elements of the tension between a desire (conscious or subconscious) and a refusal to be absorbed or protected by another that we find a clue to Courtade's future. While at the close of the novel Adam may believe that he has achieved freedom, we know from the past that this is only one stage in a cyclical pattern that sees him search for and return to some kind of security. The appeal but then terror of the unknown has to be balanced against the equal appeal and terror of being protected and suffocated. It is no coincidence (though Courtade may not have been aware of its significance) that the closing scene of the novel should take place near a stream and waterfall, and that Adam should throw the letter he tries to write to Irène ending their relationship into the water. This pattern, what Vailland later and in a different context would refer to in his own case as 'agir ou être agi', would remain with Courtade to the end of his life and would never be completely resolved. The tension that resulted from it would cause him much personal anguish, but at the same time stimulate journalism and imaginative writing of high quality.

Courtade's situation in general terms was not unique; many in a whole generation of writers and intellectuals experienced to some degree or other a tension between independence or individual activity and commitment or alignment with others. Courtade was soon to join them. Before the end of the school year 1939-40 his life began to move in a new and significant direction. Initially, and with a career in teaching in mind, he began to prepare himself once again for the *agrégation* under the general guidance of Jean Thomas in Lyon. In 1939 the theme for the first part of the English literature course had been 'L'inquiétude et la *mélancolie* dans la littérature de la Renaissance anglaise' (my italics); it could hardly have been more aptly named. It summed up a decade of uncertainty in Courtade's life, and *Hamlet* (a prescribed text) would remain influential, and eventually provide him with a model for *Elseneur*. A year later the new course, entitled 'Les débuts du *réalisme* dans la littérature élisabethienne' (my italics again), seems with hindsight to have been prophetic. But it was not so much the intellectual demands of study as the material circumstances of his life which were decisive. Through the efforts and recommendations of Georges Altmann and Jean Thomas Courtade would secure a post with the major regional paper *Le Progrès de Lyon*. From the world of journalism he would in turn find his way to the Resistance and beyond to the ranks of the PCF.

NOTES

1. In his diary 14 October 1958 Courtade would reflect on the fear which he and his sister felt for him and on 'le sentiment de bonheur dans la maison les soirs où il n'était pas là.'

2. The spelling and punctuation of these letters have not been corrected.

3. Before his early death in 1962 Courtade's son Serge showed some talent as an artist.

4. La Bibliothèque française, Paris, 1949, pp. 43–4. Full bibliographical details of Courtade's work will be found in the Bibliography (pp. 239–240); page references are given in the text.

5. Gallimard, 1972, Paris, pp. 402–3.

6. Quoted in Yves Courrière, *Roger Vailland, ou un libertin au regard froid*, Plon, Paris, pp. 199; 358.

7. It is worth recording Julien Gracq's remark: 'Comme tous les lycéens j'ai écrit des alexandrins, fort mauvais vers ma treizième et quatorzième année', *Julien Gracq. Qui êtes vous?*, La Manufacture, Paris, 1986, p. 119.

8. According to Génia, Courtade's parents took every opportunity to send him abroad on school visits.

9. For them to write to one another in English was not unusual.

10. In a letter to Jacqueline Dyard (19 December 1932) Courtade had written: 'Je crois que la chose la plus sotte et la plus insupportable dans la vie c'est de prendre parti.'

11. Born out by reports in the local Austrian press.

12. Brother also of Pauline. The father, like Courtade's, was a freemason – hence, according to Jean-Jacques de Meyenbourg, their friendship.

13. On 29 October [1933] Courtade wrote to her: 'je sens tellement las ma pauvre Line, c'est tellement *bête* le *métier* que je fais – je suis tellement dégoûté que ça ne me fait plus rien, je nage dans la résignation, après tout, quelles choses ont de l'importance? Ce n'était *pas* la vie que j'avais rêvée, et puis après, tant pis, tant pis – Je m'en fiche systématiquement. Voilà pourquoi je n'entrerai jamais à l'école!!'

14. For some discussion of this issue in the 1930s see my *Literature and the Left in France*, Macmillan and Methuen, London, 1983 and 1985, Chapter 5.

15. See Karl-Anders Arvidsson, *Henry Poulaille et la littérature prolétarienne française des années 1930*, Kungälv, Goterna, 1988, pp. 88–90.

16. Editions Grasset, Paris, 1935, p. 42.

17. Ibid., p. 13.

18. Dated 12 November 1935, the letter is signed P. Tiouch.

19. In his letter to Montherlant Courtade writes: 'Je suis ce qu'on appelle "un intellectuel", je prépare une "grande école", je ne suis pas sportif parce que [quoique bien portant et assez bien fait – crossed out] je suis très vite fatigué, et mon souffle m'abandonne.'

20. I have not been able to trace it.

21. Letter to Génia 25 March 1939; 'je suis définitivement reçu au diplôme et déjà inscrit pour l'Agrégation (j'ai eu 14/20 à l'écrit du diplôme!).'

22. Some of this experience would be reworked in 'La Bonne Brebis' in *Les Circonstances*.

23. 'Eric' appears as 'Erik' and 'Erick'; I have standardized the spelling.

24. Letter to Génia dated by her 18 July 1939: 'Ce matin j'ai trouvé une lettre de Cazamian m'informant que j'avais été récalé à l'Agrégation à 1 point/un), il fallait 39 et j'ai eu 38. 16/20 en dissertation française, 12.5/20 – anglaise, 5½/15

en thème et 4/15 en version!!!! Il est évident que je ne sais pas l'anglais!'

25. There are notes for a short story 'Le Drame', seemingly based on these experiences, dated 9 June. This was never completed, but the experience may well have contributed to 'L'utilité des miroirs' in *Les Animaux supérieurs* and to Part III of *La Place rouge.*

26. The earliest date in the packet of notes relating to the novel is 19 August 1940. The end of the typescript has 'FIN. Thiers le 15 août 1940, La Cluse le 6 juin 1941'. Added below is 'Lyon Nov. 1941.'

27. There are hints of anti-Semitic sentiments in the manuscript and two marginal drawings of the star of David.

28. There are at lease seven references to this idea.

29. An interesting echo of Dyard's reference to his 'vie de moine'.

– 2 –

From Apprenticeship
to Commitment

There is no record of Courtade's having attempted to find a publisher for *Eric et Irène,* and it is unlikely, in any case, that it would have been accepted without substantial modification. He also recognized its weaknesses himself. In a letter dated 20 June 1942 he writes to Génia: 'il m'est devenu impossible de reprendre mon roman parce qu'il était de l'adolescence [...] je n'ai pas encore trouvé les moyens et l'expression de mon âge mûr – et en même temps je suis obligé de lutter par un grand travail intérieur pour garder ce qu'il y avait de mieux dans la jeunesse.' But the novel was important for him on three counts in particular: first because he had at last found the self-discipline and stamina to finish a work of this size; second, because certain sections of it proved beyond all doubt his talent as an imaginative writer; third, and perhaps most crucially, because its completion in a way represented an exorcism of much (though not all) of his past. Courtade was now ready to move forward on three interrelated fronts – journalism, politics and imaginative writing – and embark on a career that would single him out as one of the most talented writers of his generation.

As for so many of his contemporaries, the catalyst in all this was Lyons. As we have seen Courtade's chances of securing a post with the *Progrès de Lyon* were good. Georges Altmann had already been instrumental in making his name known to Henri Brémond, editor-in-chief of the paper, and Jean Thomas arranged for Courtade to be interviewed in May 1941. He appears to have begun work in August, though according to both Génia and a fellow journalist Georges Grappin his responsibilities were modest. His principal task was to cover news items of local interest for the 'rubrique régionale', his first assignment being a report on a Fête des Compagnons ('tout à fait ridicule et sans intérêt') at Francheville.[1] Even so, his position gave him the right to attend the paper's main editorial meetings, and he appears to have made a sufficiently favourable impression on Brémond to have been asked to assist Altmann in an interview with the publisher Bernard Grasset.[2]   The interview was never published, however, since Grasset, who had retained the right to vet what they intended to write, withdrew his permission, but it was Courtade's first glimpse of the kind of work which was to become the norm for him within only a few years.

But it was not only the introduction to the invigorating world of journalism, with its editorial meetings, its dead-lines and last-minute changes of copy, which was important to Courtade. In Lyons he also found, as Vailland had done only months before, an intellectual, literary and political climate quite different from anything he had previously experienced. Already through Jean Thomas he had made the acquaintance of Auguste Anglès, who wrote in *Combat*, and with whom he was to become involved in the Resistance. He also met René Tavernier, editor of the review *Confluences*, in which several of the stories to appear in *Les Circonstances* would first be published. Aragon and Elsa Triolet too were soon part of his circle of intimates. And in addition Courtade frequented the former brothel and now restaurant 'Chez Antoinette', which had become the meeting-place for the journalists of the newspapers and magazines in the *Paris-Soir* group of publications – *Paris-Midi*, *Sept-Jours*, *Marie-Claire* and *Match* – which had left Paris and was under the general control of Jean Prouvost. Here, in what Hervé Mille has described as the 'cantine du groupe',[3] he mixed with those who would continue to play important (if sometimes conflictual) roles in his life – Jeannie Chauveau, Georges Szekeres, Roger Vailland, Jacques-Francis Rolland, Edgar Morin, for example – and rediscovered his erstwhile Lakanal friend Pierre Hervé.

The *Progrès de Lyon* had never proclaimed a single political line, and had employed journalists whose political allegiances ranged across the spectrum from the PCF to the Action Française.[4] When, in November 1942, the editors refused to obey a directive issued by the Nazi authorities to print an article denouncing British and American policies, however, it was forcibly closed down.   Some of the journalists found employment elsewhere; others committed themselves wholly to the Resistance. Courtade did both. Precisely when he became involved in any organized form of clandestine activity is not clear.[5] His friendship with the *Confluences* group would have provided him with the opportunity to commit himself from an early date, and Georges Altmann was certainly active from late 1941 or early 1942 in the activities stemming from *Franc-Tireur*. Secrecy was and remained paramount, of course. In a conversation with Yves Courrière, René Tavernier commented: 'Dans notre milieu tout le monde faisait de la résistance [...] mais on ne se posait jamais de questions sur nos probables activités clandestines. Ça ne se faisait pas. Chacun effectuait son boulot dans le secret [...] on restait discrets.'[6]

While Courtade's precise role remains unknown, therefore, it seems probable that he was eventually engaged as a messenger in Paris and between Lyons and the capital – a responsibility reflected in 'Occupations' and 'Une douzaine d'huîtres', two of the stories in *Les Circonstances*, and in Part IV of *La Place rouge*. In 1943 he was also involved in the creation of an underground organization (of which the principal member was Anglès), the Agence d'information et de documents, which was linked in particular with *Combat* and *France-Tireur*. How and why the Nazis bcame suspicious of his activities is not known; but on 6 June 1944, having resettled in Paris, he was arrested, together with Annie Hervé and Pierre Grappin, in a café in the Rue de l'Abbaye and taken to Fresnes. Courtade was released after four days, but Annie Hervé was deported, and spent several months in concentration camps.[7]

Whatever the precise details and chronology of his activities Courtade had also begun to write for a Vichy publication, *Compagnons*, a year before the enforced closure of the *Progrès de Lyon*. While it seems reasonable to accept the explanation given by Génia and others that such work gave the impression of a political 'correctness' and acted as a cover for his Resistance activities, it is also likely that with his growing family responsibilities[8] Courtade needed the extra money.

A weekly paper, *Compagnons* was the official publication of the Compagnons de France, an organisation masterminded by Henri Dhavernas, who had already been active in the scouting movement, and Paul Beaudoin, Minister for Foreign Affairs in Pétain's first government. Their concern was twofold. They wished to provide some kind of social structure for those people who had fled the occupied zone, and they targeted in particular young men between 16 or 20 in whom a sense of pride and belief in Pétain's 'Révolution nationale' would be encouraged to flourish. Not surprisingly, their project met with immediate approval, and Weygand expressed himself willing to release officer-class soldiers to assist in the first stages of the movement's organization. The Compagnons de France officially came into being on 27 July 1940, and a first mass meeting was held between 1 and 4 August at Randan just south of Vichy.

Three kinds of *compagnies* were established. The *compagnie autonome* was for young unemployed people, groups of whom would be settled near a town or village, where they would receive basic instruction in agricultural and artisanal work and assist local people. They would receive board and lodging and a loan of one franc per day. The *compagnie normale* grouped together those already with employment, and encouraged a sense of discipline and pride. The *compagnie itinérante*, as its name suggests, was composed of young artisans who would be sent to communities where local workers had either been killed or were prisoners of war. Each camp had a strict hierarchy; camp-life was organised, with periods of recreation and communal activities. For all official functions a uniform, with beret and scarf, was worn. Recruitment was made without concern either for class or for education, and the movement's aims were described in *Compagnons*, 21 December 1940.

> Remettre aux jeunes de travailler et de choisir un métier, non pas selon le hasard des circonstances, mais selon leurs aptitudes, leur goût et leurs forces, tel est le but immédiat des Compagnons. [...]
>
> Ils lui enseignent l'amour et le dévouement à la Patrie, ils lui apprennent à développer sa personnalité, à approfondir sa foi, à respecter la famille. Le Mouvement Compagnon est une école de discipline et d'enrichissement moral. Il est aussi une école de perfectionnement physique. Le Compagnon développe sa santé et son corps par l'éducation physique (méthode naturelle) et par les sports, le Compagnon devient un homme ardent et fort dans son travail. Prêt à se dévouer pour sa famille et la grandeur de la Patrie, tel est le Compagnon.

By 1943 the movement claimed a membership of 28,000 and the annual rally at Randan in August was said to attract 7,000. From the early stages, with its 'ton rude et prolétaire', an organization had emerged in which the *cadres* of the 'new' France were being formed. In this respect one section in particular was significant, the compagnie d'Uriage at the Château Bayard on the outskirts of Grenoble, where various intellectuals gathered (Raymond Aron, Emmanuel Mounier,

Julien Benda for example), and from which a significant resistance movement grew.[9]

Compagnons had then been in existence for a year, and had clearly set out its values and allegiance to Pétain before Courtade began to contribute to it. Given his attitude at Nantua and the contacts he had already begun to make in Lyons any sympathy on his part would seem impossible. But Courtade had yet, publically at least, to confirm a political position. Like Vailland in 1940–1 he must have appeared to most as at best apolitical and at worst disinterested. Just as there is little or no record of his reactions to the events of February 1934 or to the establishment of Blum's Front populaire two years later, so there is nothing about the event which split the extreme left in France in 1939, the Nazi–Soviet Pact. Only on 4 July 1941, when events had changed and Hitler had attacked the Soviet Union, do we find a statement (written in red ink...) suggesting a new conviction:

> Jamais la défaite n'a été si certaine, et jamais la révolution si proche. Cette immense armée invincible perdue dans un pays qui n'est pas à la mesure de l'Europe, détournée de sa tâche essentielle qui est d'abattre la Grande-Bretagne, cernée dans quelques mois par la neige et par la famine perdra sa jeunesse et sa foi dans l'hiver Russe [*sic*]. En même temps les peuples de l'Europe, lassés, reprendront de la liberté. Les anciennes querelles se tairont, les partisans harcèleront l'ennemi et le frapperont partout où il sera. L'immense machine se disloquera. De la Sibérie à la Bretagne les vainqueurs désespérés ne seront qu'une poussière de forces. L'aviation anglo-américaine fera le reste. Dans un an le monde sera en pleine insurrection.

Significantly this is followed by a note: 'Conduite personnelle: observance stricte de la légalité', and by the familiar list of resolutions.[10] The whole is concluded by: 'Ce jour-là mon âme est définitivement sortie de l'enfance. *Mon destin est fait.*'

If such reflections truly indicate Courtade's position by the summer of 1941, then the suggestion that his involvement with *Compagnons* was a cover may indeed be correct. His articles for the paper are varied and show no signs of conforming to a particular orthodoxy. Only the first 'Le langage des bêtes' (18 October 1941) is signed by his real name; and, while it is just possible that it could be interpreted as an allegory about clandestine communication in a controlled and supervised society, its pompous tone and pedestrian conclusion that the topic offers a rich field for further scientific investigation suggest that it is little more than a space-filler. Thereafter, between 6 December and June 1942, five articles signed by Pierre Aimery were published – the pseudonym being confirmed by the manuscripts of several. Again they appear to be random and disparate pieces. The first is an enthusiastic tribute to the American writer Jack London, 'L'Homme au grand air et de la grand'route tel était Jack London qui, il y a 25 ans, mourut au bout de son rêve.' The others are: 'Le brave générale Cambronne est mort il y a cent ans', in which the soldier's gallant and heroic exploits at Waterloo are described; 'Quand Japonais et Hollandais célébraient leur amitié', a historical survey of the relations between the two countries; 'Le père au foyer', which, in a tone entirely typical of *Compagnons,* extols the virtue of men who have had to bring up their children single-handed; and finally a piece of escapist travelogue writing on the French West Indies, 'Voici les îles de nos rêves'.

By the issues of early 1942 two changes in particular to *Compagnons* are evident. First, there are more unsigned articles (though they still represent a minority); and second, the cover from 14 February until the last issues in January 1944 bears the subtitle 'L'hebdomadaire courageux d'une époque difficile'. Whether either is significant is difficult to say, though increasingly the various *compagnies* of the parent organization were becoming centres of Resistance groups and suspected as such by the Nazis. Courtade's involvement after June 1942 remains a matter for speculation. Pierre Aimery no longer features amongst the names of contributors, but a new column by Henry Lapierre appears for the first time on 26 September. No manuscripts have been found to confirm the suspicion that once again Pierre Henri Courtade resorted to a *nom de plume,* and, superficially at least, the subject of these articles – sport – was hardly one associated with him. Their coverage is wide. The first article is about the Swedish distance runner Gunder Haegg ('Gunder Haegg est-il un phénomène?'); and thereafter, at approximately weekly intervals, Lapierre writes about athletics, swimming, cycling, football, basket-ball and boxing, as well as about more general issues such as the harmful effects of professionalism, the participation of women or the danger of exposing the young to fierce competition too early in their sporting careers.

Throughout these articles three themes are constant: the value of the effort involved, a preference for a kind of classical amateurism in the face of the growing corruption of professionalism and the important formative influence of sport on the young. On the opening of the new cross-country season in November 1942, for example, we read: 'De tous les sports, le cross est certainement celui qui fait le plus appel à la seule valeur physique d'abord; dans cet effort prolongé qui veut du courage et de l'endurance, avant tout, le jeune sportif trouve la meilleure leçon qui se puisse donner d'énergie et de volonté sportive' (28 November). Two months later on 9 January 1943, Lapierre writes: 'un examen de longue haleine, qui n'est certes pas indispensable à la vie, mais qui contribue singulièrement à l'embellir'. Such remarks are, ostensibly at least, entirely orthodox. Moral regeneration through sport was one of the prime objectives of the Vichy régime, initially pursued by Pétain's first minister for youth, family and sport Jean Ybarnégaray, who was in turn enthusiastically supported by the tennis star Jean Borotra. Read more closely, however, a large proportion of these articles, with their emphasis on *courage* and *endurance*, could be interpreted as thinly coded messages of support for the struggle against the occupying forces, which grew substantially during 1943. Equally interesting is the fact that these particular qualities which are highlighted are those demanded by the few physical activities to which Courtade himself was attracted in earlier years – swimming, running and cycling.

Henry Lapierre also contributed one other article quite separate from his usual *rubrique sportive*. On 6 November 1943 he wrote an obituary for the theatre director André Antoine, whose particular value was that 'il arrivait à une époque où le théâtre français, insensible au réalisme qui gagnait la littérature et les Beaux-Arts, se confinait dans une fadeur et une fausse préciosité, generalisatrices d'un laisser-aller dangereux.' Towards the end of the nineteenth century Antoine had tried to make the theatre more accessible to the general public, and in 1887 had created the Théâtre Libre, which, before it had to close as a result of financial difficulties, had promoted naturalist plays and farces. Lapierre's comments are certainly accurate, and can be read as a generous tribute; but they also reflect a general theory about the need for art and for literature in particular to be socially and politically relevant. Courtade was beginning to formulate such ideas, and would express them with growing conviction after the Liberation. A claim on the basis of this single obituary that Lapierre and Courtade are one and the same person would patently be absurd; but when the piece is read in conjunction with the articles on sport and given the practice of anonymity or pseudonyms, the identification seems probable. It is also certain that Courtade was being paid by *Compagnons* during 1943: a note to Génia indicates that he is to receive a salary increase (to 4,300 francs per month plus bonuses) from 1 June. And on 2 September Génia writes to him: 'Je comprends que *Compagnons* te barbe mais que faire ...' Whatever the precise truth there can be no doubt that Courtade's journalistic experience with *Compagnons* was invaluable. He clearly had a freer hand than at the *Progrès de Lyon* and if the identification with Lapierre is correct we can see both how his writing gained in subtlety and control and how his political position was becoming more defined. By 1944 he was ready for a major role in *Action* and for the last stage in his apprenticeship as a journalist before he immersed himself totally in the ranks of the Party's scribes.[11]

Courtade was certainly already familiar with *Action* in its first, clandestine form. It appeared in October 1943 as a weekly paper and as the voice of Action Ouvrière, an offshoot of the Mouvement de la Libération National, encouraging resistance to the Nazi policy of the Service du Travail Obligatoire by which French workers were forced to go to Germany. The group had centres in major towns in the southern zone like Toulouse, Montpellier and Lyons, where the paper was begun by Emmanuel D'Astier de la Vigerie. For six months it was distributed clandestinely, until April 1944, when the premises where it, *Combat*, *Franc-Tireur* and other resistance papers were printed, were discovered and destroyed by the Nazis. A decision was taken to move the headquarters of the paper to Paris, a task given to Victor Leduc, a philosophy teacher sacked by the Vichy authorities and already a member of the PCF for ten years. For four months he produced it virtually single-handed on an ancient manual press in Montreuil, taking an entire week, so he claimed,[12] to print 10,000 – 15,000 copies. With the Liberation *Action* could be found new premises, and by September had acquired the sumptuous offices at 3 Rue des Pyramides formerly occupied by Alphonse de Chateaubriant's collaborationist weekly *La Gerbe.* On 9 September 1944 the first number of the 'new' *Action* appeared, describing itself as the 'hebdomadaire de l'indépendance française'. Firmly on the Left,

With Jacques-Francis Rolland in 1945.

its political stance was underlined in this issue by the reproduction of a poster depicting two Resistance fighters, one firing a rifle, the other standing against a wall firing a revolver. On it five dates are written: 1789, 1830, 1848, 1871, 1944. Designed by Paul Colin, the poster had been banned on the grounds that it could be interpreted as an incitement to civil war; but as a banner for the new weekly paper it supported *Action*'s first editorial admirably: 'Les hommes torturés, les femmes déportés, ceux du maquis et ceux des barricades continuent leur action. Ce journal exprimera leur volonté et dira leur effort.'

The hard core of the editorial team comprised a principal editor, Maurice Kriegel-Valrimont, who had been involved with the original *Action* in Lyons, Victor Leduc, Pierre Hervé, Joinville, Fauché and Courtade. The paper quickly attracted important contributors, and from early issues articles appeared over such names as Claude Roy, Edgar Morin, Jacques-Francis Rolland, Simone de Beauvoir, Sartre, Aragon, Vailland, Jacques Duclos and André Wurmser. Francis Ponge had responsibility for the cultural section, and it was here that a young photographer Robert Doisneau first began to make an impression.

While the paper continued to be financially supported by the PCF it was not yet subject to any form of political control or interference. To use Claude Roy's phrase, this was 'un journal communisant vivant, sans jargon [...] un journal ouvert';[13] Hervé has written about its 'atmosphère fraternelle' and 'tribune de discussion'.[14] Nor indeed were all who formed part of the editorial team Party members. Hervé and Leduc were intransigently so; Jean-Jacques de Meyenbourg joined in 1944, to Courtade's scorn. Vailland, Roy and Courtade himself had still not committed themselves. Such a lack of conformity hardly mattered. All of them shared a belief in the need for a regeneration of society based on popular revolution, and Party leaders had nothing to be alarmed at in the tone of the early issues. Opposition – ironic in view of the subsequent Stalinism of several of *Action*'s writers – to the personality cult of De Gaulle was overt. In the first issue Leduc rejects the cult with some violence:

> Ce qu'il faut à la France disait récemment un journal du matin, c'est une mystique et un chef. [...] Non, il n'est pas besoin d'une mystique pour

galvaniser un pays qui s'est rué aux barricades. Sa volonté d'être libre lui suffit [...]. Ce qu'il faut à la France, ce n'est pas une mystique, c'est une pensée lucide et audacieuse, ne reculant devant aucune solution neuve aux problèmes politiques et sociaux. Ce n'est pas un chef: c'est des millions de chefs, capables d'initiative et admis aux responsabilités.

A month later, on 6 October, the editorial was even more pointed:

Il y avait dans nos campagnes ceux qui gardaient des photos de Pétain. Après la libération ils ont enlevé les photos de Pétain. Ils ont mis à leur place les photos du général de Gaulle, mais ils ont conservé les mêmes cadres. Ces cadres conservés sont l'image d'une France vieille et impuissante. Ceux qui ont accepté Pétain et la trahison – sans être les traîtres – sont prêts à accepter toute politique nouvelle. On ne fera pas une politique française forte et indépendante en s'appuyant sur les branches mortes d'un pays qui renaît.

In the main part of the paper Pierre Hervé produced a series of articles in which he repeatedly called for a collective action based on and inspired by the achievements of the Resistance. On 29 September, for example, we read:

Il s'était créé dans notre pays une magnifique unanimité nationale, qui avait entraîné de gré ou de force ceux qui, par intérêt ou par calcul, avaient la tentation de s'y soustraire. Il s'agissait de maintenir cette unanimité. Il fallait que tous, ceux de la Résistance extérieure comme de la Résistance intérieure, des cercles du gouvernement comme des milieux plus populaires, entreprennent de la maintenir, non dans un ordre figé, mais dans un mouvement qui devait redonner à la France la justice sociale dans une indépendance nationale reconquise.

Early the following year, on 26 January, in an article entitled 'La mort de la Résistance ou son union', the theme is repeated. What is required above all is '(une) union pour amener le peuple français à conquérir son indépendance nationale, tout en se libérant des servitudes économiques et financières. Union à longue échéance, qui associera la classe ouvrière et tous les Français animés d'un esprit de justice sociale.'

The message was a popular one, and *Action* did well. Every week 50,000 copies were printed and quickly sold.[15] Yet the paper owed its success more to the enthusiasm and conviction of the contributors than to journalistic experience. Of those writing in the early issues Courtade was the only one to have had any of real note; and, if Rolland is to be believed, he often had to take responsibility for chivvying his colleagues and putting an entire issue together at the last minute.

Courtade's personal contribution to *Action* began in the first issue with a column 'Les événements internationaux', a direct anticipation of the role he would fill for *L'Humanité* two years later. This was a different Courtade from the one who wrote in *Compagnons*. Assured and authoritative, his articles over the weeks analyse international events in keeping with the general spirit of the paper. Criticism is directed instantly at financial trusts, at economic and political imperialism, at the Catholic church and the politics of the Vatican, and at all signs of any attempt either to reformulate the idea of a French nation through a projection of De Gaulle as a kind of mystical leader or to express nostalgia for the values which had underpinned Pétain's policies. Above all there are constant warnings about the ever-present threat, of renascent fascism. When Mussolini is executed by the Italian people in May 1945 Courtade argues for the values of popular justice (4 May 1945); Franco is seen as a continuing threat and as someone with whom all ties should be broken (13 July 1945).

While he grudgingly recognizes the need for political alliances in the immediate post-Liberation months (23 February 1945), we find an increasing mistrust both of the United States and of Britain. On Roosevelt's death Courtade's warm tribute to this 'champion d'une démocratie agissante' also contains dark hints of an alternative political climate which would prove to be only too accurate: 'les appels et les directives de Roosevelt ne visaient pas à autre chose qu'à mettre le fascisme et le nazisme en face de leurs responsabilités et, par la démonstration éclatante de leur fourberie, à ruiner leur crédit auprès d'une fraction de l'opinion américaine encore égarée.'[16] Churchill receives plaudits on several occasions. On 13 October 1944 Courtade admires his diplomacy at the Moscow conference; on 2 March 1945 he is approved for not questioning the Soviet Union's good faith. Once the Labour Party has been returned to government in Britain later that year, however, the tone changes: 's'il [Churchill] fut absolument loyal dans la guerre, il fut aussi jadis l'un des ennemis les plus acharnés de la jeune république soviétique et l'un des inspirateurs de la coalition mondiale contre le pouvoir des soviets.'

Over Germany Courtade argues strongly for the perpetrators of Nazism to be brought to justice, but at the same time underlines the need to re-educate the German people. On 29 September 1944, in 'Que faire de l'Allemagne vaincue', he writes: 'Quelle que soit la répugnance qu'on éprouve à gagner la confiance d'une population que son apathie a rendue complice des crimes de ces chefs, la nécessité politique imposera, tôt ou tard, de compléter des mesures de répression par une persuasion intelligente et appuyée sur les faits.' Six months later his tone is much harder, even if the policy is more sharply defined:

> il faut donc que chaque Allemand soit d'abord vaincu et qu'il le sache, c'est le commencement de son salut [...]. Tout cela ne servirait à rien si ses ennemis principaux, le prussianisme et les trusts n'étaient pas irrémédiablement réduits à l'impuissance. C'est ici qu'on voit qu'un traitement rigoureux de l'Allemagne vaincue concorde exactement avec les intérêts du peuple allemand lui-même.

Such faith in the essential probity of 'le peuple' and in their regenerative capacities not surprisingly is voiced especially in articles on the Soviet Union, whose integrity in the aftermath of victory cannot be questioned: 'Seule, la propagande ennemie peut laisser croire que l'Union soviétique abusera de la situation.'[17] In the kinds of statements that would become the norm in the Communist press, Courtade argues that, unlike other Allied countries, whose imperialist ambitions could already be seen in their negotiating positions over east European countries and the Middle East, where the democratic voice of the people was being ignored, the Soviet Union was planning for the future 'sous la direction d'un gouvernement qui a l'approbation des 9/10 de la population.'[18]

Ideas such as these dominate articles that often appear to have been written to a preconceived formula: an opening proposition of a general nature, followed by a description of the immediate circumstances that occasion it, which prompt questions to be debated. Underlying the whole is a wariness and even refusal of generalization, abstraction and idealization. What must dictate decision-making should be the active constraints of a given situation; only then can a pragmatic and historically-guided course of action be adopted. This general pattern is one that will dominate Courtade's foreign affairs articles as his technique is honed and perfected through the columns of *Démocratie nouvelle*, *Les Cahiers du Communisme* and above all *L'Humanité*. A tone is established. The reader is flattered. An appeal to his or her reasonableness – and reason – is carried by a judicious sprinkling of questions, to which answers are then provided as though there could be no sensible alternative. Possible counter-arguments or objections are voiced and met. Structurally the articles are normally made of paragraphs containing a single point each; and if sentences appear occasionally to be overlong, it is often because an argument is being developed through a series of clauses. At the same time the short sentence is used where necessary to good effect usually to underline a conclusion or to claim triumphantly a self-evident truth that is finally brought out into the open.

But Courtade was not only developing the skills required by a journalist obliged by his paper's schedule to produce concise politically instructive articles in every issue at short notice. He also wrote longer pieces, which, while having the same political framework and direction, revealed his descriptive and narrative skills. One illustration of this is an article he wrote in November 1944 describing a visit to London, where he claims to have found a society economically transformed by the war and on the verge of fundamental change.[19] But beyond the political point is a concern for detail and atmosphere of the kind already occasionally glimpsed in *Eric et Irène*. He observes, for example, Victoria station and people as they return home from work:

> Les visages sont penchés sur les journaux, un peu moins épais qu'avant la guerre, et la vieille odeur anglaise du tabac de Virginia, le parfum entêtant des drugstores flottent dans l'air humide de novembre. Les courts taxis haut perchés virent sur place. Au-delà des kiosques à journaux, éclatants de couleurs vives, le black-out enveloppe la ville. Pas tant d'uniformes qu'on pourrait croire. Ici et là, le pompon rouge d'un marin français met une note gaie dans un cône lumineux.

In the same article he describes the effects of the *blitz* on south London:

> Derrière les façades miraculeusement préservées, les ruines ont déjà la patine des années, des pissenlits ont poussé dans les salles d'opération des hôpitaux détruits. C'est un décor de la campagne de Rome au bord de la Tamise. Ou mieux, ces ruines élégantes qu'aimaient les peintres français du dix-septième siècle. La mort est propre et tranquille comme un cimetière de la campagne anglaise. Dans les quartiers ouvriers, d'immenses espaces ont été entourés de murs bas qui portent le nom des anciennes rues. Le sol a été nivelé, les papiers peints arrachés.

Equally striking is the description of a German town that he and Claude Roy visited in May 1945, which he will adapt for 'La Carpe', the final and one of the grimmest stories in *Les Circonstances*: 'On n'imagine à quel point une ville détruite est immense. Partout l'air et du ciel. C'est la campagne sans verdure. Un lieu géométrique. Le silence de la campagne sans le chant des grillons un chant de mort.'[20]

This pattern of contributions by Courtade – concise, pithy articles on major international events interspersed with the occasional and more discursive *grand reportage* on a foreign town or country[21] – would be maintained, albeit with increasing irregularity, until the end of his collaboration with *Action* and the paper's disappearance. That *Action* should find itself eventually in conflict with the PCF was perhaps inevitable, given the disparate political nature of its staff and the consequent occasional expression of opinions that did not wholly reflect Party orthodoxy at a time when it was beginning to enjoy real influence.[22] Courtade, we should remember, was not yet a Party member; but the tenor and rigour of his articles on international events – not only in *Action* but in *Les Cahiers du Communisme* for which he began to write in July 1946 – attracted the attention of Maurice Thorez who, though Kriegel-Valrimont, would invite him to join the staff of *L'Humanité* in the same month, at which point membership was both essential and automatic. But if Courtade had given unequivocal evidence of his faith in Communism in his articles and the various talks and discussion groups organized by *Action*,[23] one incident in November 1946 briefly threw a shadow across events in a way that would be repeated more seriously in almost identical circumstances a decade later.

By the summer of 1946 Stalin's Minister of Culture Andrei Zdanov began to issue his directives on the need to promote the values of socialist realism in art and literature. In France opposition to such rigidity was voiced by Roger Garaudy (whose political credentials could not be doubted) in *Arts de France*. In *Action* Pierre Hervé pursued the same line in an article entitled 'Il n'y a pas d'esthétique communiste' (22 November), calling for diversity and opposing the 'rôle sacerdotal' of the artist. Such views provoked an instant reply from Aragon in *Les Lettres françaises* and when Hervé went further and claimed to find in works by Aragon and Elsa Triolet elements which would be anathema to Zdanov the incident threatened to explode. A further article by Hervé was withdrawn after Thorez personally intervened.[24]

Ten years later Hervé would challenge Party orthodoxy in much the same way, and his essay *La Révolution et les fétiches* would see him subjected to bitter, violent attack and eventual exclusion. As we shall see, Courtade would experience considerable anguish in 1956, at a time when both personally and politically he was in a state of some crisis; but in 1946 matters were different. He already enjoyed Aragon's friendship and patronage, and professionally could ill afford to antagonize him by showing any public support for his friend. He tried to adopt a tone of conciliation, and even reminded Aragon of his own turbulent, iconoclastic past with the Surrealists; but, unlike others – Leduc and to some extent Vailland – he refused to be drawn further. In a letter to his first wife, Andrée Blavette, Vailland wrote of the whole affair: 'Bagarre qui est aussi l'occasion d'éprouver les hommes et m'a confirmé ton intuition de la faiblesse de Courtade.'[25] The point is a fair one. However compelling the professional reasons were for remaining cautious, Courtade, in public at least, bowed to Party discipline. The incident was enough to warn the PCF that *Action* was potentially dangerous. Interference with editorial policy increased, financial support was removed during the course of the following year, and the paper was obliged to close down. For Courtade this quickly became history. Within a year he was well on the way to establishing himself as one of the Party's outstanding journalists, and had taken the first steps along a path that would lead to a prestigious career; but that career would also bring its moments of tension and crisis.

In addition to his essays and his increasing workload in journalism, Courtade continued to work at his fiction. The few papers from the early 1940s contain fragments of short stories that suggest that he was still preoccupied by sentimental tales of adolescent romance or exotic escapism. Probably with the help of Jeannie Chauveau, working as a journalist with *Marie-Claire*, he published his first short story in the magazine on 1 May 1942.[26] 'Ecrit en marge' is a slight piece, a tale of disappointed teenage romance with echoes of his relationship with Jacqueline Dyard. He would publish another four pieces in *Marie-Claire*, but his first major breakthrough in fiction came with the acceptance by Tavernier for *Confluences* of 'La Salamandre' (a story later to be incorporated in *Les Circonstances*) in November 1943. In July of the following year 'Une bonne brebis' appeared in the review; in January 1945 'Occupations', and in August of the same year 'Un Vichy allemand', an early version of 'La Carpe'.[27] Courtade owed this success in particular to Aragon, whose enthusiasm for 'La Salamandre' was extended to *Les Circonstances* as a whole, whose publication in 1946 he greeted as a major literary event.

Les Circonstances (1946)

'Pierre Courtade nous a donné avec *Les Circonstances* la plus forte *surprise* littéraire depuis l'*Enfance d'un chef* ou le *Voyage au bout de la nuit*.' Thus wrote Claude Roy in *Europe*.[28] Eight years later, when the stories were republished in a new edition illustrated with powerful, sometimes strident drawings by Edouard Pignon, Roy reviewed them again, and no less enthusiastically, in *L'Humanité*. And yet, perhaps because he relied overmuch on memory and wrote his review hurriedly or because the passage of time caused him to recall specific features at the expense of others, the thrust of what he had to say in 1954 does *Les Circonstances* less than full justice. In essence said Roy the collection was simply about the war: ' *Les Circonstances*? Une seule: la guerre, l'occupation, le fascisme au moment de son triomphe.' And yet the title alone seems rather to deny this. While there is no evidence that Courtade considered an alternative, the plural surely does invite us to look outside the immediate circumstances of 1940–1944, even though these may be dominant and draw our attention above all else. To be sure, six of the ten stories do relate closely to the events of this period; the others, superficially at least, have little or nothing to do with them, and in two cases are strongly autobiographical. 'Une bonne brebis' has a setting clearly based on Courtade's year's experience in Southampton; 'Les Cheveux coupés en quatre' draws substantially on his time in Nantua.

All, whatever their subject, are interrelated by recurrent narrative devices and motifs, and illustrate certain preoccupations that we have already noted in his various papers and diaries and which will feature in Courtade's subsequent fiction – individual freedom, chance, choice, death, identity, love, responsibility, sincerity and so on.

In the opening story 'Occupations' we have the description of the ambushing of a Nazi car in Paris, resulting in the death of the officer in it, followed by the Nazis' response to the incident. The event has its basis in fact. The Nazi general Von Schauernburg was killed in this way early in 1943, and Courtade later wrote about it in *Action*, 6 October 1944, in an article 'Julius Ritter et le Général von Schauernburg étaient exécutés'. The account of the narrator's arrest, brief imprisonment and interrogation also undoubtedly contains more than an echo of Courtade's own experience four months earlier. Like the title of the volume as a whole, 'Occupations', with its plural, is also inviting. This is a story that takes us beyond the mere physical presence of the Nazi forces in France, and even beyond the kind of mental control that is imposed as a result, to the different 'occupations' of ordinary life which suddenly assume new significance as they are threatened with extinction – the taste of a cigarette or of bread, the sight of new buds on a tree, the glimpse of a barge on the Seine, recognition of the temporary nature of many relationships.[29] But it is also and more importantly a story that illustrates the growing realization that passivity is not sufficient, and that to escape once from the clutches of the Nazis is reason enough to embark on a life of positive commitment and continue the struggle against them. The remaining five stories dealing specifically with aspects of the Resistance will develop several of the various 'occupations' that are here held out as possibilities. They will also examine the role of fate, as well as the theme of war and brutality as particular manifestations of evil.

Just as we can only speculate about the title, so the absence either of any manuscript or of notes about *Les Circonstances* makes it impossible to say with certainty whether or not Courtade had given any serious consideration to the volume's internal organization. But there are signs, especially in the stories concerning the Occupation, that he did. In terms of simple chronology the fact that 'La Carpe', in which the action is set *after* the Allied drive into Germany is under way, should come last is appropriate. Sometimes a precise reference, it is true, seems to have significance. In 'Deux douzaines d'huîtres' a mention of the Nazis' 'dernier hiver' (p. 126) can only suggest late 1943 or early 1944; in 'Personnes seules' their presence in the south of France means that the earliest possible date for the action is the summer of 1943. But in neither case does this appear particularly relevant for the placing of the story. In the case of 'Occupations', events ought to dictate that it appear towards the end as well; but, as we have seen, the fact that it illustrates the necessity of being committed to a struggle against the Nazis demands that it should in fact come first.

After it come four stories dealing with themes and issues for which the Nazi presence on French soil has no direct relevance; in fact various autobiographical hints suggest that they belong to the pre-war decades. 'La Salamandre', the story recommended by Aragon for publication in *Confluences*, is stylistically the most adventurous. But behind Courtade's inventiveness seem to lie echoes of his childhood and adolescent years, and of his relationship with his father (here a 'receveur de l'enregistrement') and possibly with his mother as well, cast in this story in the role of the *receveur*'s wife. The couple live in a house 'fournie par l'Etat' (p. 45), a mixture perhaps of 13 rue du Chemin de Fer at Sceaux and the property provided for his parents in Auch. The narrator's decision to allow his moustache to grow could also be an amusing allusion to Courtade's attempts to do the same in the mid-1930s 'pour faire plus âgé'. More clearly in 'Une bonne brebis', Southernborough, complete with its port, Central Park and Regal Cinema, its beer and darts, is based on Southampton; James Craigg and the mental picture the narrator has of him drowning (p. 59 and p. 67) owe something to René Jammes and his death at Seeboden. The Booth family with whom they lodge recalls the one Courtade had stayed with in Norwood in 1930.

In 'Identités' there appear to be no links of this kind. It is the story of a small provincial aristocratic family, the Comte and Comtesse de Marboz-Garenzac, obsessed by their position, appearance and name, which will be immortalized by their tombs in the family vault. The comte's secretary is in love with the comtesse, and sets out (and with success), like Julien Sorel in Stendhal's *Le Rouge et le Noir*, to seize her hand and have her admit her true feelings for him. No doubt the rich peasants whose children attended the school at which Courtade taught in Nantua (as well as the parents of some of his private pupils in Paris) are in part responsible for his description of this family;

but the more direct autobiographical echoes are of a cultural kind – his fondness for Stendhal's novels together with their petulant, 'misunderstood' author, and for *Hamlet* (p. 83 and p. 85). Finally, 'Les Cheveux coupés en quatre' – the most 'autobiographical' of them all – draws heavily on his teaching experiences in Nantua. In addition to such echoes and allusions as these, there are others to a number of formative experiences of earlier years – to America and to Southampton (p. 105), to Seeboden (p. 106), to the Compagnons de France (p. 110) or possibly to the early years of his relationship with Génia (p. 112).

In broad terms there does appear to be therefore a chronological development across these four stories leading us to the point in Courtade's own life where he would leave indecision behind and commit himself to the Resistance. Clear or veiled allusions to specific events or experiences in his past are of limited interest, however, being no more than convenient points around and on which he can build a number of key themes. Even so, the positioning in particular of 'Les Cheveux coupés en quatre' as the last of the 'non-Resistance' stories is important. The title itself suggests indecision and procrastination, and at one point, when a local dignitary voices the opinion that some parents are worried about Savoy's influence on their children and that he is likely to be attracted by the vaguely radical political ideas of another colleague, Peloux, the principal's reply shows little concern: 'Savoy est incapable de faire du mal à une mouche. C'est un coupeur de cheveux en quatre. [...]. Peloux est plus vaseux que l'autre, ce sont des intellectuels' (pp. 109, 110). Elsewhere, in a passage where Savoy is (indirectly) shown to be reflecting on his response to world events as reported in the press, his own mocking self-doubt is clear:

> Il se mit à lire le journal. Il était content. Mais d'une certaine manière. Il cherchait derrière les assassinats, les bombardements et les déportations, des infrastructures. Sa perspicacité lui suffisait. Mais pas toujours ! Il s'interrogeait alors sur l'efficacité , le sens et les conditions de l'action [...]. Le journal le fascinait. Cette reconstruction graphique du monde tranquille, assurée; personne ne répondait! Personne ne disait publiquement: non, ça n'est pas vrai ! et peu à peu l'image du monde se décollait de la réalité [...] (pp. 98, 99).[30]

It is precisely the discovery of this reality – or of a particular reality – and the need to respond to it in a positive manner that provide the principal thrust of the five remaining stories. In this respect, within the collection as a whole 'Les Cheveux coupés en quatre' is pivotal.

The first of the last five, 'Deux douzaines d'huîtres', deals with the transmission and diffusion of clandestine material (again probably based, as we have noted, to some degree on Courtade's own activities), with the risks taken by those involved, with their courage, and perhaps most of all with the arbitrary nature of fate. (In his 1954 review of *Les Circonstances* Claude Roy quite properly singles out Claire, whose task it is to reproduce for distribution the material she is brought, as one of the true unsung heroes of the Resistance.) 'Personnes seules' tells the story of a small café-hotel in southern France caught up in the violent interchanges of Resistance fighters and Nazis shortly before the arrival of American forces and the Liberation. The question of what precisely the political positions of the victims are is not the issue, even though the absence of political commitment is by implication significant. The hotel owner and his friend appear *pétainiste* to a degree; the group of two young people – of whom one, Rosenbaum, is a Jew with false papers – are self-centred, bored and concerned only with their own survival. The hotel owner's friend is killed by stray bullets; he himself is shot by Nazi soldiers, who then take the young people prisoner. Two of the soldiers leave to search the rest of the hotel, and in their absence the Jew, sensing this is his only opportunity to act in some kind of meaningful way, manages to seize the remaining one's gun. Not knowing how to use it he inadvertently shoots his three companions, but when he turns it on the Nazi has run out of ammunition. The two other soldiers return and he is brutally killed. Courtade's point, once again, is that when violence comes it does so in a totally arbitrary manner. Fate is not to be controlled.

Of the last three stories the first, 'Le Médecin de campagne', is an illustration of the ways in which the *milice* infiltrate resistance networks. The doctor, himself in hiding, is called out one night by a member (Le Chat) of the local *maquis* to attend to someone who has fled there and has apparently fallen sick.[31] The whole episode is of course a trap, and the doctor is captured and led away to certain torture and death. Only by the end do we realize that he has been betrayed, even though hints are given from the beginning that all is not well. It is not clear, for example, whether Le Chat has betrayed him, and if so whether he has been forced in some way to do so, or whether the *milice*, through their own efforts, have in fact managed both to capture the doctor and to break the resistance network. Such uncertainty not only invites the reader to speculate; it also once again underlines the role of chance. But it also introduces and poignantly addresses such issues as the cynical exploitation of fellow human beings in the name of political ideology, the reliability of human nature and the capacity truly to resist. In this respect the position of 'Le Médecin de campagne' in *Les Circonstances* is significant, and is perhaps another indication that Courtade did deliberate on the collection's overall organization. For whereas it deals with a triumph, however minor, for the forces of fascism, 'Le Système', the following and penultimate story, is a tribute to a human being's capacity to resist and to survive under even the most appalling conditions.

Written as though it is based on a true account, 'Le Système' describes the fate of prisoners in Nazi hands. From first interrogation and torture we are taken on an ever-worsening nightmare journey to a concentration camp, a hard-labour colony, an underground munitions factory known simply as 'le tunnel' and eventually an extermination centre. The 'system' of the title is the sustained, brutal attempt to destroy the human spirit, to reduce human beings to a position in which they have no hope, in which life is absurd and empty of all values and in which at the end only bestiality remains. The world described is one of indiscriminate continuous violence. Darkness, bitter cold, mud and excrement are the norm relieved only occasionally and callously by interrogators ('des hommes polis' (p. 189)), the SS or the camp commandants, as part of the whole reductive and destructive process. Eventually, as he awaits death in the extermination camp, the narrator manages to escape with a handful of survivors after a bomb attack by the Allied forces. In a German village they are initially greeted with sympathy, only to be handed over to some SS officers as soon as these reappear. (Such opportunism recalls 'Personnes seules' and anticipates 'La Carpe'.) Only when it becomes quite clear that an Allied victory is at hand are the prisoners finally abandoned. The irony of the narrator's closing words is savage: 'Le dernier jour, ils nous emmenèrent sur la route à un croisement. Ils ne savaient plus de quel côté nous emmener. Ils nous rangèrent le long d'un petit chemin en nous recommandant de nous mettre à l'abri des avions. La vie est précieuse' (p. 205).

If, for all the hellish qualities of the experience recounted in it, 'Le Système' is a witness to the spirit of true resistance and indeed an illustration of the view held at the time (by writers like Sartre or André Chamson) that words could be a form of arms, it leaves us nonetheless with the feeling that little is required for the process to be repeated. There is of course, in this story more than in any other in *Les Circonstances* a kind of Brechtian parable of class struggle. But that is not Courtade's principal concern: he would deal more explicitly with such issues in his second collection of stories, *Les Animaux supérieurs*. Here the focus is on evil – in the form of fascist brutality and oppression – which, unless vigilance is maintained, is likely to manifest itself again at any moment. Such, too, is one of points made in the final story, 'La Carpe', which is the only one to deal with events after the Allied drive has begun, and is set in Bavaria.

The story opens with the discovery by two French soldiers of four dead Germans in a forest clearing. In the wallet of one of them are some photographs of atrocities, in particular of a group of civilians who have been hanged and of a woman, raped and viciously bayoneted, lying on a table surrounded by smiling Germans. One of the dead soldiers has a medallion bearing the effigy of the Virgin Mary; an identical one is worn by the French sergeant. When, shortly after, they arrive in the nearby village they find a young German woman who claims to have been raped four times; but blame is immediately attributed to Moroccan soldiers, two of whom have been executed. Such incidents as these are clearly intended to show that in war distinctions are not always easy and clear-cut, even if right is generally held to be with victors.

But from this initial idea Courtade develops two points in particular: first, a critique of the attitude of the majority of French citizens to the invading Germans in 1940; and, second a final reminder of the ever-present threat of war and evil. When the Allied forces take control of the village 'Les gens [...] parlaient français et les drapeaux flottaient aux fenêtres' (p. 221). In particular, the local *pharmacien*, whose house is *above* the village, '[qui] n'avait jamais été membre du parti national-socialiste' (p. 222) and who claims he has always voted social-democrat and lays the blame for the war squarely at the door of the Prussians, is depicted as the archetypal, sycophantic opportunist, whose 'affection' for France is limited to French cigars and a collection of racily illustrated eighteenth-century books. He invites the two French soldiers to dinner; but confronted with the photographs he collapses into embarrassment and bluster. Not only his guilt but his pusillanimity are underscored. The parallel is clear. But more significant still is the presence of the carp. When the soldiers arrive for dinner they notice that the fountain in the fishpond (like the one in the hotel in 'Personnes seules') no longer works. The water is effectively lifeless. When they leave they see the fish again 'lourde et noire comme un sous-marin à l'affût' (pp. 232, 3), and when one of them tries to disturb it by throwing a pebble into the pond the carp remains unmoved; as the soldier observes: 'Ça vit vieux, ces trucs-là [...] et c'est bête' (p. 233). War with its attendant horrors and the evil of which it is a particular manifestation is a permanent threatening presence, ready, like the carp, to resurface at any moment and without warning. While, as we shall see, there are echoes across and between the ten stories in this collection, the open-ended nature of the conclusion is important. Nothing can be anticipated with certainty. As the narrator of 'Occupations' observes early on: 'On ne sait pas d'avance' (p. 31).

Clearly the predominant theme of *Les Circonstances* is the need for commitment, an acceptance of responsibility and a rejection of all excuses or forms of *mauvaise foi*. Reflection and intellectual speculation alone are insufficient; they must be converted into action, however difficult and whatever the danger. In his treatment of this issue even within the relatively narrow spectrum of political engagement Courtade was by no means alone, of course. Writers, and especially but not exclusively those of the Left, had from the early 1930s, returned to it in a variety of ways. Towards the middle of the decade Aragon and Paul Nizan had warmly embraced the new directives from the Soviet Union concerning socialist realism and expressed the view that the writer's duty was not to entertain but to instruct. While, as we know, Courtade first appears to have begun to form ideas about imaginative writing as a potential vehicle for political ideas through his study of the works of Shaw, there is no evidence to show that he even remotely shared such a view as the one expressed for example, in Nizan's 'Pour une littérature responsable' or in Aragon's *Pour un réalisme socialiste*. Nor, in spite of considerable evidence to the contrary, is there any to suggest that he would be influenced by the new wave of socialist realism that dominated much left-wing theorizing on art and literature in the 1950s, when he produced his two most blatantly political novels *Jimmy* and *La Rivière noire*.[32] Nonetheless, even if he did not go this far, there is no doubt that in all his published fiction he sought to illustrate a particular thesis or preoccupation which, in the main, was constructed around personal experience.

Not all characters in *Les Circonstances* are guilty to the degree that Courtade suggests those in 'Personnes seules' are, of opting out of responsibility or choices, or of blaming others for the present state of France. In several cases there is an acknowledgement of the attraction of a private world normally centred around an existing or potential emotional or sexual relationship with a female companion – Fleur in 'Occupations', Aline and Claire in 'La Salamandre', Lily in 'Une bonne brebis' and Anne in 'Les Cheveux coupés en quatre'. (Interestingly enough, only Claire in 'Deux douzaines d'huîtres', whose commitment to her resistance activities has destroyed her femininity and has resulted in her being known impersonally as 'La Gestetner', escapes the otherwise seemingly blanket categorization of women as fickle, unreliable and self-centred.) There is also recognition of the force of habit and the ease with which it deflects any need to take decisions or positive action. Jacques in 'Occupations' acknowledges the appeal of the life led by those 'qui suivent le courant de la vie comme des bouchons' (p. 35); in 'Une bonne brebis' the narrator and Craigg return to Surinam Street and warm themselves by the gas–fire: 'Nous sommes restés un bon moment à écouter les déclics dans la machine et le bruit du gaz qui fusait. On a entendu des pas dans la rue, des pas d'homme, puis des pas de femme, puis plus rien, puis des gens qui se traînaient, puis une chanson. Puis le silence est devenu bruissant de pluie. En dix minutes les plus incroyables banalités de l'attente et de l'angoisse' (p. 67); the young man who ensures that there is continuous music for the *thé-dansant* offered by the principal in 'Les Cheveux coupés en quatre' 'changeait les disques sans s'occuper de savoir ce qui venait, mais simplement qu'il y ait du son, du rêve et qu'on parte, qu'on ne soit plus là' (p. 105).

But there is a difference between such automatic, unthinking acceptance of routine and the witting retreat into a mode of life and a closed world which then serve as a protection. The most obvious example of this is in 'Identités'. The count is challenged one day by the local policeman to produce his identity papers.

Because of his name and distinctive social position in the community he has never thought it necessary to have any. When they are now issued his image, status and self-esteem are destroyed: 'Il lit à haute voix: *Nez*: moyen. *Front*: moyen. *Bouche*: moyenne. *Signes particuliers*: néant.' (p. 86). The count is of course both a contributor to and a victim of a particular class system; not that this is an excuse. But he has been passive.

Far worse is the case of Savoy, whose training as an intellectual has rendered him quite incapable of coming to decisions which might threaten to disturb the normal course of his life – a theme to which Courtade would return in much greater detail in *Elseneur*. Early on in the story, following a passage in which we are given Savoy's reflections on his life at the school and on his ideal alternative ('être enfoncé dans un fauteuil crevé habitué à mon corps et (d')écouter le déchirement des pages d'un livre par la femme que j'aime' (p. 95)) the narratorial voice provides us with a commentary: 'Ainsi passait dans le crâne de cet intellectuel universitaire, à intervalles irréguliers, ce courant de rêverie. [...] Tout cela suivait avec un léger murmure les méandres du cerveau [...] et finalement allait se perdre derrière les yeux dans le parfait silence du regard' (pp. 96, 97). Not only has Savoy learned to reduce everything to abstraction, he does so wittingly. And at the same time as he protests he is powerless to do otherwise, he feels guilty. Craigg voices the same dilemma in 'Une bonne brebis': 'Je ne me pose pas de questions [...] pour ne pas me répondre des mensonges' (p. 62). In each case this is the height of bad faith.

At the heart of *Les Circonstances* is the issue of having the courage to reject the comfort of habit and a life with no real purpose (what the narrator in 'Une bonne brebis' calls 'une forme vide' (p. 58)): not to claim like most of the characters in 'Personnes seules' that external circumstances are all-powerful, not in other words to remain passive, but instead to act and to resist with and on behalf of others, in the full knowledge that in the context of the Occupation defeat and even death may result. Here again Courtade's placing of 'Occupations' as the opening story appears to have been deliberate. Chance arrest suddenly makes Jacques realize that his life hitherto has been purposeless: 'la simplicité de s'être fait prendre par hasard m'écrasait, et que le destin, il y a quelques minutes si vacillant, se fût figé si vite' (p. 12). More significantly still, on his release by the Gestapo he reflects on his newly discovered sense of responsibility: 'J'étais le délégué des hommes et des femmes qui n'avaient pas eu ma chance' (p. 34).

As we have seen, the remaining stories in the volume then illustrate the two possible responses: denial or acceptance. But while a preference is indicated clearly enough, there is neither self-righteous approval nor unbridled optimism when it is followed. Present circumstances are special, creating an aberration, 'un monde déroutant, absurde' (p. 192). Scattered across the stories are allusions to a normality beyond which must be rediscovered: 'l'autre côté de la vie' (p. 24); '(un) dehors très loin au-delà de la nuit' (p. 121); 'l'autre côté du monde' (p. 122); 'le monde [...] avant qu(il) fût totalement empoisonné jusque dans les détails' (p. 171); 'comme avant, quand les choses avaient leur visage ordinaire' (p. 178). But, as we have seen, it is evident from the last lines of 'La Carpe' that while the present aberration may be corrected, there is no guarantee that another will not reappear at some point in the future. Moreover, acceptance of responsibility and a commitment to struggle will not necessarily and automatically result in success. Just as chance can oblige even the most neutral of bystanders to become involved, so it can favour or thwart the most active. The narrator of 'Deux douzaines d'huîtres' is fortunate; the doctor in 'Le Médecin de campagne' is not, nor is Rosenbaum in 'Personnes seules'.

In terms of its principal themes and the way in which the general organization of the volume supports them *Les Circonstances* shows considerable merit. But that is not enough. Any collection of short stories will depend for its success on more than simple thematic consistency. In Camus' *L'Exil et le Royaume*, Sartre's *Le Mur*, Aymé's *Le Passe-Muraille* or Tournier's *Le Coq de Bruyère*, for example, recurrent themes are underpinned from story to story by certain stylistic features – tone, narrative voice, use of image, cross reference or intra-textuality and so on. Courtade's achievement in this respect, one can also find in large part impressive, but not without certain reservations. No doubt the principal reason why 'La Salamandre' found favour with Aragon was its allegorical, allusive and elusive qualities. We have to try to make sense of a text that appears to be at once narrative, reflection and dream. A similar technique appears in Jacques' thoughts about Fleur in 'Occupations', where Courtade attempts to convey through an association of ideas and sounds his realization of what was happening to him:

> Quand je levais les yeux, je voyais les petites feuilles vertes et velues des marronniers qui éclataient dans les bourgeons gluants, brillants, si brillants qu'on croyait y voir les reflets du fleuve et au-delà des canaux, des péniches, de grands plans d'eau où couraient des nuages, des images d'oiseaux blancs, des lignes de peupliers, des musiques, un bonheur déchirant, et la bouche de Fleur, des mots, des mots, des mots enfilés, des perles, des perles fines, fines herbes, herbes folles au sommet d'une colline couverte de marguerites, fleur penchée sur la colline, il est mort l'ami Lénine. (p. 12)

In 'Une bonne brebis' the narrator reflects on the dubious sexual charms of Lily: 'elle était d'une pièce, musclée, sans grâce. Douce et duvetée mais dure, perdue dans une rêverie qui tourne court, retombe comme ces vagues' (p. 60). While this precise example may appear forced (or over-indulgent) and out of place within the tone generally, it does at the same time remind us of the successful manner in which Courtade has the multiple meanings of the title resonate throughout this story. (The phonetic similarity of *pécher*: to sin, *pêcher*: to fish and *pêche*: here, peach (*duvetée*); themes of sinning and saving, of sheep-like behaviour and an inability on the narrator 's part to do more than dream.)

Another obvious stylistic weakness is Courtade's tendency to shift his narrative viewpoint, sometimes accompanied by changes in tense, in order to be both inside and outside his character, and thereby to provide a more rounded version of events and to write or prompt the reader to take a more distanced view. There are also occasions, as in 'Identités' (p. 85), when by recording what is not spoken but only thought Courtade approaches in a rather primitive way the technique of the *sous conversation* to be found in the novels of Sarraute or Claude Mauriac. In striving for effect details can also be annoying. Despite its context, the reflection on music-lovers in 'Occupations' ('La faiblesse idéologique des mélomanes est le trait le plus démoralisant de leur caractère' (p. 27)) is unnecessary. When Banting drinks his cup of tea he does so 'd'un trait, retrouvant d'instinct le geste de Socrate' (p. 70). Camuflet, in 'Les Cheveux coupés en quatre' sees the pianist's face 'comme une lumière de fenêtre lointaine au flanc d'une montagne' (p. 113). And in 'Deux douzaines d'huîtres' a moment's attention to continuity would have helped. As the narrator climbs the stairs to Claire's flat he is confronted by the

Gestapo. The barrel of the sten gun is described as 'un tube d'acier bleui percé de trous comme une poêle à marrons'; moments later (though arguably the narrative voice has shifted) he notices 'l'éclat bleu du réfrigérateur de la mitraillette' (pp. 131–2).

Nonetheless, while these and indeed other devices, such as for example Courtade's stereotypical presentation of Nazi soldiers and officials, may be highlighted, they should not draw our attention away from the considerable stylistic merits of *Les Circonstances*. In terms of detail the unfortunate examples just quoted can be balanced by wholly appropriate and, in context, striking ones. In 'Occupations' the Jew instantly arrested by the Gestapo after the car has been blown up 'portait l'étoile de David pour aller acheter du pain' (p. 10); the link here between the awfulness of the stigma, his consequent fate and the banality of this necessary activity requires no gloss. When Banting's story about how he has spent the evening is challenged in 'Une bonne brebis', both it and the hypocrisy in general of bourgeois life in Southernborough are 'crevée d'un coup, ouverte comme une poche de papier pleine d'eau' (p. 69). As Chapuis lies dying on the threshold of the hotel Amour Joufflu in 'Personnes seules', his body makes 'les lents mouvements du dormeur ou du foetus' (p. 151). But where in a more general way style and theme come together with particular success is in Courtade's use of images based on passage, on neatly circumscribed and usually artificially lit scenes of action reminiscent of a stage set and, more extensively, on water.

Quite deliberately, it would seem, all three are introduced in the opening story. In particular Jacques' forced transition from a position of relative unconcern into the dark world of Nazi activities and his consequent acceptance of new responsibility is a passage of initiation; a step which demands both conviction and courage. In 'Deux douzaine d'huîtres' every time the narrator passes through the doorway and entrance hall of Claire's block of flats he risks arrest by the Gestapo, who may be lying in wait: 'Les entrées des maisons étaient devenues, pour lui, des défilés pleins de menaces qu'il fallait passer vite en détournant la tête [...]' (p. 124). For Rosenbaum in 'Personnes seules' the decision finally to take action into his own hands can only be realized literally by crossing the threshold between the café and the courtyard (p. 153). The doctor leaves the security of his safe house only to walk into the trap laid by the militia. Whatever the outcome, what is important is the passage from one way of life ('un autre monde') to another with the ever-present threat of torture and death. To describe or indicate this second world Courtade frequently has recourse to the second of these key images, linking it with the first. Once again from the very beginning we have in 'Occupations' 'le cercle dans le soleil' (p. 10) highlighting the spot where the German car has been blown up and heralding the new and decisive turn in the action. The device is especially well deployed in 'Deux douzaines d'huîtres': 'Il traversa la rue pour échapper au vague rond de lumière de la lampe bleue [...]' (p. 126); and, a moment later, on his arrival at Claire's apartment block we read: 'La porte cochère était ouverte sur une large entrée: au fond commençait l'escalier et au-dessus une lampe suspendue faisait un cercle sur les premières marches' (p. 127). A group of Gestapo are there, and the scene is complete: 'On les voyait bien, éclairés comme dans un décor de théâtre, étroitement groupés sous la lampe' (p. 128). In 'La Carpe' the forest clearing, with its corpses and final reminders of Nazi atrocities, is like the closing scene in a play. On this occasion, however, the light is natural.

At this stage it should be noted, perhaps, that Courtade appears to be at his best as an imaginative writer in his handling of limited scenes, a characteristic certainly attributable to his experience as a journalist. He rarely attempts, even in his longer fiction, extensive descriptions of places, people or events, for example, and when he does so there is always a motif running through them as a constant reminder of their purpose. While, therefore, this quality is well suited to Courtade's aim in *Les Circonstances* of drawing attention to the limited and aberrant nature of the Nazi occupation, it is used to good effect elsewhere as well. In 'Les Cheveux coupés en quatre', for example, the principal's reception, or in 'Identités' the scenes in the family vault or at the dinner table all have a forced artificiality about them, with the characters playing parts that are required of them by society. In 'La Carpe' the *pharmacien*'s house sharply focuses attention on the question of collective guilt; in 'Personnes seules' the hotel, bathed in the light and heat of the southern French sun, is a 'set' not only from which no one will escape alive, but in which each individual will be made to face up to the reality of his or her isolation in moments of choice.

However successful Courtade's handling of images associated in this way is, those relating to water are far more numerous, and are integrated in the texts so as to create a metaphoric framework spanning all ten stories. Water appears in the opening sentence: 'Le soleil s'était levé sur un jour béni: beau printemps, belles rives tranquilles d'un petit fleuve sacré' (p. 9). Here the river is part of a scene that reflects Jacques' initial *insouciance*, but it quickly becomes a frontier (almost Styx-like) between his present life, thereby linking with images of passage, and the new one into which he is about to be violently thrust by circumstances. An echo of this occurs after he has been released by the Nazis and re-crosses the river in search of Fleur (p. 34). Thereafter the notion of water as an emblem of innocence or purity or as an indicator of better times is reaffirmed throughout. In 'Le Médecin de campagne' the sound of the rushing stream is one example:

'Le bruit du torrent les transportait déjà dans le monde d'en haut où ils étaient les maîtres, où la terre déjà avait repris la couleur qu'elle avait jadis avant que toutes ces choses commencent, avant que le monde fût totalement empoisonné jusque dans les détails' (p. 171). Minutes later the doctor remembers that 'Il avait entendu ces bruits toute son enfance' (p. 171). The river in 'Les Cheveux coupés en quatre', especially as it approaches the sea, flows through a world which 'était resté ce qu'il était jadis' (p. 93) and 'où il n'y avait que du ciel et la légèreté insaisissable des nuages' (p. 99). In 'Une bonne brebis' the sea offers escape from the dreariness (the rain and the 'lumière d'aquarium' (p. 58)) of Southernborough, while in 'Deux douzaines d'huîtres' 'le goût de la mer était le goût de la liberté' (p. 122). (Even in 'Identités' the comtesse and the secretary can anticipate swimming together while the comte is away in Toulouse.)

But even if the distant sea remains unsullied, all other forms of water are threatened. Thus as the doctor approaches the shed in which he will be trapped, the sound of rushing water fades (p. 171). In the town the river in 'Les cheveux coupés en quatre', once a home for herons, now attracts only sparrows and is full of debris and abandoned boats (p. 93) even if an unseen undercurrent still flows strongly towards the sea (p. 99). The water in the moat around the château in 'Identités' is motionless; and in 'Personnes seules' and 'La Carpe' the fountains no longer work. In the former 'la vase [...] sentait les vieilles pourritures' (p. 150), while in 'Le Système' showers are a prelude to head-shaving and delousing, snow turns to jagged ice which lacerates bare feet, and the prisoners eventually are forced to exist almost permanently, as we have already noted, in rivers of mud or excrement. In *Elseneur* water will be a source of imagery providing one of the main keys to the book's meaning, while the title alone of Courtade's second novel *La Rivière noire* already suggests corruption and evil.

The persistent allusion to water in a variety of forms in a volume of short stories such as *Les Circonstances* suggests not so much a planned strategy as an unconscious preoccupation or even obsession. Possible reasons for this will be examined later, but it has to be acknowledged that it does provide a form of subtext that, while it helps bind the stories together and keep Courtade's immediate concerns in focus, also invites consideration of more general issues such as light and darkness, life and death, good and evil, public and private and so on. In this way, as in all worthwhile examples of committed writing, Courtade succeeds in *Les Circonstances* in blending private concerns with public ones; yet there is no suggestion that he sets out to demonstrate the need to act or even the advisability of acting in accordance with a particular philosophy or political creed. (We should remember that whatever his sympathies, Courtade had not yet become a member of the French Communist Party.) Most immediately the stories in this collection are about the realization – in both senses of the word – of individual responsibility and in consequence about sincerity, authenticity and relationships with others. In those stories in particular that relate specifically to the Occupation and Resistance there is a clearly preferred mode of conduct, but there is no strident disapproval or dismissal of those who fail to follow it. Courtade's tone remains modest and tempered throughout. Moreover the effect of irony ('Identités'), of self-observation ('Les Cheveux coupés en quatre'), of doubt ('Le Médecin de campagne') and above all the recognition of the arbitrary nature of chance give several of the stories a striking degree of complexity and subtlety, and also serve to throw into sharp relief the moments of true horror such as we have in 'Le Système' or 'La Carpe'.

One risk for any writing that deals predominantly if not wholly with contemporaneous events or with those of a recent past as traumatic as the 1940–44 period is that it may lack a sense of perspective and objectivity. Another is that in an attempt to be 'real' the author will indulge in excessive detail and unwittingly stifle the creative process by which some features are given more prominence than others, which in turn leads to artistic balance.

There are further problems relating to interpretation as well. When an imaginative writer (or historian) writes about events still vivid in the minds of his readers he does so sharing with them the full knowledge of how those events have evolved and how the problems they produced have been resolved. In this way he contributes directly to a particular historical interpretation that gathers credence the more frequently it is articulated. But when he writes about them in order to *re*interpret them, and does so – as did Courtade in his first novel *Elseneur* – within the perspective of a political belief to which he has only come *after* they have taken place, he immediately challenges orthodoxy, and in consequence risks accusations of partiality or distortion or simplification. This in turn provokes the question raised by several and at length by Sartre: 'Pour qui écrivez-vous?' The politically sympathetic reader will enthuse about the fresh – or different – account that is being proffered; his opposite, if he bothers to read the book at all, will not. More publicly professional critics will follow the same pattern.

For Courtade the problem would be posed not only in the 1940s in connection with the Occupation but also in the following decade as France experienced the horrors of colonial warfare and as American influence and interference grew. With *Les Circonstances* he showed himself on the whole more than capable of dealing with it, the concise, limited nature of the successful short story not only focusing sharply on a particular event but allowing the reader a degree of free, undirected reflection. In a novel, altogether more discursive and complex, the problem is presented differently.

Elseneur (1949)

Quite when Courtade began work on *Elseneur* is not known, but it is more than simply a historical or political novel. We know from several letters that *Hamlet* continued to fascinate him after 1938, and the themes of indecision and procrastination had already appeared in *Eric et Irène* and in 'Les Cheveux coupés en quatre'. But the framework is clearly that of the Occupation and Liberation, and there is a constant interplay in the novel between events of the previous few years and the evolution of his protagonist.[33] As we shall see, there are occasions when Courtade's authorial hand is too evident, as though he is afraid to let his story carry its own significance; and there are others when he indulges in excessive autobiographical reflections. Neither characteristic will disappear from his imaginative writing; but *Elseneur*, like *Les Circonstances*, was ample evidence of a writer with considerable talent.

While Shakespeare's Denmark is situated somewhat vaguely in the mists of northern Europe, Courtade's Elseneur is specifically next to Poland. Its political allegiance, its size and character are noted at an early stage: 'une principauté germanique grande à peine comme la moitié d'un département français et de moeurs très provinciales' (p. 95). It is headed by an anonymous puppet prince who came to succession after the death of his brother Charles in doubtful circumstances during a hunt six years earlier. Power, such as it is, rests in the hands of the primeminister Julius Horn, with his bevy of sycophantic and stereotypical secretaries, policemen and spies. He has a son Oswald (Laertes) and a daughter Clarissa (Ophelia). Courtade's Hamlet is Karl, who, incited by his father's ghost, has for these six years been contemplating revenge. He has also studied at the university in the neighbouring state of Wittenberg, where he has been deeply influenced by the philosophical teaching of Herion. His sole confidant (Horatio) is Haeling ('sa conscience, sa raison' (p. 190)) and in his own way he is in love with Clarissa.

Within this broad framework there are a number of quite specific allusions to features of Shakespeare's play. Karl writes and has enacted a play depicting the circumstances of his father's death (pp. 74; 97–102). Horn and the Prince arrange for Karl to represent Elseneur on a diplomatic mission to Wittenberg, accompanied by Niederhaul and Ollenberg (Rosencrantz and Guildenstern), who have orders to kill him (p. 105). Clarissa dies by drowning (pp. 232–4); Oswald and Karl shoot one another in a final confrontation (p. 260). There are also precise echoes of the text. Behind 'Valait-il mieux se soumettre ou se révolter? La crainte des punitions dans l'au-delà ...' (p. 38) is Hamlet's most famous soliloquy in Act III Scene 1. When Karl sees Horn immediately before his departure with Niederhaul and Ollenberg he shies away from killing him, on the excuse that 'c'était lui donner une chance, comme de frapper un homme en prières, si criminel soit-il, dans un moment d'innocence ou de naïveté' (p. 160). Again Hamlet's hesitations in Act III Scene 3 are echoed. And above all Marcellus' key phrase in Act I Scene 4 that 'Something is rotten in the state of Denmark', a theme carried throughout

Shakespeare's play by repeated images of corruption and putrefaction, is as central to *Elseneur*, where it finds its precise echo, as it is to *Hamlet*. In their first conversation together Haeling observes: 'il y a quelque chose de pourri dans la principauté d'Elseneur' (pp. 68–9), and hours later Karl 'regardait ce corps du monde et n'apercevait pas un seul endroit qui ne fût pas pourri' (p. 121).

In order to have *Hamlet* suit his immediate purpose Courtade also had to adapt and add. Within his general presentation of the characters are two significant modifications. First, Horn emerges as an amalgam of Claudius and Polonius; second, Gertrude has been eliminated entirely, thus removing the whole dimension of sexual jealousy and allowing Karl's indecision to be centred in the political context of the novel and in the philosophical issues which that raises. These matters in turn have also been braced by the introduction of new characters and by the development of one (Fortinbras) whose appearance in *Hamlet* is only marginal. In *Elseneur* he emerges as Heydrick, dictator of the neighbouring state of Wittenberg, whose territorial claims on Elseneur give the novel its focus and more than any other element locate it firmly in 1939–40. Courtade also introduces the common people, who will challenge Heydrick's advances and Horn's ready acquiescence, and whose principal spokesman is Hans Peter. Two other characters who have no forebears in *Hamlet* owe their existence to Courtade's early years. Herion, the philosophy teacher at Wittenberg, who is seen as being largely responsible for Karl's uncertainty, is based on Jean Guéhenno. Peffik, a political journalist, has ideas on the provision of plots of land for working-class people to build their own homes that are a caricature of the scheme masterminded by Louis Loucheur.

Where and why Courtade decided upon what he would like to define to Vailland as the 'solution Elseneur' for his first novel is not known. Certainly some of the stories in *Les Circonstances* have an underplayed allegorical quality ('La Salamandre' or 'La Carpe', for example); but this adoption and adaptation of a universally known work, albeit in a different *genre*, was a new venture, of which there is no hint in his private papers. It is also possible that while he had little time for Camus as a political thinker, the recent example of *La Peste* had not been without influence, especially in its treatment of Occupation of various kinds. Anouilh's *Antigone* and Sartre's *Les Mouches* and *Les Mains sales* (in which Hugo can be seen very much as a 'Hamlet' figure) may also have made their mark. Whatever the reason, the appropriation of *Hamlet* as a model or basis for his perception (from the late 1940s) of the French response to Nazi aggression during the previous four years, which invited at the same time wider consideration of such public matters as commitment, the need for decisive action or class struggle, also allowed Courtade to explore a number of private concerns.

Even when we permit a degree of licence both in the treatment of individuals and in the handling of time, the immediate allusions to France's position in 1939 and 1940 are evident. Heydrick 'is' Hitler; Horn with his 'Mouvement de la Régénération' is Pétain;[34] Severing is possibly Gaston Bergery. In Albrecht, Hans Peter and their comrades we have the nascent Resistance, which if not Communist in name is so in inspiration. Interestingly, their movement is only twice referred to as 'la résistance' (pp. 175; 249); its more usual designation, which is precisely that of the period, is of *insurgés*, *terroristes*, *rebelles* or *perturbateurs*. And while De Gaulle and the Free French appear not to be alluded to after Heydrick's invasion has begun, there is a thinly disguised reference to the former's radio broadcasts from London: 'les gens, rassemblés autour des postes de radio, dans les cafés, écoutaient les commentaires de l'étranger' (pp. 223–4). Atrocities committed by Heydrick's soldiers are rumoured (p. 223) and his anti-Semitism is accepted and put into practice by Horn (pp. 60; 218). Although he is ostensibly demanding only the right of passage in order to settle his six-year-old dispute with Poland, Heydrick is using this request as a pretext for occupation. His terms, like those presented to Pétain by Hitler, are clear; there shall be no hostilities, and the maintenance of law and order is to be the responsibility of the government; 'des actes d'hostilité [...] ne seraient pas tolérés' (p. 59). After an initial show of doubt and reserve Horn capitulates; he decides privately that the policy he will advocate will be one of 'collaboration mutuelle sur un plan d'égalité, (p. 37) and has a *communiqué* published in the *Gazette du Nord* appealing to the people of Elseneur to grant to 'nos alliés l'accueil qu'ils méritent' (p. 209).

Beyond such parallels and allusions as these Courtade has blurred and merged others in order both to generalize about the nature of society and government in Elseneur and to make his critique that much sharper. Like Shakespeare's Elsinore, his is also a northern, Germanic land; it is near the sea and possesses an extensive waterway system, both of which assume growing symbolic significance as the novel progresses. The names too are Anglo-Saxon or Nordic rather than French, with Oswald and Severing hinting at two notorious fascists, Oswald Mosley in Britain and Vidkun Quisling in Norway.[35] These two features – geographical position and names – and the fact that Heydrick's expansionist policies have been in operation for six to seven years (p. 36) combine to give the novel another interesting dimension. Hitler came to power in 1933 and Courtade is suggesting that since that date capitulation has been inevitable: '... on ne voyait pas très bien ce qui pourrait l'arrêter [...]. On s'accusait mutuellement d'avoir manqué de fermeté quand il était temps encore' (p. 224). So intent has Elseneur been on living in its glorious past ('le temps où Elseneur avait presque dominé les pays du nord' (p. 177)) that its citizens have become powerless to resist. Refuge in institutionalised religion, in traditionalism and in conservatism on all fronts (p. 65) has resulted in an inward-looking, impotent nation that has collapsed into self-pity (pp. 15–16) and self-analysis (p. 12).

While Courtade does not dwell on them at length, such observations as these were, of course, the exact opposite of the view held by many in France at the moment of defeat. For such people it was precisely a turning away from traditionalism and allegiance to the past and Catholicism, encouraged by left-wing and internationalist ideas, that had fundamentally weakened the country and brought about its downfall. As Paneloux would say to the citizens of Oran in his first sermon in *La Peste*: 'Vous l'avez mérité.' All that remains is a façade of prosperity and strength. When Horn returns to Elseneur from his meeting with Heydrick he is greeted by a handful of well-appointed soldiers. The commentary is telling: 'Horn félicita l'officier commandant le détachement pour la belle tenue de ses hommes. Il n'y en avait pas deux cents comme eux dans Elseneur, mais on aurait pu croire et on essayait de faire croire que toute l'armée était sur ce modèle' (p. 20).

A contrast between the bright superficiality associated with those in authority and the dark brooding strength of those from whom resistance will eventually spring underpins the novel from the beginning. As Horn's plane approaches Elseneur, the appearance of the town is at once revelatory: 'Horn reconnut Elseneur au rayonnement des avenues lumineuses qui partaient de la place de la Constitution. Là les feux des voitures faisaient une ligne presque continue. Mais au-delà la ville était médiocrement éclairée' (p. 18). The port, once the source of the country's greatness, now has only a handful of boats and a single lighthouse. In Chapter 4 we have a long description of Elseneur (pp. 64–7) with its ornate, pompous and anachronistic air, dominated by the presidential palace and gardens. From its terrace there are views across the sea; but these are ignored ('Tout ce monde tournait le dos à la mer' (p. 67), possibly another echo of *La Peste*) as the palace and its occupants turn self-protectively and self-indulgently in upon themselves. Elsewhere, the 'beaux quartiers' of the town exude an air of hostility to any intruders (p. 136).

By contrast, the working-class areas close to the port form 'un réseau protecteur' (p. 136), and despite an imposed uniformity of building, and hence anonymity, have a human warmth that is echoed in the more distant rural parts. A reminder too of the contribution made to Elseneur's past by ordinary people is the cemetery that lies in the shadow of the palace, a symbolic statement that their spirits live on (pp. 65–6). While this division – 'D'un côté la lumière et de l'autre les ténèbres' – is indisputable, the significance commonly (officially) attributed to it, and ironically summarized by Haeling as 'La vertu côté cour et le vice côté jardin' (p. 68), is the precise opposite of the true state of affairs. Nowhere is this more evident than in Courtade's descriptions of the palace and of the *soirée* held on the night after Horn's return from Wittenberg. In the first, Karl finds himself in the main entrance: 'La lumière d'un lustre de cristal, mille feux en biseau multiplées par les reflets décomposés de l'arc-en-ciel brillaient au-dessus de sa tête. Sur un mur, le prince régnant, fraîchement peint, resplendissait dans l'hermine. Karl s'attarda un instant à considérer cette ordure vernissée' (p. 75). In the second the gluttony, glitter and superficiality of the 'polichinelles dorés' (p. 89) are lambasted in a kind of Flaubertian tirade (pp. 87, 8). And finally, in the following chapter, two images filtered through Clarissa's consciousness herald the ultimate collapse of this brilliant but shallow society. The first: 'L'orchestre avait recommencé à jouer, comme sur un paquebot qui coule' (p. 107); the second, more surreal: 'Les fenêtres du château s'enfonçaient, vraiment de biais, une à une, dans une boue silencieuse qui se refermait sans une ride' (p. 109).

Such emphasis on light and brilliance in descriptions of the bourgeois and governing classes of Elseneur leads in turn to a studied presentation of representative individuals as though they were in a play. The result is a hierarchy of characters of increasing complexity, but all essentially wittingly complicit in the roles demanded of them and conscious of their performance. At the base there are Niederhaul and Ollenberg, petty spies whose double act reduces them to near-clowns. Reynaldo the policeman, whose task is to report on Clarissa's activities, and who, hovering uncertainly between official informer and voyeur, has so convinced himself of the justness of denunciation that it has become like a religion: 'Son goût de la dénonciation s'apparentait à un goût de la confession' (p. 181). Although marginal to the main plot, he is clearly intended to be the archetypal policeman, concerned only with law and order ('Tout était propre, net' (p. 181)) and ready to offer his services to whatever regime is in power. In a small way he recalls the infinitely more sinister Massart in Nizan's *La Conspiration* (one of several echoes of the older communist writer's work) and anticipates Vailland's Marchand in *Un Jeune Homme seul*, whose very name is indicative of his relationship with those in authority. So lacking in complexity is Courtade's presentation of Reynaldo that he verges on caricature, as does Jansen, a vacillating colonel in Horn's army, who is drawn into resistance in spite of himself when he automatically arrests four officers sent to Elseneur by Heydrick. Nor do the Prince, 'cet oiseau prétentieux', who mouths only generalities (p. 94), and Oswald fare any better, though the latter, glimpsed as a smaller version of his father, pompous and lacking in human feelings, is not in the final attack without courage.

With Perceval and Severing Courtade's presentation is slightly more developed. The former has risen through the ranks of the officer class on the strength of his ability to act the part well and of a book justifying the Prussian victory over the French at Sedan in 1870.[36] Devoid of real ideas (p. 50) and suffering from an inferiority complex (p. 49), he sees Horn's willingness to negotiate with Heydrick as a threat to his authority. His response is not to indulge in rational argument, but to put on an act once more; only, however, to someone who is equally adept: 'Perceval s'était composé un visage d'une naïveté calculée que Horn admira en bon connaisseur' (p. 55). By the close of the novel he manages to convince people that he has been instrumental in arresting Heydrick's approach. Severing equally has merged with his position. He is 'l'homme fichier' (p. 18), devoid of any real personality, vulgar, has a 'visage de clown' (p. 25) and speaks a language full of 'généralisations à la mords-moi-le-doigt [et] les vues profondes comme un miroir. Un curieux mélange du vocabulaire officiel et de ces familiarités qui donnent l'air d'être dans le secret des choses' (p. 15). After the occupation of the palace he is captured by the resistance fighters. Momentarily his mask has slipped; but, like Perceval, he has a ready and confident explanation of how he has helped their cause. This instant shift of allegiance in order to save his own skin in fact destroys him: 'Sans cravate, pas rasé, le cheveu dérangé, il avait quelque chose d'humain qui commandait que son cas fût examiné. Mais d'avoir voulu pousser trop loin son avantage en proposant immédiatement ses services, le perdit d'un seul coup' (p. 265).

The principal actor in this part of the cast is obviously Horn. He has cultivated his appearance through years of practice in the service of different political regimes to the point where the official mask *is* the man – 'un masque inséparable de l'habit de cérémonie, du piquet d'honneur et de l'hymne national' (p. 9). The benign smile, 'que Horn déclenchait dans les cérémonies officielles' (p. 11) and which is popularized by the 'imagerie officielle' (p. 21) is what brings him his support. Yet from the beginning we are allowed glimpses of the fragile human being behind the public figure, who fears flying and who is old. Shortly before landing he falls asleep; the mask temporarily dissolves as the muscles of his face slacken and 'il ne restait plus que la chair flasque d'un visage quelconque [...] un air d'usure profonde' (p. 10). Again, when he meets Albrecht, while he is waiting for the presidential car to be repaired, he is secretly ashamed of speaking only in the language of his official position. Fundamentally he is alone, trapped within his role: 'L'espèce de solitude dans laquelle il s'était lui-même enfermé lui était de plus en plus pesante' (pp. 26, 7).

These preparations in the opening pages are necessary for the role Horn is to play in the rest of the novel. Browbeaten by Heydrick, he has to justify his agreement to his cabinet colleagues, and readily slips back into the 'personnage automatique' (p. 129), with his hyprocisy, compromise and language of half-truths. When he talks to Karl before the latter's departure with Niederhaul and Ollenberg, sincerity quickly gives way to official-speak: 'Le son de sa propre voix l'émouvait. Au bout de quelques phrases, elle eut l'ampleur balancée d'un discours' (p. 191). This assurance is finally and irrevocably shattered, first, by the news of the imminent attack on the palace and by Heydrick's indifference, and second, by the discovery of Clarissa's suicide note. In the first case, as in the plane, the mask dissolves: 'il ne se voyait pas, mais il percevait sa pâleur, la décomposition intérieure de ses traits jusqu'à la profondeur de la chair, jusqu'aux os frêles et creux' (p. 235). In the second, despair and terror destroy him; but even in his grief he is able to think only in clichés (p. 251). The human figure is unquestionably there, but such has been his life as a 'comédien politique' (p. 250), as he defines himself, that any expression of genuine emotion is denied him.

Having drawn up a range of characters of this nature, whose very shallowness is a commentary upon the regime they serve, it would be both tempting and easy for Courtade to have presented the representatives of the opposition as being worthy, incorruptible and far-sighted. While he does not entirely avoid this trap, his political vision also pushes him in a rather different direction. The opposition movement is divided into two camps: liberal intellectuals and workers. The former hold clandestine meetings, in which their sense of moral superiority *vis-à-vis* both invasion by Heydrick and spontaneous uprising in opposition is expressed in a language no less cliché-ridden than that of Horn and his colleagues. In particular the phrase 'avoir le droit' recurs like a motif:

> Il est évident que nous approuvons cette réaction patriotique saine, mais il est tout aussi évident que nous avons une responsabilité. Nous n'avons pas le droit de laisser les choses aller si loin, qu'elles aboutissent à un massacre inutile. Ce n'est même pas une question politique, ou, plutôt, c'est mieux que cela, c'est une question de morale. On n'a pas le droit d'utiliser ainsi l'enthousiasme d'une jeunesse qui est prête au sacrifice. On n'a pas le droit de jouer avec les hommes. (p. 119)

Ultimately they are incapable of translating this sense of outrage into meaningful action, and see the only influence possible to be to facilitate 'l'entrée dans le gouvernement d'éléments sains' (p. 120). They are at best *attentistes*, and at worst defeatist.

Real resistance is expressed by the workers, and not in words but by instinctive actions accompanied by a profound sense that, even if in the short term defeat is inevitable, their commitment must be to the future (p. 135). Courtade's presentation of them is no less careful than it is in the case of the government. The flat, unemotional description of their preparations for initial conflict or the matter-of-fact account of the undisciplined (because they have no training) but enthusiastic attack on the presidential palace are essential (p. 239). So too is the emphasis on the darkness (Haeling's reference to 'les ténèbres') and depths of the countryside from which they emerge. Albrecht is 'l'homme de la nuit' (p. 28). Like Zola's miners in *Germinal*, or more particularly like Barbusse's soldiers at the beginning of *Le Feu*, they emerge from an elemental world in order to create anew. But precisely because they are innocent and inarticulate Courtade glosses his descriptions with 'explanatory' passages for his reader or imposes his authorial voice on a character. For example, indirectly Hans Peter recognizes that 'pour le présent cela ne changerait pas grand-chose [...]. Mais il fallait penser à l'avenir. C'est pour cela que ce n'était pas inutile' (p. 135); or: 'Ce n'était que très lentement qu'ils avaient commencé à s'apercevoir qu'il était possible de changer leur vie par un travail patient, en luttant courageusement pour de petites choses qui, d'abord, paraissaient sans importance' (p. 138). This kind of interpretative intervention becomes more prominent at the end of the novel as the significance of revolutionary (*sic*) action is discussed. As we shall see, it is just one of the ways in which Courtade controls his text and moves out of the specific focus on the resistance to the wider perspective imposed by his new political faith.

Surrounded by these various attitudes are Karl and Haeling, who, in spite of the former's predominant role, form a kind of joint hero. In the closing scene Haeling, having finally committed himself fully to the cause of the resistance, reflects on his past life and anticipates the future: 'Je suis en train de me demander si je n'ai pas passé des années à rêver, dit-il enfin [...] il brûlait d'agir' (pp. 268 and 270). This is precisely the immediate (1940) subject of *Elseneur*, the step from indecision to commitment. Although he has had links with the *conspirateurs* (p. 39) for some time, his unwillingness to join them completely has been as much for intellectual reasons as for those of class. He is *équilibré, précis, complexe* (p. 39) and lucid (p. 190) – qualities for which Karl has hated him. Unlike his friend, he has not been misled by the teachings of Herion (p. 48) and as a result has realized that his life is not to be spent debating the potential effect of hypothetical action. Even though Hans Peter reminds him at the end of the novel that 'il vous reste du chemin à faire' (p. 267), this 'fanatique des idées pures' (p. 14), as Horn describes him, now sees the importance of collective action and responsibility. This is the lesson he attempts to make Karl understand: 'En ce qui vous concerne, vous vous en moquez; très bien. Mais vous n'êtes pas seul, que vous le vouliez ou non!' (p. 91). With no personal experience of working-class life, the transition is difficult: 'Il les croyait d'un autre espèce et désespérait de parler jamais le même langage' (p. 173). When he is arrested, however, he is finally pushed into a position of opposition, and at once feels solidarity (pp. 183–4). The last barrier has been crossed.[37]

Reflecting on his friendship with Karl after the latter's death and from his own newly discovered position of certainty, Haeling realizes that it had amounted only to an 'échange de rêveries inconsistantes' (p. 265), and that, while he had eventually chosen to participate in the struggle, Karl had essentially remained 'ce perroquet de l'idéal' (p. 248), still incapable of committing himself uncompromisingly. In death Karl's face and hands are limp (*mou; mollesse tiède* (pp. 263–4)), a physical manifestation, as in the case of Horn, of his fundamental nature.

Like his Shakespearian forebear, Karl is defined in advance of his first appearance in person. Horn remarks that he is 'un personnage nul dont l'utilité était finalement contestable' (p. 17); Oswald dismisses him as 'fou [...]. Un halluciné' (p. 24); Niederhaul and Ollenberg report on his 'véritable crises de folie' (p. 38). In addition, so totally has he absorbed the teachings of Herion that he is 'un pot-pourri de toutes les doctrines' (p. 25), 'complètement possédé par ces chimères' (p. 46). As Haeling comments when Karl does eventually enter upon the scene: 'La philosophie de l'école vous a pourri jusqu'à la moëlle' (p. 68). At the same time, while like Hamlet he is not mad, and is on occasions sufficiently lucid to know that his behaviour is totally inadequate (p. 69), he has become the victim of his assumed role.

For his introspection and self-indulgence to be turned into something positive he has to be put into a position where he is obliged to act positively. He has several opportunities. First he kills Niederhaul: 'Une grand joie l'envahissait et il regardait autour de lui avec la curiosité gaie et enfantine d'un malade désespéré, rappelé miraculeusement à la vie' (p. 200). Second, he heroically puts the government troops' machine-gun post out of operation. Yet even now his first thoughts are for the image which such acts will convey of him: there remains a dislocation between them and their contribution to collective effort. Hans Peter rightly observes: 'L'idée d'être dans le rang n'importe où lui était insupportable' (p. 266). Karl is still essentially 'indifférent [...] à tout ce qui se passait' (p. 245), still part of what he can only regard as a piece of theatre in which he can participate whenever he feels so inclined. The battle in the palace gardens therefore remains unreal (like Waterloo for Fabrice), 'une féerie. Que tout d'un coup le rideau se lève, et la représentation pouvait reprendre' (p. 245).

For complete engagement, at least in personal terms, to be achieved Karl has to kill Horn, as Hamlet had to kill Claudius. And this (again like Hamlet) he fails to do directly, sending a group of soldiers back to Clarissa's room, where only minutes before he had had ample opportunity as he and her father had talked together. Nonetheless, this does seem to act as some kind of release, and in his final scene, when he is on the point of meeting Oswald, we read: 'Pour la première fois peut-être il lui semblait que sa comédie ne se jouait pas sur un théâtre' (p. 260). But the *peut-être* is significant, and in any case his death relieves him of making the important step that Haeling has taken. Purely in terms of what he accomplishes there is no evidence that Karl could or would have had the will-power to commit himself unequivocally to the working-class resistance in the immediate struggle against Heydrick and ultimately for a better society. To the end he remains 'un héros de roman' (p. 172), and Hans Peter's reflection on his first participation in the resistance movement remains valid: 'Je ne sais pas ce qu'il cherchait' (p. 263).

Where we find a different but telling dimension to Karl's role is in his relationship with Clarissa. Ostensibly his treatment of her (like Hamlet's of Ophelia) has the same cavalier and cruel self-centredness which he displays elsewhere. But Clarissa also represents other qualities. Already a clue that Karl somehow has the potential to share these is provided by the phonemic echo between their names – *Karl/Clar*. The implied superlative in the suffix *-issa* is a further hint of her purity and powers of perception alike. The latter are evident from her *journal intime*, in which she reflects on the games she and Karl have played together in the maze in the palace gardens, seeing it as a symbol of their relationship: 'vous voyez comme ce labyrinthe est une bonne représentation de notre vie' (p. 80); she recognizes too that 'cette tyrannie que Karl prétendait exercer sur elle était le signe même de sa faiblesse' (p. 81). But the indication throughout the novel of her real significance is the way in which she is consistently associated with water. The first physical description we have of her signals this link unambiguously: 'Quand elle les [ses cheveux] peigne, ils volent, frémissent, se dressent et s'accrochent comme les fines tentacules d'une tête marine dans une poussière d'eau et de soleil' (p. 79); she also likens herself to 'une mouette posée sur une bouée flottante' (p. 79). She imagines death by drowning (p. 109), and in her farewell note to her father she writes: 'Je voudrais être sur la plage de Norreport, j'ai besoin d'eau claire et de repos' (pp. 227, 8). When she finally commits suicide, the water 'la reçut avec un éclaboussement lumineux' (p. 234), an image which resonates almost religiously with purity and joy. Moreover, she leaves this life on 'ce premier jour de vrai printemps' (p. 234), the selfsame day (described with the same words) that has already witnessed the outbreak of popular uprising (p. 204).

Yet a problem remains. Suicide is normally a result of selfishness, resignation and defeat, and is hence incompatible with the spirit of resistance, especially as the latter implies a collective action. This would, of course, seem to echo Karl's egocentric role, and is what Courtade is anxious to warn against. In his procrastination Karl is not alone; he is like 'mille jeunes gens à Elseneur' (p. 174). Fundamentally to blame for this state of affairs is the teaching of Herion – 'Il ne s'agit en aucune façon de doctrine d'action' (p. 39); 'un enseignement destiné précisément (et consciemment) à perpétuer la confusion mentale' (p. 46); 'Herion avait sans cesse le mot "pur" à la bouche' (p. 70). The result is inertia. Elseneur is 'ce pays esclave' (p. 117), and the willingness of the ruling class to capitulate in the face of Heydrick's aggression is a kind of moral suicide. Fortunately, through their experience of living, those elements from which the resistance will rise have recognized the danger. In a passage at the beginning of Chapter 8 in which he describes Albrecht's developing political and social awareness, Courtade writes: 'Vivre c'était changer la vie. Un homme qui s'abandonnait et qui acceptait la vie comme elle est s'endormait et mourait' (p. 131).[38]

How then, in view of his 'performance', can Karl – and Clarissa – be considered, if only potentially, to be on the 'right side'? The answer is to be found in their relationship with the elemental world, and in particular the *thématique de l'eau*. They are not, like Hamlet and Ophelia in Shakespeare's play, in some way misfits whose deaths release them from their torments in this world; they may leave others to carry on the struggle, but they remain linked with them spiritually and elementally. From the very beginning of the novel it is stressed that Elseneur is surrounded by 'des paysages élémentaires composés de terre, d'eau et de vapeurs' (p. 7). When he is shot by Oswald, Karl falls forward, 'son visage enfoui dans l'odeur de terre mouillée' (p. 261). Elseneur is, we should also recall, a port; the working-class districts of the town are near the sea; Albrecht, Hans Peter and the others come from a countryside cut by canals and frequently buried in mist; Karl's father is described in the play as glimpsing the sea from the forest (p. 101); when Haeling is arrested he can smell the sea air (p. 182); Oswald just before his death 'sentait le flot monter autour de lui' (p. 260); Haeling, struggling to come to terms with his new colleagues, 'brassait une eau contraire [...] remontait le courant d'un large fleuve' (p. 269). Nor should we forget the most significant point of all, namely that Horn and those associated with the presidential palace have turned their backs to the sea. In all there are over fifty references to water in some form or other in the novel, creating a unifying presence for all that is pure and a source (*source*) of optimism and potential regeneration.

It is at this point that we should reconsider the double focus of *Elseneur*, Courtade's views on the efficacy of imaginative writing and his own manipulative procedures to achieve certain ends. Published in the fifth year following the Liberation and in the early stages of the Cold War, Courtade's (and the novel's) perspective is by definition a very particular one. As a novel about the invasion of France and the initial stirring of resistance it has distinct qualities. The descriptions of the hesitations and hypocrisy of those in power and the determination of others in opposition, of the skirmishes with Heydrick's troops or of the attack on the presidential palace are accomplished. Equally well-captured are the responses of individuals – Horn's moments of despair, Karl's brute fear – or realistically observed details – the shattering of Albrecht's head by a stray bullet, for example. And with the knowledge of the eventual outcome of these years there is, as in all such novels, a dynamic of unspoken optimism that underpins the entire narrative. But Courtade's concern is as much, if not more, with France beyond 1949 as it is with France in 1940, or even in 1944. After the invasion of the palace has taken place one of the chandeliers is left shining 'de feux ironiques' (p. 262). In the context of 1940 this is a nice detail. Nazism, and more especially collaboration were not stamped out at once, and would assert themselves with the most barbarous consequences. In 1949, however, its significance is somewhat different. Courtade would appear to be saying that, despite all efforts, culminating in the Liberation, those evils, symbolized throughout *Elseneur* as we have noted by artificial light and brilliance, have not been completely extinguished. The struggle has to continue.

The emphasis on collective action is linked *thematically*, as we have also seen, to the elemental world, with its possible echo of Zola's *Germinal*, and hence of the Revolution as well. This is a powerful directive in any reading of the text. It is further supported by the *structural* use of a part-hidden dramatic form. Chapters 1–5 could be seen to constitute a first act, in which essential information is conveyed and the principal characters are introduced. Chapters 6 and 7, dealing with the reception and developing the relationship between Karl and Clarissa, might be a second. The pivotal and critical short third act would be Chapter 8, in which members of the resistance are introduced. Act IV (Chapters 9–12) charts the unravelling of the situation, and contains Karl's first positive gesture – his killing of Niederhaul. Act V (Chapter 13) describes the attack, and closes on a positive note as Haeling finds his way into the resistance movement. This (r)evolutionary pattern leads to what Roger Vailland four years later, in *Expérience du drame*, a unique contribution to the debate about socialist realism, would term 'une nouvelle situation, radicalement, qualitativement nouvelle.'[39]

Summarized in this way, it would appear that *Elseneur*, appearing just two years after the major publication in France of Zhdanov's directives about art and literature, has an important illustrative contribution to make. Unfortunately, and for whatever reason, Courtade appears not to have had the courage to allow his adaptation of *Hamlet* to speak for itself. A combination of wanting to ensure that his interpretation of events should not be misconstrued and a fundamental uncertainty about the simple efficacy of words on the page results in the inclusion of material not all of which is directly related to the plot, and in some heavy-handed authorial intervention. In the first case autobiography is in part sometimes responsible. While the attack on the teachings of Wittenberg is surely directed at the post-war existentialists as much as it is at Jean Guéhenno, the latter's presence is too intrusive. Similarly, while Peffik's scheme to provide workers with plots of land in order, according to Courtade, to distract them from political activity raises an interesting socio-political issue, it resonates too strongly with his own embittered memories of the rue du Chemin de fer at Sceaux. Sometimes popular conceptions are to blame. The portrait of Heydrick as hysterical (p. 57) and racked by sexual fantasies (p. 60) follows those accounts of Hitler's life which by extension could be made to discredit all who showed themselves sympathetic to his policies. More limited or irrelevant still is the episode in which an analogy is made between garden slugs and subversive political elements (p. 176) or the report of the brutal treatment of a black American worker by the whites (pp. 149–152).

None of Courtade's fiction suggests that he was either aware of or bothered by the kind of distinction that Sartre had made in 1939 in his celebrated attack on Mauriac between characters as objects and as subjects. His authorial voice mixes with theirs, developing and glossing their thoughts and observations in order to ensure that a particular interpretation should prevail. There are occasions as well, especially when he wishes to underline the positive message of the novel as it may apply in 1949, when he stands quite outside his characters and openly sets out his own views. In his presentation of Albrecht and Hans Peter and on the need to struggle for an improved life we read: 'Certainement, ni Hans Peter, ni Albrecht ne pensaient à tout cela. [...] Ils ne pensaient à tout cela, pas de cette façon en tout cas [...]' (pp. 138–9). Earlier Albrecht's thoughts develop into the reflection by Courtade on inaction being a form of death (p. 131). After the palace has been captured there is a long authorial section on the legitimacy of revolution and the destruction of the aggressors' possessions:

L'expérience a prouvé que les révolutions font très peu de victimes innocentes. Le juge peut se tromper, mais non l'homme qui depuis des années a jugé à chaque heure du jour et de la nuit et qui a tenu, inconsciemment le plus souvent, un compte implacable et fantastiquement précis des humiliations qui lui ont été infligées.

[...]

Il y avait parmi les groupes qui parcouraient le château des hommes qui pendant cinq ans n'avaient pas vu la lumière du jour, qui avaient ramassés des excréments avec leurs mains nues, qui avaient été giflés sans pouvoir répondre, et d'autres dont les chevilles étaient encore sanglantes du poids des chaînes. Il est légitime de briser à coups de crosse le piano du bourreau, et cela finalement vaut mieux que d'en faire un usage honnête.

[...]

Les révolutions trop raisonnables sont à bien des égards suspectes. Celles qui furent grandes et durables dans leurs effets eurent leurs commencements marqués par ces exces que la morale réprouve. Mais la volonté générale d'effacer jusqu'au souvenir de la tyrannie est réconfortante. (pp. 253–4)

Technically there is nothing new in such a narrative procedure, but it does take us into the heart of Courtade's problem, once again raising questions about literature, its effectiveness, and its audience.

In Courtade's last novel, *La Place rouge*, the autobiographical hero is at one point stopped by a Nazi control. In his luggage is found a copy of Malraux's unfinished *La Lutte avec l'ange*, and the official asks him: 'Vous connaissez quelqu'un qui a changé d'avis à cause d'un livre, vous? C'est pas ça qui fait que les gens changent d'idées.' In *Elseneur* the same doubts are already expressed. After the performance of Karl's play Haeling poses virtually the same question: 'Mais en quoi cela avance-t-il nos affaires?' (p. 102). Earlier, in a passage that again strongly recalls Nizan in its thoughts on the subject, novels are dismissed as boring and empty in which 'D'éternels personnages de chevalerie, différemment déguisés selon les époques, y pourfendaient les éternels moulins à vent de la passion. La littérature d'Elseneur n'exprimait plus depuis longtemps que des sentiments déliés dans une langue sybilline [*sic*]' (p. 81).

Nor are newspapers necessarily any better. This is due essentially to their being subject to political control and to their coverage of events which are either irrelevant or sanitized in a way to which the public has become accustomed and which it now expects. In contrast 'Un journal qui avait donné une image fidèle et comme photographique de la réalité aurait été un véritable puzzle' (p. 153). But it is not just a question of a socio-political or indeed cultural climate. When writers attempt to describe events retrospectively language itself proves somehow inadequate, and what should have been the true thrust of the work is threatened if not lost altogether: 'la connaissance qu'ils croyaient avoir des événements, dans la petite fièvre de la création, leur apparaîtrait, la page écrite, dérisoire. Les mots sans le halo qui les entoure avant qu'ils aient été choisis et ajustés, désespéraient les témoins les plus sensibles et les plus sincères' (p. 155).

With *Elseneur* Courtade encountered and in part solved this problem. His recourse to Shakespeare's play for his treatment of the Resistance has distinct merits, even though as a technique it is perhaps not developed as fully and as subtly as it could have been. Unfortunately, his uncertainty that it can serve equally well to carry the revolutionary message that by the late 1940s he clearly considers it to be his political duty to express leads to the kinds of authorial control and intervention we have noted. And it is presumably this lack of faith in his original idea and the hybrid form that results that will prompt him in a letter to Vailland in 1962 to talk of 'mon espèce de fuite'.

In his essay *Nous* Claude Roy talks about Courtade's 'liberalisme esthétique', which, he claims, was a safety-valve for the growing fanaticism of his belief in Stalinism. Roy also claims – as did many others – that in private Courtade was opposed to Zhdanovism and to the socialist realist novels of André Stil or the paintings of Fougeron. This may indeed have been true; but it seems that his public role – like those played by so many of his characters in *Elseneur* – was already becoming too demanding.

NOTES

1. 'Je fais tout l'édition de l'Ain', letter to Génia, 23 August 1941. The articles are unsigned. The reference to Francheville is in a letter dated 26 August.

2. Letter to Génia, 26 August: '[un interview] qui portait sur l'édition à Paris et la collaboration intellectuelle Franco-Allemande. Pendant 1h 30 nous avons travaillé absolument d'arrache-pied pour mettre au point quelque chose dont le patron a été content. Mais cela n'a pas fait l'affaire de B.G. non pour des raisons techniques (de ce point de vue il était content et m'en a promis de m'envoyer des livres 'en souvenir'). Mais d'un autre point de vue, qu'il m'est difficile d'expliquer dans une lettre et qui touchait à des questions d'une importance politique assez grande.'

3. Quoted in Courrière, *Roger Vailland, ou un libertin au regard froid*, Plon, Paris 1991, p. 255. Described too by René Tavernier in his unpublished *Des Ecrivains m'ont parlé* [? 1982] as 'l'ancien bordel devenu à Lyon, près de la place du Pont, le restaurant des journalistes travaillant dans le groupe Prouvost'. I am grateful to Olivier Corpet of IMEC for having allowed me to consult Tavernier's typescript.

   In her obituary for Courtade (*Lettres françaises*, 16 May 1963) Jeannie Chauveau recalls Courtade at their gatherings: 'Je me rappelle les incroyables après-midi de fou-rire au bistrot de nos habitudes, où Pierre, plus sérieux qu'un vieux pion, rédigeait en 175 formules différentes, toutes aussi percutantes que celles de Félix Fénéon les 3 lignes d'informations locales qu'il titrait invariablement "vol de clapiers à Taccin-la-Demi-Lune". Cela tenait de la magie. Quel talent, déjà, pour ces malheureux lapins disparus.'

4. The paper's archives were removed and destroyed by the Nazis.

5. His notes contain a reference to his being in Annecy in 1941 for the *Progrès de Lyon*. François de Menthon had organized a resistance group in Annecy, and from November 1940 had published a paper, *Liberté*.

6. Courrière, *Roger Vailland*, p. 270.

7. Undated letter to Génia: 'J'ai été arrêté mardi à midi par la police allemande à la suite d'un concours de circonstances absolument abracadabrant. Figure-toi que j'avais rencontré ce jour-là par hasard une petite journaliste que j'avais connu à Lyon autrefois, Annie le Chevallier, qui travaillait à "Compagnons". Elle venait d'arriver à Paris et comme je n'avais rien de mieux à faire ce jour-là je suis allé déjeuner avec elle. Il n'y avait pas 10 minutes que nous étions dans le restaurant qu'on nous a arrêtés et emmenés [...]. Il y a surement erreur pour elle comme il y avait pour moi; enfin moi on m'a relâché, il était tellement évident que je n'y étais pour rien dans des histoires dont j'ignorais le premier mot que ça soit allée se mettre dans des histoires aussi bêtes'. And a letter dated 7 September to his parents: 'Mon camarade Pierre Grappin qui avait été arrêté en même temps que moi le 6 juin a réussi à sauter du train qui le transportait en Allemagne, mais la pauvre Annie, elle est toujours déportée et nous avons appris qu'elle avait été cruellement battue mais nous ne l'avons pas dit à Pierre.' Jeannie Chauveau (*Lettres françaises*, 16 May 1963) again recalls the event: 'Il avait joué les imbéciles, ses faux papiers avaient inspiré confiance, et on lui avait recommandé de venir prévenir cette obligeante Gestapo, si jamais il avait vent de quelque complot.'

8. Serge Courtade was born in January 1942; Sylvie would be born in July 1944.

9. For further information see in particular the works by Bourdin, Halls and Tissier listed in the Bibliography.

10. 'endurcissement et maîtrise de moi-même: / ne plus fumer / lecture / travail assidu / marcher dans la campagne / étudier la maîtrise du *visage / du sommeil / de la parole*.'

11. Courtade did have a short spell with the Agence française de presse which grew out of the clandestine AID. My inquiries for precise information hve been met with silence.

12. See Victor Leduc, *Les Tribulations d'un idéologue*, Syros, Paris, 1985, Chapter III.

13. *Nous*, p. 20

14. *Dieu et César, Sont-ils communistes?*, La Table ronde, Paris, 1956, p. 24 and *Lettre à Sartre et à quelques autres personnes par la même occasion*, La Table ronde, Paris, 1956, p. 20.

15. According to Courrière (*Roger Valland*, p. 351) this reached 100,000, though he gives no reference. In an undated note, probably to his parents, Courtade wrote: 'Quand nous aurons du papier et que nous pourrons tirer 100,000 à 16 pages nous aurons gagné.'

16. 'Roosevelt devant son peuple', 20 April 1945.

17. 'Conséquence diplomatique d'une victoire', 26 January 1945.

18. 'L'Homme au cigare entre les dents', 15 March 1946. A deliberate echo, of course, of the image of the communist threat as a savage with a knife clenched between his teeth, which had been so basic to much right-wing propaganda from the 1920s and had been particulrly prevalent during the Occupation.

19. 'Pour l'observateur averti, l'Angleterre en guerre a accompli une profonde révolution sociale qui se marque par une extraordinaire égalisation des conditions' and 'la guerre a laissé sur l'Angleterre des marques si profondes, si impitoyables, que les chances du Ritz de s'imposer à nouveau sa conception du monde sont faibles'!

20. 'Un morceau de l'Allemagne', 4 May 1945.

21. For example, on Yugoslavia (23 November 1945), Poland (24 May 1946), Italy (15 August 1947), and the Soviet Union (2 May 1947).

22. According to Leduc (*Les Tribulations.* p. 76) Thorez was sympathetic to *Action*; but some, like André Marty, were opposed to the paper's open-mindedness.

23. Another publication from this period should be noted. In 1945 the Editions françaises nouvelles published Courtade's first work of any length, an essay *Pour connaître la pensée de Darwin*. He had first come across Darwin's work, it seems, when he had been working for his *dîplome* on Shaw. The essay was for a series, to include others on Schopenhauer, Bernard, Nietzsche, Bergson, Renan, Alain and Péguy. I have not been able to discover how Courtade became involved, but his contribution, after an orthodox survey of Darwin's life and the reception of his theories, quickly develops into a political statement. Darwinism, he argues, has been adopted by those who see poverty and unemployment, for example, as natural consequences of capitalist market forces, about which therefore nothing can be done. But not only is capitalism attacked; socialism too has become seduced by a misreading or a misapplication of the scientist's theories: 'l'idée que la vie économique est régie par les lois de la jungle, peut cadrer aussi bien avec les conceptions socialistes qui voient, dans le rapport économique, une lutte entre exploiteurs et exploités, et dans la condition du prolétariat moderne une survivance de l'esclavage né de la guerre elle-même, loi fondamentale qui a présidé à la formation des sciences humaines. C'est pourquoi le darwinisme social plut aux "socialistes", comme il avait plu aux capitalistes. Il offrait aux uns une justification scientifique de leur hégémonie, aux autres une explication biologique de la "lutte des classes"' (p. 91). Such a radical view was not likely to have passed unnoticed. Courtade's political credentials were also boosted by the publication of another book, *Essai sur l'antisovietisme*, the following year. Here, adopting his position developed through the columns of *Action* and *Démocratie nouvelle*, he argues that by investing in the regeneration of Germany the Allied governments are really defending themselves against

what they perceive to be the Soviet threat. Allied policies are idealist and self-interested. Only in the Soviet Union does a hope for truly democratic, revolutionary socialism lie. Courtade's orthodoxy in this essay is exemplary. At one point, for example, we read: 'la Russie n'avait jamais, à aucun moment, fait cause commune avec Hitler et, en vérité, les milieux diplomatiques et gouvernementaux d'Europe occidentale ne l'ignoraient pas' (pp. 48–9). It is hardly surprising that an anonymous reviewer in *Les Cahiers du Communisme* (8 February 1947) should speak of 'ces 160 pages nettes, précises, implacables, où le raisonnement est sans faille et l'expression sans faiblesse, d'une traite, comme si l'on courrait vers un dénouement'.

24. See Leduc, *Les Tribulations*, p. 89.

25. From the archives of Frédéric Vailland, quoted in Courrière, *Roger Vailland*, p. 355.

26. See my 'Un inédit de Pierre Courtade: *Ecrit en marge*', *Cahiers Roger Vailland*, No. 2, Novembre 1994.

27. See too 'La Torture du "pourquoi",' June–July 1945, which had first appeared in *Action* (27 April).

28. *Europe*, mars 1946.

29. The first edition of the collection has a kind of preface a quotation from Melville's *Moby Dick*, which describes the two sides of a tortoise's shell – the upper one dark, the 'belly' shining and colourful: 'La tortue est à la fois noire et claire.' This quotation will disappear from the 1954 edition but one of the ideas running through the stories is indeed of the unexpected, the unusual or the hidden.

30. For a more extensive discussion of the problems of truly and objectively representing events in the press see in particular 'Le sang-froid professionnel' in *Les Animaux supérieurs*.

31. The device was common enough. For a more recent illustration see the scene in *Lecombe Lucien*, the film by Louis Malle with a scenario by Patrick Modiano, in which a member of the *milice* arrives at the house of a doctor

suspected of being a member of the Resistance, claiming to have been wounded in a skirmish with the local 'terrorists'. It may be entirely coincidental but, according to Genia, Courtade hated cats.

32. For further discussion of socialist realism in these two periods see my *Literature of the Left*, Macmillan, London, 1983, and Methuen, London, 1985, Chapters 5–7.

33. Interestingly, the film of *Hamlet*, with Olivier in the title role, opened in Paris in 1948 to general acclaim.

34. Horn appears not to have had any personal experience of war and armed combat: 'il n'avait jamais vu un cadavre et n'avait respiré l'odeur de la poudre qu'à la chasse ou aux manoeuvres' (p. 226). This would, of course, diminish the image of Pétain, whose initial popularity was due in large part to his successes in the First World War.

35. The fact that Karl is the Germanic form of Charles, his father's name, may also be intended to indicate the degree of infiltration.

36. In the character of Perceval Courtade may be making a reference to Michel Mohrt, whose essay *Les Intellectuels devant la défaite de 1870–71* (1942) condemned democracy as it had developed during the nineteenth century as something that had fundamentally weakened France.

37. The character of Haeling is almost certainly based on Pierre Hervé.

38. This is another, especially strong, echo of Nizan, whose perception of death as a form of total capitulation to an oppressive capitalist system is expressed most powerfully in *Antoine Bloyé* and *Le Cheval de Troie*.

39. In *Oeuvres complètes* (Editions Rencontre, 1967), Vol. V, p. 137. See too a letter in *Ecrits intimes* (p. 445) to Pierre Berger, where, in discussing *Un jeune homme seul*, Vailland talks about the need to create 'une situation nouvelle radicalement, ou en language dialectique qualitativement différente de la situation initiale'.

$$- 3 -$$

Party Scribe

The role played by the PCF in the immediate post-Liberation years and beyond through the period of the Cold War has been so abundantly charted and analysed (and from all angles) that there is little need for the detail to be repeated here. We should not, however, forget or in any way underestimate the reputation and status that the Party had acquired by 1946. By that year it enjoyed a membership of close to one million, and the support, especially from the under-40s, of more than five times that number. Between 1945 and the mid-1950s it would consistently take between 20 and 25 per cent of the votes at national elections. The principal reasons for this popularity are well known. The Resistance record (real or claimed) of many of the Party's leading members and its confident championing of the underprivileged, bolstered by a solid theoretical base for its policies, drew to its ranks a wide swathe of support, not just from the working class but from bourgeois liberal intellectuals as well. Nor must it be forgotten that Communists world-wide allowed themselves to be inspired – hypnotized would be a better word, perhaps – by a leader whose name had been immortalized by the decisive, heroic battle of Stalingrad in 1943 and whose image as a giant of wisdom and political genius was carefully cultivated in committee rooms behind the walls of the Kremlin. This personality cult, as it became known, was as prevalent in France as elsewhere, leading to what Tony Judt in a typically pithy phrase has termed 'the sanctification of the absurd Maurice Thorez, a surrogate local Stalin.'[1]

At the elections for a Constituent Assembly that followed hard upon the Liberation in the autumn of 1945 the PCF obtained the highest score of any party, with 151 seats, a clear indication of its strength and potential influence. After considerable, but for the PCF inconclusive debate with the Socialists and the MRP a tripartite government was formed; but

De Gaulle initially refused to give the Foreign Affairs, Defence and Interior portfolios to Communist ministers. After more manoeuvring (and an offer by De Gaulle to resign) the cabinet formed in November contained five Communist ministers, with Charles Tillon being given responsibility for the critical armaments portfolio, but under De Gaulle, who personally took charge of national defence as a whole. By 1946 and after De Gaulle's eventual resignation in January this number of ministers increased to six, with Thorez as deputy prime minister, and subsequently to seven – the highest ratio of participation in government by the PCF ever. In the general election of November for a legislative assembly the PCF took 169 seats. When the Socialists (101 seats) refused to meet to draw up a joint programme the Communists produced their own, proposing as well that Thorez should become prime minister. In spite of the latter's claim, in his much-publicized interview with *The Times* newspaper in London in the same month, that it was possible 'to envisage the road to socialism by other paths than those taken by the Russian Communists', and that the PCF would respect the French parliamentary system, it soon became clear for a large number of parliamentary colleagues that the spectre of bolshevism was still a real issue. The PCF's programme was attacked from all sides, and a compromise was preferred. In the governments headed first by Blum and then by Ramadier early in 1947 five of the ministers were Communists, with François Billoux being entrusted with Defence. None the less, the process of marginalization had already begun.

Throughout the spring and summer problem followed problem as France attempted to right herself at home and abroad. Internally, wage negotiations and strikes were critical. Late in April the PCF leaders – in danger of alienating much of their support base if they did not do so – openly approved the strikers' actions, and in so doing provoked a crisis.[2] Ramadier claimed a split in his government, and called on parliament for a vote of confidence. This he got (by 360 votes to 186), and he seized the opportunity to dismiss his Communist ministers. But if it was an internal issue that finally pushed the PCF into isolation, it was events on the world stage that had already created the necessary climate. When in March a vote was taken on military credits to increase the offensive against Ho Chi Minh in Indo-China, the PCF ministers abstained, in order to maintain their anti-imperialist policy and also in order not to be seen to be willing to wage war against fellow Communists. But over and above this the first moves in the process that would essentially split the world between the so-called free democracies and the Communist block had been taken. In April the government signed an agreement (with Britain and the USA) by which it surrendered France's claim on the Ruhr. This was the first step in what would be seen by the PCF as the renaissance of Germany, approved by the Allies and opening the way for that country's revenge, and even more significantly for America's expansionist policies. With their allegiance torn, the events of early May came as a relief for many Communists. From now on the PCF moved into opposition, and, despite a moment of renewed popularity in January 1956 when Thorez again appealed for a 'Front Populaire' government, it would never be so close to shaping government policy as it was in 1946–7.

That Courtade should have been invited in the early summer of 1946 at Thorez's insistence to join the staff of *L'Humanité* at that high point in the PCF's history is hardly surprising. As we have seen, his credentials as a talented journalist had already been established, and while he was not yet a card-carrying member of the PCF his analyses of world events in the pages of *Action* were strictly orthodox. Once at *L'Humanité* he assumed the column hitherto contributed by Marius Magnien, but in essence was seen (and liked to see himself) as the successor to Gabriel Péri.[3] With his contributions to the major papers and reviews of the PCF press he would, over the next fourteen years, faithfully and predictably release the PCF's line on foreign policy in editorials and more general articles alike. His knowledge of English was of considerable advantage, giving him direct access to the British and American press. This is particularly noticeable during the first two years of his career with *L'Humanité*, when scarcely a week passed without there being at least two translations from newspapers or from statements made by British and American politicians. As his responsibilities grew and he travelled more widely[4] there is no doubt that his command of the language eased his way in the numerous international conferences he was asked to cover.

It was a period of intense, almost at times frenetic, activity. Scarcely a year passed without at least two or three major visits abroad, and with his various journalistic commitments Courtade found himself obliged on occasions to produce seven or eight articles and essays per week. Some of these, such as those on Albania or on China, which were the fruits of protracted visits, or others on De Gaulle's policies, were extracted from the pages of *L'Humanité* and *L'Humanité-Dimanche* and published separately, either as supplements or by the PCF's publishing house, the Editions sociales.[5] During this period he also wrote and had published two further novels and a volume of short stories, and began work on *La Place rouge* and *Le Jeu de paume.*

In public, therefore, Courtade gave the appearance of being a fully committed PCF intellectual whose orthodoxy and discipline were exemplary. Even though he was not active in his local Party cell he was rewarded by being elected in 1954 to the Central Committee of the PCF, at whose meetings, according to Gaston Plissonnier, his contributions, if relatively few, were always probing and sometimes disturbing. From the late 1940s a number of events already called for an official reaction – the Kravchenko case, the denunciation of Tito, the trials of Rajk and Kostov, the question of the Soviet Camps. The problems these caused for left-wing intellectuals and for Communists in particular have been elegantly dealt with by David Caute. As he has pointed out, Courtade's position remained utterly orthodox, and indeed when, in the changed climate of 1956, Tito would be welcomed back to the Communist fold and Rajk rehabilitated he would continue to articulate the Party line, seemingly without difficulty. With that in mind a quotation from his preface to *L'Affaire Rajk* makes amusing, instructive and nicely ironic reading: 'Un jour il paraîtra monstrueux que l'authenticité de ces aveux ait pu être mis en doute comme, inversement, il nous paraît monstrueux aujourd'hui que l'innocence de Dreyfus ait pu être contestée. Il faut à la vérité un certain temps pour s'imposer.'[6]

As Caute and others remind us, drawing on the memories of the likes of Edgar Morin or Claude Roy, it is virtually impossible to know whether Courtade (along with others at the time) was genuinely convinced of Rajk's and Kostov's guilt, or whether he was merely voicing the view expected of (or dictated to) him.[7] In his private diary, 29 March 1956 Courtade notes: 'Appris à 13h par *France-Soir* la réhabilitation de Rajk en Hongrie. Bien sûr je m'y attendais. Je sais que *ce que j'ai fait je l'ai fait honorablement* – parce que je le croyais [...] utile à la cause de la révolution mais quelle autorité puis-je avoir? J'ai été trompé. Je voudrais aussi la certitude que tout le monde a été *trompé* comme moi (et que certains n'ont pas été d'*ignobles cyniques*).'

That there were two standards or positions here is evident; they are to be found too in his behaviour towards two individuals with whom he had enjoyed close friendship: Georges Szekeres, whose courage in executing dangerous resistance activities he had much admired, and Pierre Hervé. The former, a Hungarian who had played an important role in the Resistance, came to know Courtade in Lyons. After the war he worked for the Hungarian foreign affairs department in Rome, and at the time of the Rajk trials was summoned to Budapest as a witness and to answer questions about his own activities. Fearful of what could happen to him he left Rome for Paris, where he hoped to find work and enjoy the support of his erstwhile French Resistance friends. Instead he was met with blank indifference, even hostility.[8] Eventually he was handed over by the French to the Hungarian authorities, with the result that he was imprisoned for seven years before being freed in 1956. He refused thereafter to meet Courtade again.

The required public front was also to be seen at the time of the *affaire* Hervé. Although he too had been forthright in his denunciation of Rajk and Kostov, Hervé was not always willing to accept PCF pronouncements uncritically. As we have noted already, rumblings of his discontent had already been heard in *La Libération trahie* (1945) and *La Politique et la Morale* (1946); but in 1956, and only weeks before the Twentieth Congress of the Party, he openly attacked its authoritarian attitude and blinkered policies in his essay *La Révolution et les fétiches*.

The tone of this is set early on. The Party leaders, Hervé claims, 'voudraient tout ramener au culte des chefs et de l'autorité, aux cérémonies commemoratives et à la récitation d'un credo de citations consacrées.'[9] Throughout he argues – frequently quoting Lenin in support – that Marxism has a degree of flexibility in its application all too often ignored by modern theorists; that it offers guidance, 'une méthode pour rechercher les solutions et notamment une méthode pour orienter consciemment l'idéologie en fonction d'objectifs politiques déterminés';[10] even, that it can and should admit pluralism and relativism. Political activity driven on by an uncritical acceptance of an ideology rapidly degenerates into fanaticism. In the third and final section of his essay Hervé turns his attention to the role of Party intellectuals and writers, claiming that they must be allowed a degree of freedom in order to be of benefit to the working class. Again his target is the narrow interpretation and inflexible imposition of dogma, and the preference for orthodoxy of content over artistic form and expression. Without refering directly to Zhdanov or to Kanapa and Casanova, Hervé clearly has in view here the tenets of socialist realism and what he sees to be the deliberate reduction in the critical and constructive role of the intellectual in the face of a narrow ideologically-driven *ouvriérisme*: 'La pensée, l'esprit critique, le raisonnement ont été trop humiliés. La foi du charbonnier, l'autorité et la discipline ont été trop exaltée [*sic*].'[11]

La Révolution et les fétiches caused considerable outcry. Not surprisingly, it was roundly condemned for its revisionist proposals and idealist position by PCF critics – Victor Michaut in *Les Cahiers du Communisme*, Guy Besse in *L'Humanité*, André Voquet in *France Nouvelle*. In February in *Les Temps modernes* Sartre was less dogmatic, arguing that while Hervé had been wrong to publish the essay, the Communist Party should have been more ready to enter into the kind of discussion it invited. Only in a climate of openness could the Party hope to benefit fully from its intellectuals: 'Nous voudrions en vérité que vous établissiez pour les intellectuels communistes des conditions de confiance et de sécurité telles qu'[ils] [...] puissent retrouver l'envie d'entreprendre des recherches concrètes et d'apporter leur contribution au marxisme, c'est à dire à notre culture.' Sartre's article was of course more a reflection of his own position *vis-à-vis* the Communist Party at this time than a commentary on Hervé's essay; but even if it was also an attempt to stimulate discussion and at least in part an invitation for compromise or reconciliation to be reached, it was to no avail. Hervé was disciplined and formally excluded.

Ten years later *La Révolution et les fétiches* would hardly have caused a murmur. In 1956 its author was publicly condemned for heresy, but in private his remarks struck more than one sympathetic chord with not a few Party members, even though their public role would not allow them to admit it. Apparently Courtade was privately furious that Hervé had not seen fit to discuss his ideas with him, feeling that his friend had in a way betrayed him. The diaries contain no reference to such feelings, but the problem of the book's publication is given some consideration. Courtade's sympathy is clear, and in an entry for 21 January he writes:

J'approuve presque chaque ligne et en même temps je comprends pourquoi le principe de la publication d'un tel livre est intolérable pour le Parti. Mais il sera utile et quel *autre* moyen Pierre avait-il de dire ce qu'il avait à dire (et que des milliers pensaient avec lui, clairement ou confusément).

He then continues to considere how he should respond:

S'il est critiqué une critique d'idées – *bien*. Je me tais. Il est assez grand pour se défendre – et ce serait simple.

   - S'il est exclu – je proteste *dans le parti*.

   - S'il est sali, traité de policier etc. ... je dois protester publiquement et par conséquent risquer toute ma vie – mais mon bonheur est à ce prix. Le silence ferait de moi un être veule – et par conséquent inefficace.

But such resolution came to nought, and silence was in fact what followed.

Courtade's reaction to *La Révolution et les fétiches* tells us a good deal, but it has also to be set in the context of his private situation. As we have seen, his obligations as a Party journalist through the early 1950s, together with those of his other writing, were considerable, physically and intellectually demanding. To this was added from March 1953 a crisis in his personal life when the film director Louis Daquin introduced him and Génia to Nicole Chatel. Never one to have been overkeen in his observation of strict marital fidelity,[12] Courtade soon found himself drawn to a woman twenty years younger than himself, and, while there is no direct evidence for it, the additional tension this created undoubtedly contributed to a heart attack that he suffered in October 1955. It was during his convalescence, spent between two hotels in St Germain-en-Laye, that he reacted to the *affaire* Hervé. He would not return to the matter for several years, and then only in *La Place rouge*, in which Hervé is unflatteringly portrayed in the character of Cazaux.[13] Courtade would never be forgiven by his former Lakanal schoolmate.

The absence of any *journal intime* before 1955 makes speculation about Courtade's private thoughts on PCF policies and directives difficult. According to Claude Roy his reactions to those issued on the role of art and literature acted as a safety-valve or counterbalance to those on political matters: 'Son *libéralisme* esthétique affermissait son dogmatisme politique. Les incartades qu'il s'autorisait dans ses goûts, et en littérature, étaient la soupape de sureté qui l'ancrait dans l'acceptation fanatique du *Credo* stalinien.'[14] Others who knew him confirm this, and recall that he found the intellectual and aesthetic climate of the PCF in the early 1950s rebarbative and even ridiculous. Yet, as we shall see, *Jimmy* and *La Rivière noire*, both indubitably 'engaged' works, display not a few qualities which set them squarely in the context of socialist realism.[15]

Convalescence in the hotels and in a series of houses belonging to various friends provided Courtade with a time to reflect and write. From the autumn of 1955 through to the early months of the following year he completed or wrote the stories that would appear under the title of *Les Animaux supérieurs*. Diary entries refer frequently to them, and to a need for his fiction to be rooted firmly in reality: 'rechercher systématiquement dans les faits divers la *trame* de la nouvelle ou du roman.' This is a theme he would return to, and which would find full expression in *La Place rouge.*

Not surprisingly, entries during these months are dominated by references to the complexities of and the anxiety caused by his relationships with Génia and Nicole, and by reflections on his achievements and future. All hinge on the need to act decisively, to 'sortir de soi-même'. Given the circumstances this is little more than we might expect; but one entry in particular has more than an echo of preoccupations and inhibitions from earlier years as well: 'Pourquoi je repousse avec violence le "petit minet" (qu'est-ce que c'était que le petit minet?) Les [?], l'enfant peureux, ignorant de la vie. Si seulement il avait été pur ... mais même pas ! G[énia] déteste *l'homme* en moi. Elle me veut soumis etc. etc. [...] voilà la question pour moi maintenant, la question du choix [...] ce n'est *pas* le choix entre N[icole] et G[énia]. C'est le choix entre deux manières d'être pour moi.' This desire to liberate himself and to start afresh is expressed as well in a number of references to his writing, journalism and fiction alike: 'J'ai donné mon temps (et en fait 10 ans de ma vie) à la fabrication d'articles quotidiens que d'autres auraient pu faire aussi bien – et mieux peut-être' (23 November); 'Je serais sauvé si j'étais capable du *moment d'énergie* nécessaire pour me mettre à un travail *vrai.* Mais probablement tout ce que j'ai écrit jusqu'à présent et *que je n'ose plus regarder* ne vaut rien. Là est la clef' (13 December).

As so frequently in the past, however, resolution and determination were not to be realized in actions; by February Courtade had already accepted the offer of writing three articles for *L'Humanité-Dimanche*, and by April he would once more be contributing regularly (if less frequently) to the PCF's two main papers.[16] During the next two years he would continue as their principal international affairs specialist; but by May 1958 he would increasingly focus on the Algerian problem, on the role of De Gaulle, and on what the PCF decried at every opportunity as a renewal of fascism. With the success of *Les Animaux supérieurs* and a promising beginning on *La Place rouge*, in January 1959 Courtade signed a contract with the publishers Julliard guaranteeing him forty thousand francs per month from January to May. During this period he ceased writing for *L'Humanité*, but continued to do so for the Sunday paper, producing a new and substantial column, 'Le tour d'horizon de la semaine politique', intended to be the equivalent of or answer to Mauriac's celebrated *bloc-notes* in *L'Express*. They continued virtually without interruption for over a year. By the end of 1959 he had asked to be sent to Moscow as *L'Humanité*'s permanent correspondent. He eventually left with Nicole in July of the following year.

However high a public profile Courtade had between 1955 and 1960, and however fully reintegrated he appeared to be in the PCF's intellectual machinery, the unrest and more importantly the doubts remained. Having recovered from his illness he would not return to live with Génia in their apartment in the Rue de Verneuil, claiming as an excuse the danger of the effort required in climbing the stairs to the fourth floor. For a year he led an itinerant existence, living sometimes alone, sometimes with Nicole in the south of France, on the outskirts of Paris and in the capital itself in various houses and flats borrowed from close friends. Eventually they settled in a small flat in the Rue de Varenne in 1956, where he began work on *La Place rouge*.

But physical separation from Génia in no way made the break an easy one.[17] On several occasions entries in his *journal intime* return to the theme of the 'petit minet', and project Génia's influence over him as an extension of his mother's. In October 1956 he writes: 'je coupe le long cordon ombilical qui m'a rattaché de ma mère à G[énia] dans une enfance secrètement *prolongée*.' Four months later (6 January 1957) we read: 'Ma seule chance de devenir un homme était naturellement – vingt ans plus tard de couper le cordon ombilical', and shortly after (1 February) he blames Génia for not having accepted 'ma transformation naturelle. Je n'étais pas devenu un autre homme comme elle l'a cru, mais homme. Elle aurait dû comme ma mère m'aider à couper le cordon ombilical qui l'attachait à moi. Devenir un complice et mon amie. L'esprit petit bourgeois l'en a empêchée.' Two years later the situation, while much improved, has still to be resolved: 'Grand progrès dans mes rapports avec Génia. J'ai pour la première fois l'impression que je vais réussir à me délivrer *d'elle*. (Non pas de son souvenir, non pas de son amitié, mais de la *domination* qu'elle exerçait sur moi, encore maintenant à distance)' (14 February 1959). At the same as entries of this nature there are others in which Courtade also claims a continuing *need* for Génia. Both appear to be a classic demonstration of a subconscious desire to admit finally and fully to his own guilt.

Without doubt deeply disturbing in its own right, this problem remained also inseparable from Courtade's continuing uncertainty about his relationship with the Party (but not with Communism) and about his obligations and qualities as a writer. The first long general reflection on this comes three months after his release from the clinic:

> Continuer de vivre comme je le fais me conduit immanquablement à la destruction, à la neuresthénie en tout cas – à l'impuissance et probablement à la mort. J'ai revisé toute ma vie – artificieusement justifié d'aller *au fond* des choses – cela doit cesser. Pour cela je dois me soumettre à une règle simple. Il fallait – je l'avais souhaité – qu'elle me soit donné [*sic*] en terme d'une souffrance authentique. Comme une lumière – cela est venu: la règle sera de tout faire au service de la *vérité*, aussi bien pour ce qui concerne ma vie personnelle que pour la vie publique. Mais pas la vérité pour la vérité (il n'y a pas de règle enfantine, de "recette") la vérité pour la justice (ce qui implique parfois le silence), la vérité pour l'humanité (ce qui implique – dans la vie privée certains accommodants). (26 March 1956)

This need for absolute truth as a standard against which personal and public achievement or utterance should be measured is of particular concern in Courtade's relationship with the Party. While he does not refer to it directly in his private diary, the Khrushchev report on Stalin's regime is here relevant. As we shall see, Courtade's public treatment of this in the pages of *L'Humanité* is orthodox.[18] In the diary entry quoted above, however, even though there is an acknowledgement of the need for a controlled or partial truth ('parfois le silence'), it appears to be at odds precisely with this absolute standard.

Only two weeks later (6 April) the problem re-emerges: 'sur le plan politique j'ai, dans une grande exaltation, inutile sans doute, essayé de convaincre la direction du journal qu'il fallait combattre pour la vérité etc. ... Mais je suis *las*.' (According to his close friend and colleague Max Léon, Courtade argued for the publication of the report in full.)[19]

These last few words are no doubt telling, but Courtade seems to be caught in an insoluble dilemma. On the one hand is his need to bear witness publicly to his faith in Communism, on the other is the recognition that certain revelations may destroy its credibility. The only way to avoid this is to hide behind the carefully rehearsed formulations of party-speak, and of this and of the mentality and attitudes that it reflected Courtade would become increasingly impatient, at least in private. Party officials are dismissed on more than one occasion as members of a sect, guilty of self-delusion ('un parti qui se croyait fort' (8 October 1958)), and even of ignorance resulting from a willing but unthinking submission 'au devoir conçu comme un impératif absolu interdisant tout jugement sur ce qui est commandé' (28 September).

The same problem is posed, if to a lesser degree, in his reflections on his aims and ambitions as an imaginative writer, though it is little more than a reformulation of the content versus form question that left-wing intellectuals had been debating in various ways for the preceding twenty-five years in particular. For Courtade it was not enough to be '*à la fois* un militant communiste et un écrivain qui a "franchi" le barrage', as he wrote in October 1956; the problem for him presented itself as the need to have within the *same* book a demonstration of Communist values (making of it 'un livre de vérité'), but cast in a form and style of intrinsic merit free from any kind of prescription or directive. That this remained a fundamental problem for him, however, even after the completion of *La Place rouge*, can be seen from the long letter Courtade wrote to Vailland in 1962.

Clearly what Courtade needed as much in his private life as in his public one was some kind of enforced change. The period of reflection, even though occasioned by illness and convalescence, had been valuable. But while questions had been raised, few had been adequately answered. His own basic faith in Communism seems not to have been shaken, even if he had increasingly little time for many of those charged with the responsibility of carrying it to the world at large. But despite a determination to produce a piece of imaginative writing of substance, and despite the success of *Les Animaux supérieurs* and Julliard's mark of confidence, doubts clearly lingered. And he was already haunted by 'la fatigue de la vie' and by thoughts of death. On 24 November 1958 he notes: 'j'apprends que je suis assez sérieusement malade,' a confirmation of lingering suspicions recorded regularly in his diary in early January of the previous year. All of this would be projected into the pages of *Le Jeu de paume*.

The tone of his diary throughout 1957 and 1958 is in general one of pessimism and uncertainty. Every so often a moment of conviction or decision gives rise to Vailland-like expressions of confidence ('Ma fierté d'être avec la petite phalange *des hommes debout'* (28 September 1958)), and he contemplates writing a short story to be entitled 'Héros'. But neither is there, nor will there be, any resolution. Moscow and the Soviet experience would certainly bring new dimensions and allow Courtade a happiness he had not known for many years; but the last three years of his life will continue to have running through them the same fault line of uncertainty and increasing anxiety.

The Journalist

Courtade's immediate responsibilities on joining the ranks of the Party scribes were to cover the government's European policy and to draw his readers' attention to the threat that the PCF considered was being posed by that policy to national identity. The PCF argued, not without some justification, that France's (and indeed the Allies') acceptance of America's Marshall plan showed signs of indecent haste. This inevitably threatened not just economic autonomy, but what in the early 1990s it would become fashionable to call 'national sovereignty'. France, with Bidault as spokesman, would become simply another American colony: 'Accepter, défendre ce plan, c'est se ruer dans la servitude, c'est faire bon marché de l'indépendance et de l'honneur de son pays' (11 November 1947).[20] The tone of the argument against was frequently quite unambiguously xenophobic, with the spectre of a renascent, belligerent Germany under American protection a regular theme. What is more, it was a policy which reflected the vested interests of those in control right across the Allied powers, and ignored the feelings of millions of ordinary people. As the PCF became

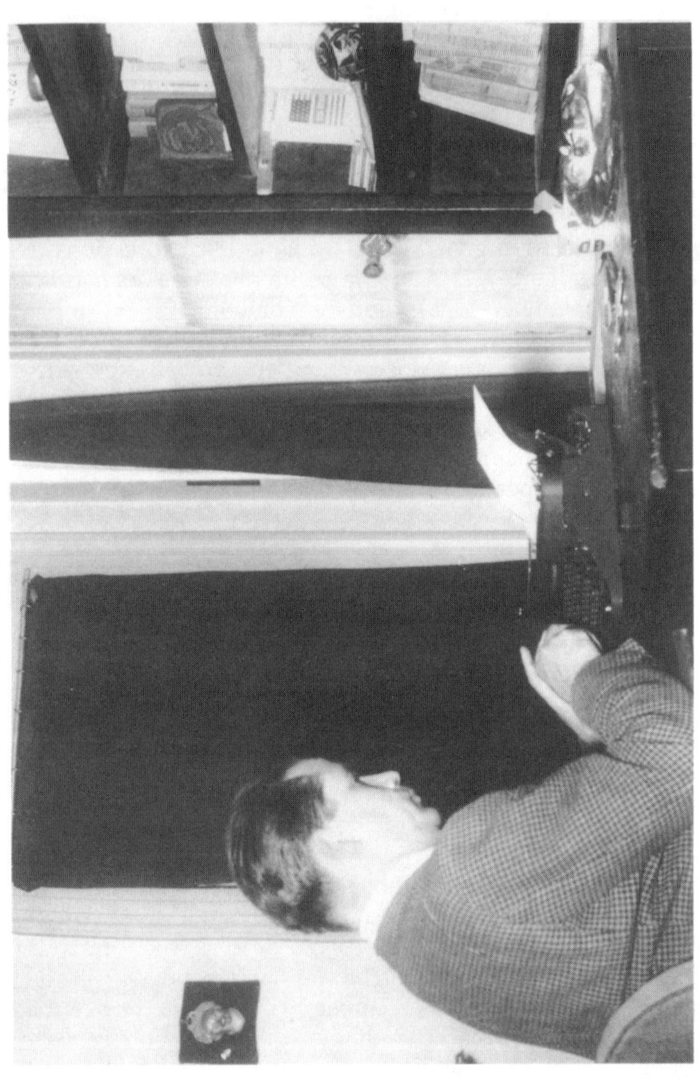

Rue de Verneuil, 1951.

increasingly marginalized the arguments were rehearsed daily. A piece Courtade wrote for *L'Humanité* 7 October 1950 is typical:

> Ce problème est de faire accepter au peuple français *qu'une fois de plus* soit reconstituée à ses frontières la force qui, trois fois en moins d'un siècle, a ravagé notre sol. Et cela cinq ans à peine après la victoire, quand les ruines ne sont pas balayées, quand le deuil est encore brûlant dans le coeur de centaines de milliers d'hommes et de femmes de ce pays!

Five months later, in one in a series of articles devoted to Adenauer's overtures to the Allied governments, the tone is even more bitter:

> Enfant chéri de M. Truman, il sait qu'il n'a rien à redouter des autres gouvernements satellites et en particulier du fantomatique gouvernement français trop heureux d'offrir, avec promesse de le fournir, le moment venu, du sang français.
>
> Tout cela, bien entendu, au nom de la 'défense' de l'Europe et de ces valeurs de la civilisation chrétienne que Mgr Feltin exaltait l'autre jour dans la chaire de Notre-Dame, aux applaudissements des collabos. (1 March 1951)

The criticism of a spineless French government ('les muets du sérail américain' (14 May 1953)), all too willing to capitulate to American demands, had already appeared in his articles in the *Cahiers du Communisme* and in *Démocratie nouvelle*. So too had allusions to the increasing American presence as another Occupation. This was a theme which featured increasingly in PCF discourse and was echoed extensively in the press (see for example *Les Lettres françaises*) and in imaginative writing. André Stil's trilogy *Le Premier Choc* (1951–3) was a particular example. In February 1948 Courtade drew the parallel between American and Nazi policies; later that year he demonstrated how in the USA what was presented as 'une démocratie capitaliste' quickly turned into 'un Etat déjà policier et presque fasciste' (*Démocratie nouvelle*, May 1948).

And the theme continued. Six years later the Nazis were the 'maîtres spirituels' (8 September 1954) of the American government; beneath the camouflage of European unity was to be seen 'la gueule d'acier des canons de la nouvelle Wehrmacht'

(9 September 1953). When, in March 1957, the Rome Treaties on Europe and on nuclear armaments (Euratom) were about to be signed Courtade's invective burst out: 'L'Europe dont on vous propose d'être les fourriers, c'est l'Europe [...] héritière de la sanglante Europe hitlérienne. Cette "civilisation" c'est celle de la guerre à l'Est et de l'hégémonie de l'Allemagne revancharde à l'ouest' (23 March).   In strict accordance with PCF views Courtade reminded his readers that in any case the Europe that was being formed ignored Moscow, Prague and Warsaw, with their histories and culture; it was an American-led block, and no more than a colony, or more vulgarly 'le croupion de l'aigle américain' (30 July 1954).

Inevitably such clear aggression and indications of a policy of imperialist expansion since the end of the war had obliged the Eastern block to adopt a defensive position. Such was the determination of the Soviet people and such had been the progress made since the Revolution that by the late 1950s the Americans were obliged to realize that they could no longer enjoy a superiority in nuclear capability. Fortunately the Soviet people, like all working-class populations, were dedicated to peace. Even someone as blinkered as Foster Dulles, dismissed on his appointment as Dean Acheson's military adviser in the spring of 1950 as a 'fanatique glacé' and a 'partisan acharné du réarmement de l'Allemagne réactionnaire' (8 April 1950), was aware of this:

> [il] sait très bien que l'Union Soviétique n'attaque pas parce que l'Union Soviétique n'attaquera jamais parce que la guerre d'agression est entièrement contraire aux principes de son gouvernement, parce qu'il n'y a, en URSS, ni capitalistes, ni trusts qui auraient intérêt à la guerre, parce que l'Union Soviétique n'a pas besoin de la guerre. Parce que son intérêt comme Etat coïncide avec les intérêts de tous les peuples et que les peuples, partout, veulent la paix. (21 April 1953)

Such insistence on the inherent peaceful aspirations of 'les peuples' was again part of official policy, of course; it would cause considerable embarrassment to a large number of PCF members and sympathizers three years later, at the time of the invasion of Hungary.

Beyond Europe, American policies, seen by the Communist Party as being entirely interventionist, remained a focus for attack. Activities in Korea, Formosa and North Africa, for example, demonstrated the ways in which the United States attempted to establish not simply pockets of influence, but bases from which, if necessary, attacks could be launched on the Communist world – hence the (regrettable) need for the defensive measures taken by the Soviet Union and, after the formation of the People's Republic in 1949, by China. And in order for the threat to be fully grasped Courtade, like many Communist journalists, frequently returned to the model of France and the Nazi presence. Thus, for example, on 25 January 1955 he wrote of Formosa:

> Par rapport à Formose, la Chine se trouve actuellement dans la situation qui eût été celle de la France si, à la Libération, des forces allemandes, appuyées par des collabos et grossies de soldats français enrôlés de force, s'étaient établies en Corse et y avaient installé un gouvernement Laval qui eût continué à prétendre 'représenter' la France ...

And while in several *grands reportages* on the United States Courtade showed a grudging admiration for certain aspects of American life, recalling his earlier youthful reaction in 1931, it was short-lived. In 'Choses vues en Amérique' or 'L'Amérique a peur', for example, Courtade underlined the gloss and superficiality of a society in which information was withheld and in which corruption reigned as capitalism was allowed to run riot. Ultimately his observations on America's domestic policies were every bit as vehement as those on activities overseas – racial discrimination, the conviction of the leader of the American Communist Party on charges of conspiracy in 1948 and 1949, the McCarthy purges in the early 1950s, or the execution of Ethel and Julius Rosenberg in 1953, two years after their having been convicted as atomic spies.

Such was the obligation on all PCF journalists to follow directions for a simplistic black-and-white analysis and presentation of affairs, that it is in no way surprising that the governments, and especially the people, of the Soviet Union, China, Vietnam or Algeria should have been presented as essentially peace-loving, and as the depositaries of true social and political wisdom. Any recourse to military action would always be justifiable and legitimate in the struggle against oppression. The following sentences from articles on Tito at the time of his disgrace, for example, could be taken from any of several dozen: 'C'est l'histoire, au fond assez simple, d'une petite bande d'hommes déjà liés par des crimes et des faiblesses anciennes qui, s'emparant d'un mouvement authentique, jouent la comédie de la révolution ...' (30 October 1949); or: 'Dans la lutte courageuse qu[e le peuple] mène pour recouvrer son indépendance, pour reconquérir l'héritage de ses glorieux partisans indignement trahis, il est fort de la solidarité des travailleurs animés par l'internationalisme prolétarien' (3 July 1952).

Spokesmen for and representatives of imperialist aggression are ultimately all rejected, whatever passing recognition there may have been for their political skills at any given time. Churchill, for example, is dismissed by Courtade as racist, a cynic (*Les Cahiers du Communisme*, March 1946) and as the 'gauleiter américain' (11 October 1948); Ridgway is greeted on his arrival as Allied commander in Europe in 1952 as 'l'homme du napalm' and 'ce tueur microbien' (7 May 1952); Bidault is 'une mécanique américaine' (25 April 1953), 'une autruche' (29 April 1954) and 'un des hommes qui ont fait le plus de mal à la France depuis dix ans' (13 September 1955); Félix Gaillard is 'un super Dulles' (31 December 1957). And so on. By comparison Ho Chi Minh, Chou En Lai, Malenkov, Molotov, Bulgarin, Vyshinsky, Maurice Thorez and others who work selflessly on behalf of the people for the creation of true socialist democracy everywhere in the world meet with unqualified approval. All of them, needless to say, take their inspiration and guidance from Stalin.

Thorez's return to France in April 1953 after his convalescence in the Soviet Union was greeted by Aragon in the columns of *L'Humanité* with an absurd, sycophantic poem already especially written for the occasion, 'Il revient ...'. Not everyone concerned with the Party approved. The tone at least suggested that policy had perhaps been lacking guidance, and that only with the return of 'notre ami Maurice' could things be put right.[21] Whether Courtade agreed with Aragon's gesture or whether he was instructed to do so is not known, but he too had published on 31 March a similarly ludicrous piece:

Le voici qui revient parmi nous. Jamais la France n'a eu autant besoin de lui, de sa lucidité, de sa confiance raisonnée dans le grand avenir de notre peuple. Avec lui, avec notre Parti Communiste Français, avec la confiance et l'appui de millions d'honnêtes gens qui voient clairement maintenant à quel désastre on veut les conduire, nous remonterons la pente.

Courtade's admiration of and sympathy for Thorez seem to have been genuine, but it must not be forgotten that in the PCF leader there was not simply a projection of Stalin but, now that the Soviet leader was dead, a kind of French replacement, almost a reincarnation.[22] According to those close to him at the time Courtade does not appear to have been affected by Stalin's death even remotely in the way that Vailland was, for example. For him, as for so many, Stalinism as a creed had replaced the man.[23] The 'culte de la personnalité' had taken over. When therefore the Khrushchev report on his predecessor's atrocities first became news it was almost inevitable that Courtade should have been given the task of assessing it in the light of the Party's policy drawn up at the Twentieth Congress.

It now seems certain that Thorez was shown a copy of Khrushchev's speech just before it was delivered on 25 February 1956, and that he decided to conceal it from his Party colleagues. When it was published, the PCF initially refused to acknowledge its authenticity, and reference was made regularly to 'un rapport attribué à Khrouchtchev'; but before such a position became no longer tenable (*Le Monde* would carry the text on 4 June, for example) Courtade was asked to produce some explanatory articles. As we have noted, he is said to have been against withholding the report; but in these articles he rehearsed the arguments to be deployed later by the Party in its attempted justification. That the 'culte de la personnalité' had got out of hand was acknowledged; but while unfortunate, it was almost inevitable given the nature of the evolution of Communism under such a powerful leader and because of the threat imposed by his enemies. Not only was it to the Party's credit, therefore, that the errors should have been recognized and corrected, however painful such an act was; but it was an indication of its courage, determination and general openness. 'A y bien réfléchir, les seuls qui avaient le droit de dénoncer les erreurs commises en URSS, c'étaient les Soviétiques eux-mêmes. Ce droit ils l'ont payé des plus grands sacrifices qu'un peuple ait jamais consentis, non seulement pour son avenir mais pour l'avenir de toute l'humanité' (8 July 1956). Furthermore, to have taken action earlier would have been inopportune and would have radically undermined the whole concept of the Revolution at that moment in its development. Courtade's argument was of course a standard one.

Later in the same year in October ingenuity of a related, if rather different, kind was required after the Soviet Union's invasion of Hungary. In this case the process of the erosion of Stalinism set in motion by Western imperialist forces had encouraged reactionary or counter-revolutionary activists to attempt their *coup*; Soviet intervention was not invasion, but a proper response to the appeal of the people to protect them against a fascist regime. In the wake of the Khrushchev report both the event and the attempted justification were too much for some Party intellectuals and supporters, and resulted in the letter of protest published in *France Observateur* and signed, amongst others, by Sartre, Vercors, Claude Roy, Rolland, Simone de Beauvoir and Vailland.   Although Courtade expressed misgivings in private, he could not be persuaded to add his name; and while it was André Stil as *L'Humanité*'s editor who went to Hungary and assumed the responsibility of 'explaining' the country's problems to the paper's readers, Courtade's contributions on the subject remained entirely orthodox.[24]

As he recovered from his illness he turned his attention once again to the general international scene, and especially to what he had come to term 'la Petite Europe', the Suez problem, the nuclear arms race, and Algeria. De Gaulle, the 'apprenti dictateur' as he was dubbed by the PCF, also became a special target.   As with Churchill, Courtade was not unwilling to acknowledge some of De Gaulle's past achievements. When, in late 1959, he reviewed the third volume of the *Mémoires de Guerre*, he recognized the skill with which the General had handled national policy in the face of American pressure after the Liberation.[25] But De Gaulle's weakness was to have allowed his perception of himself as the only person capable of saving France to have taken control and to have succumbed to the flattery of others. This was a personality cult of a different sort! On 2 September 1958 Courtade wrote: 'L'homme qui en août 1944 pouvait – c'est vrai – descendre à pied les Champs-Elysées au milieu d'une foule en armes en est aujourd'hui réduit à faire "monter" des manifestations à sa gloire, par le chef de ses services secrets, Soustelle en personne! ... Quelle misère! Quelle chute!'

By 1947 and the ousting of the Communist ministers from government the General and his policies were already a target for direct attack: 'De Gaulle veut la France esclave de l'étranger, parce que c'est la seule chance pour lui de s'en rendre maître' (13 November 1947). And such would be the tone of articles in the communist press for the next decade as De Gaulle hovered in the wings waiting to reintroduce himself to the centre stage. But it was through the weeks leading up to the investiture of De Gaulle as head of state in June 1958 and in the context of the bloodiest episodes of the Algerian War that the attacks were most sustained. Throughout the conflict the PCF had, it claimed, been advocating a peace settlement based on negotiation and on the wishes of 'le peuple algérien'. Courtade's articles faithfully reflected this position. De Gaulle's early manoeuvrings were seen as overtures to the vested interests of the *pieds-noirs* and the army, and as an encouragement to the Americans to continue their policy of establishing power bases in North Africa.[26]

Comparisons were made not only with Louis XIV, Napoleon or Boulanger but with Pétain, Darlan, Franco and Mussolini. This was a form of demagoguery which had to be opposed by all true Frenchmen if the Republic and its values were to be preserved: 'Le rempart de la République ne peut être l'homme qui s'est emparé des pouvoirs de la République par effraction. Le rempart de la République ce sont les républicains unis, et agissant contre le fascisme qui opère à l'ombre du pouvoir personnel' (30 June 1958). Courtade's articles from May 1958, with some additional commentary, were published by the PCF as a pamphlet in June under the title *Ecrits pour la République*, and enjoyed very considerable success. They also resulted in his receiving a large numbers of abusive letters from Gaullist supporters, and even several death threats. At this time Courtade produced as well an essay, *L'Arabe sans maître*, in which much of the same material is used. When Fasquelle rejected it early in November Courtade's note in his diary reflects a kind of tired resignation: 'Appris que mon manuscrit a été refusé par Fasquelle. Raisons politiques sans doute, mais d'une certaine manière il a raison je l'avais fait comme un *pensum* .'

With the advance from Julliard Courtade did not write again in *L'Humanité* until September 1959, when he went to America to cover Khrushchev's visit, though at André Carrel's invitation he contributed to *L'Humanité-Dimanche* his new, substantial weekly article, 'Le Tour d'horizon de la semaine politique'. In these, and indeed for the next nine months before he settled permanently in Moscow, Courtade returned frequently to the Algerian problem; but increasingly his articles focused on Franco-Soviet relations, on the nuclear threat, on Khrushchev's offers to reduce the number of atomic weapons. The Party line never wavered. In late March, Courtade headed a team of *L'Humanité* journalists to cover Khrushchev's visits to France. In a special issue of the Sunday paper (13 March), full of colour photographs, his anticipation of the Soviet leader's arrival was almost as fulsome as the one given to Thorez seven years earlier:

> Il est compréhensible que, comme révolutionnaire, vous soyez intéréssé et ému par tout ce que la France a représenté et continue à représenter dans l'histoire du mouvement ouvrier mondial. Vous êtes ici sur la terre où s'élevèrent pour la première fois les strophes de 'l'Internationale', vous êtes dans le pays de Babeuf et des communards.

It was clear from this and his other articles that Courtade's credentials – at least and once again in public – were impeccable, and that he was ready for the Soviet Union.

Any journalist writing as extensively and as frequently as Courtade did for papers so faithfully reproducing a Party line (as distinct from the broad direction of a political movement) would inevitably develop a house style. At *L'Humanité*, apart from regular editorial meetings every morning, no specific directives were issued nor, according to journalists who worked alongside Courtade, was there any form of scrutiny or direct censorship. Max Léon recalls that any doubts or potential ambiguities that could not be resolved at such meetings were fully debated with the *rédacteur en chef* and, if necessary, with the paper's editor. Last-minute alterations could be made even in the print room, and Courtade's concern for accuracy and for the right *tournure de phrase* caused more than one editor frustrating moments as he waited for final copy. One result of such procedures, of course, will be conformity in content, and to some degree in tone as well, and in terms of their political orthodoxy Courtade's articles in any of the PCF's papers or reviews were hardly different from those by Yves Moreau, Antoine Acquaviva, René Andrieu, Madeleine Riffaud or a dozen others. When Pierre Grappin once asked him in the 1950s how he was able day after day to produce a 'correct' (usually resolutely Stalinist) analysis of any events on the international scene, Courtade's reply was what might be expected – but not, so Grappin recalls, without a degree of cynicism. It was enough to collect and collate as much documentation as possible, Courtade explained, and thereafter pass it through a kind of doctrinal grille. Anything that did not conform to received wisdom would automatically be trimmed and discarded.

Yet while orthodoxy and personal conviction go a long way to establishing any journalist's reputation, it is the strategies and characteristics of an individual style that capture the reader's full attention and enthusiasm. Again, as in any political discourse, there are similarities in articles by various *L'Humanité* journalists for the purpose of emphasis or attack; but Courtade's style has a number of distinctive personal qualities. Most frequently his tone is one of dialogue; he proposes an engagement with the reader, and makes an appeal to his intelligence and good sense. Sarcasm and irony (characteristic qualities of his private conversations) are widely deployed to undermine an opponent's position or to demonstrate the inadequacy or total stupidity of a non-communist policy. Equally prevalent are understatement, scorn, derision, anger, indignation and incredulity that a given point is not self-evidently correct. His articles have a tight internal structure, they alternate between positive and negative arguments, between *thèse* and *anti-thèse*, before finishing on a challenge which either invites acceptance or urges reflection. But they are rarely 'literary' pieces; rather they display the direct syntactic forms of speech.

Points are made in paragraphs that are frequently short, and sometimes contain one sentence only. Techniques include: repetition and refrain ('Une fois encore l'Union soviétique a ..., une fois encore elle..., une fois encore elle...'); warning ('Le fait qu'ils n'aient pas recours immédiatement à la violence ne doit pas faire illusion'); concession ('Mais admettons qu'il soit nécessaire, dans des conditions nouvelles [...], admettons même que [...], il n'en reste pas moins que ...'); direct appeal ('Travailleurs français, acceptez-vous que ...') and a rallying call to the epic qualities of 'La France' or 'les peuples'. Courtade also moves his arguments forward by a series of key words and expressions – of indisputable logic (*or, donc, ainsi*), of persuasion (*autant dire que, nul doute que, une fois de plus*), of emphasis (*la vérité est que, il est clair, essentiellement, certes*) and so on.[27]

The result, almost without exception, is direct, polished and, like most good journalism, provocative, even if skewed in a particular direction. Of course, Courtade is writing for a public which almost without exception is already convinced of the rightness of the case being presented, and is only looking for an authoritative affirmation. There is therefore a complicity established between writer and reader; the latter allows himself to be engaged and positioned in a particular way, knowing in advance that assent is virtually the only response possible. And if ever there should be any possibility of lingering doubt about a policy or his interpretation of it, Courtade readily resorts to the ploys of quoting statistics or consulting the authentic witness.

As a result of his visit to the Soviet Union in the spring of 1955 he produced in *L'Humanité* and *L'Humanité-Dimanche* a series of eight articles, 'Sur le chemin de l'URSS'. In one (7 April) he discusses the sense of responsibility shared by Soviet workers and the levels of production, which all too often are said by the Western press to be deliberately inflated. Courtade's response to disprove such accusations is simply to quote a government spokesman who, by definition, must be above suspicion of not telling the truth:

> La statistique est fondée sur la vérité. Ce n'est pas là une affirmation gratuite. Cette exigence de vérité découle de la nature même du régime économique de l'URSS. Staline a dit: 'L'ajustement des chiffres sur une idée préconçue est un crime.' On ne peut pas établir un plan avec des chiffres truqués. Le recours à de tels procédés conduirait tout droit à la catastrophe.

In an earlier article (4 April) the view of the individual citizen's life in the Soviet Union as being subject to constant surveillance and control is equally a fabrication of the capitalist press. In this case Courtade cites as his witness one Vladimir Jacoumovitch Karassev, who, when questioned about freedom, expresses only incomprehension and surprise: 'Il est passé dans les yeux vifs de Karassev une lueur d'étonnement que je n'oublierai jamais.' Such techniques as these are simply the written equivalent of photographs of large happy families or smiling workers and peasants, for whom the Revolution and Communism have brought not just contentment but a sense of sharing in a collective effort for a future in which peace, freedom and economic security are guaranteed.

The Imaginative Writer

Totally in harmony with the new political orthodoxy of the Party that developed in the late 1940s was a renewal of the socialist realist theory of art. Already in the 1930s this theory, formulated by the Union of Soviet Writers in 1933, had been given some currency in France through the columns of *Commune* in particular. Broadly, such literature should be realistic in its portrayal of life in all its aspects, but should show how revolutionary socialism emerges as the natural political philosophy leading to social betterment. At this point there were no guidelines for the *form* a work of socialist realist writing should take; the theory would automatically become 'l'essence même de l'oeuvre, incarnée dans ces images.'[28] Just over a decade later a new authority would enter the debate in the form of various directives pertaining to culture as a whole issued by Stalin's minister of culture Andrei Zhdanov, whose *Sur la littérature, la philosophie et la musique*, with an introduction by Duclos, appeared in 1948 and quickly acquired the status of dogma. Zhdanov had no doubts: 'L'écrivain doit éduquer le peuple et l'armer idéologiquement.'[29]

From the militant left articles and statements of deep conviction regularly issued. In *Les Lettres françaises*, for example, Elsa Triolet wrote: 'L'écrivain public [est] celui qui épouse et devance l'événement, qui l'exprime et le commente, le devine et l'éclaire socialement et politiquement parlant' (23 June 1947). Pierre Daix in the same paper two years later claimed that 'le réalisme socialiste est l'expression esthétique de cette force politique',[30] and in an essay on Balzac in May of the same year in *La Nouvelle Critique* argued that the duty of the artist was to participate 'à la lutte réelle des hommes pour changer le monde, pour être capable d'exprimer la vérité du monde.' For more than a decade *La Nouvelle Critique* (first published in December 1948 a century after the Communist Manifesto) became the catechism for the faithful, with Laurent Casanova and Jean Kanapa as its principal Party intoners. Just as a series of talks by Aragon in the 1930s had been reproduced as *Pour un réalisme socialiste* (1935), André Stil's *Vers le réalisme socialiste* appeared in 1952 on his being awarded the Prix Staline for *Au Château d'eau*, the first volume of his trilogy *Le Premier Choc*.[31]

The climate that developed, and the kinds of imaginative writing that it encouraged may, with hindsight, seem rebarbative. Stil's work or Aragon's reworked version of *Les Communistes*, like Nizan's *Le Cheval de Troie* in 1934, are characterized by schematization and an unashamed authorial control as they try to ensure that the direction of their work is not missed. Yet not all who in broad terms accepted the Party's political orthodoxy conformed quite so slavishly to the demands of the socialist realist canon. Vailland in particular was one whose novels *Beau masque* (1954) and *325.000 francs* (1956), while possessing a clear political line, have a complexity that broadens their appeal and invites readers to work at the meaning for themselves.[32]

With his two militant novels of the 1950s, *Jimmy* (1951) and *La Rivière noire* (1953), Courtade situates himself somewhere between these two positions. As we have already seen, for all his utter political orthodoxy at no point does Courtade appear to have had any time for the directives being voiced by the Party's cultural section. Indeed, according to Claude Roy and others he was entirely scornful of them. And yet he was no more prepared in 1956 over the Hervé controversy to risk adopting a position of sympathy in public than he had been ten years previously. He had come to believe quite firmly, however, that imaginative writing had a vital role to play in alerting people to the dangers of Western imperialism and in illustrating in a more palatable and far-reaching way positive qualities of revolutionary socialism. Vailland's *325.000 francs* grew directly out of a visit he made to Oyonnax with a view to writing a series of articles about working conditions there. Instead he decided to write a novel, 'car la portée sera plus grande. C'est trop important.'[33] The words could have been Courtade's as well.

Jimmy (1951)

> Il savait qu'une vie tout à fait nouvelle commençait pour lui. Qu'il serait désormais un homme profondément différent. Que ni le bonheur, ni la vie quotidienne n'auraient le même goût.
>
> Il ne savait pas encore à quel point il serait exigé de lui, ni comme il serait difficile de garder vive dans la tempête la petite flamme qu'il avait allumée ... (p. 358)[34]

With these words and with their unmistakable authorial gloss and trite metaphor Courtade's long novel about the spread and threat of American influence in the post-war world comes to an end. *Jimmy* is a form of *Bildungsroman*, the account of the slow and painful political awakening of a young American Jimmy Reeds, who moves from a position of middle-class orthodoxy and conservatism to one where he is ready to challenge authority and espouse the causes of freedom and justice. At the judicial inquiry into his recent activities with which the novel closes he is already classified as a Communist, even though he has a long way to go before his growing sympathies and awareness can be translated into official recognition in the form of Party membership.

Jimmy enjoyed considerable success. Serialized in *Les Lettres françaises* and in *Zvezda*, a Leningrad review, it rapidly sold over three hundred thousand copies. Certainly the climate was propitious. Concern over the influence of America was widespread, and by no means voiced only by the parties of the Left in France, even if they were the most outspoken. In addition to those in *L'Humanité*, nowhere was this more popularly expressed, perhaps, than in the pages of *Les Lettres françaises*, where a series of articles and cartoons sustained an attack on all levels and features of American activity and the American way of life, frequently drawing parallels between them and those of the Nazi regime of the Occupation. Anti-Americanism was also one of the standard themes of the new wave of socialist realism, though Courtade's novel is not as blatant as some in its exploitation of it.

A glance at André Stil's trilogy *Le Premier Choc*, for example, shows the degree to which it could be taken. This novel describes the resistance of workers in 1950 – 1 to the arrival of an American arms ship in a port somewhere on the south-west coast of France. Actual circumstances and collective memory here combine to provide the material for a bitter commentary, and the volumes are studded with significant incidents. For example, one character is gratuitously killed by an American lorry as he escorts local children across a busy road on their way to school; an elderly couple whose lives have already been destroyed once by the Nazis see themselves at risk again and commit suicide; an SS officer returns to France to work as an agent for the Americans.[35] Courtade's novel is by no means as blatant as this, even when, in the second part, Jimmy spends time in Paris ostensibly studying on a GI scholarship. The same

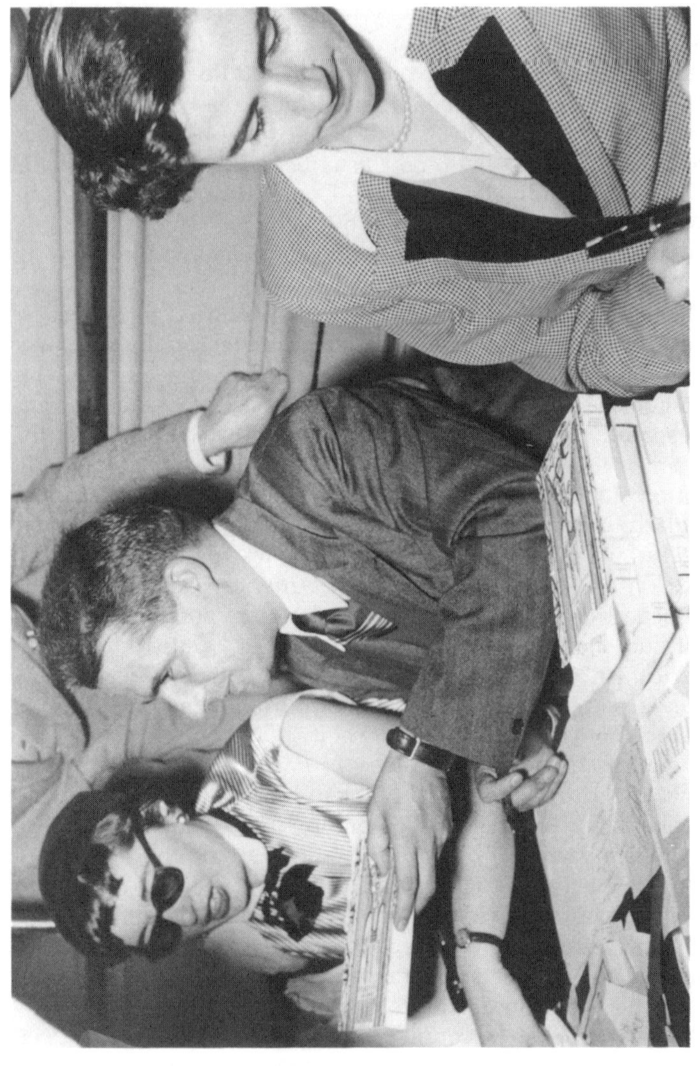

Signing copies of *Jimmy* in October 1951. (Photo Vues françaises)

intended warning is unquestionably there; but Courtade is more concerned to penetrate the American mind and to deal with broader types in order to make his political points.

After his first visit to the States as an adolescent in October 1931 Courtade had always been eager to return. His appointment to the *L'Humanité* staff provided him with ample opportunity, and he visited the country in 1947 and 1949. By the time he came to return in the autumn of 1950 anti-Communist measures in the USA were beginning to tighten, and initially Courtade was refused a visa, a fact to which *L'Humanité* not surprisingly gave much publicity. When it was eventually granted, and limited his movements to 'New York et ses environs immédiats',[36] the conditions were in fact no different from those imposed in 1947 and 1949. Nor, we should not forget, was this particularly unusual. Already in March of the previous year Paul Eluard, Jean Boulier, the former Jesuit priest and teacher, and Eugénie Cotton had had visas refused when they applied to attend the New York Peace Conference. But there could be no doubt that, as the Cold War grew in intensity, so did suspicion and paranoia, and on both sides. Courtade wrote about this climate extensively in his regular columns in *L'Humanité*, and especially in eleven major articles cabled back from New York in October and early November 1950. It and its effect on the average citizen form the focal point of his novel.

Jimmy has three sections. The first is built around a concert given by the black American singer Paul Robeson organized by left-wing pacifist groups; the second describes Jimmy's life in Paris and, through the experience of one of his friends who is a journalist, front-line action in the Korean war; the third, much shorter, has Jimmy return to the States, and describes his new political and personal awareness.

When he had first gone to the States Courtade had been impressed not only by the extremes of living conditions, but also by the brightness and gloss, especially of New York. As we have already noticed, the latter seems to have been the inspiration for several of the descriptions of Elseneur; in *Jimmy* it occurs as a motif pointing to the superficiality of a way of life that is constantly being controlled by advertising and the cinema. Early in the novel we have the description of a radio broadcast:

> (Les) commentaires enflammés sur la 'nouvelle bataille de Berlin' et les félicitations aux gars du pont aérien (l'Amérique a les yeux sur vous) étaient coupés par des publicités musicales qui ne vous laissent pas une minute libre. Bon Dieu, si on avait suivi leur conseil, si on avait fait toutes ces choses absolument *nécessaires* ou absolument *distinguées* qui consistaient à boire de la bière *mais aussi* du vin, à économiser et à dépenser, à améliorer sa chevelure grâce à la lotion Breck, à passer les vacances à Atlantic City, la Bagdad américaine, à se faire une réputation d'homme du monde en offrant à ses amis du whisky Castaris pour aller finalement terminer sa soirée au Broadhurst Theater où tous les gens bien *devaient* aller ... (p. 25)

Such publicity is also fundamentally erotic: 'Jimmy avait vécu au milieu des sollicitations d'une publicité sexuelle qui envahissait toute la vie, par les journaux, par le cinéma, par la rue. Un entremêlement fantastique de cuisses, de poitrines, de sourires, de combinaisons, de bas. Rien qui ne fût rapporté au sexe' (p. 74). This constant bombardment leads to a society in which anonymity is rife (New York is 'cette immensité [où] personne ne se connaissait' (p. 52)), and conformity and stereotypical behaviour the norm. The pattern of Lucy Reeds' life is dictated by the images presented by films and magazines, and she is 'defined' by a number of instant descriptions, such as for example 'la-femme-qui-vous-aide-dans-la-vie-et-partage-vos-soucis-et-vos-joies' (p. 26);[37] having allowed herself to be moulded by her husband she has wittingly become 'la femme douce et molle [...] fabriquée pour son usage, pour se rassurer, pour excuser sa propre faiblesse et son égoïsme' (p. 133); and when Jimmy is offered the chance of promotion to a senior company position in Albany she can only think 'que ça serait tout de même épatant d'être la femme de Mr Reeds d'Albany' (p. 43).[38] She lacks passion, takes no pleasure from sex, and is content to follow passively 'le ronron de la vie quotidienne' (p. 22).

In dress, manner and language James H. White, Jimmy's boss, is equally the stereotype of the American business man. He owes his success to having allowed an injury sustained in a minor road accident in 1918 to be taken for a serious war wound, and has thereby gained acceptance by the prestigious and influential Légion, a right-wing club originally established by ex-servicemen: 'grâce à elle il avait grimpé quatre à quatre les échelons de la Compagnie, c'est grâce à elle que deux ou trois fois par an, revêtu de l'uniforme bleu de commandant, il défilait dans la rue principale d'une ville du Middle-West derrière le bon vieux drapeau de ce régiment avec lequel il s'était à la fin persuadé qu'il avait délivré la cathédrale de Reims' (p. 27). White's life is second-hand and artificial. He speaks in clichés and unquestioningly accepts the political statements and policies of the present Republican government: 'Il y a des rouges partout, voilà la verité' (p. 76). He believes in law and order, and sees force as the only answer to civil or political unrest. He is violently racist (p. 109) (his surname alone is a clear indicator of this), and he believes that for the good of democracy and the free world Communism must be eradicated at all (and any) costs. The North Koreans should be the target of a nuclear attack; so too should Moscow.

Convinced of his beliefs and totally conditioned by the kind of life he has trained himself to lead, he fully expects others to do the same. His wife (like Lucy) tamely echoes all he says and does. Their son Tom, who has disappointed him by wanting to study psychology, only fully lives up to his expectations when he is drafted to Korea. Tom, who soon comes to realize the futility and impossibility of the American position there, is killed. White's life is shattered; but even in mourning and faced by Jimmy's bitterness about the war, he chooses to play a role: '[il] essayait de prendre le visage de la vertu offensée qu'il avait vu dans les films patriotiques quand on vient insulter le père du héros mort' (p. 337).

If such people as these are presented by Courtade as being wholly typical of the majority of contemporaneous American middle-class society, the village of Rockfield where the Robeson concert is to be held is a kind of microcosm: 'une petite ville assez artificielle [...] la reconstitution luxueuse d'un petit village anglais du XVIIe siècle' (p. 107). The staging of the concert, the precautionary measures taken by the liberals to ensure that all will be ordered and peaceful, the sabotaging of it by racist elements (including the Ku Klux Clan), the contrast between the dignity of Robeson's singing and of pieces by Bach, Vivaldi and Chopin and the blazing cacophony of the Légion's brass band and the fascists' car horns, the complicity and brutality of the police, and the subsequent total misrepresentation of events by the press are all elements we would expect in the description of a set piece such as this, with its self-evident political message.

Nor is stereotyping or weighted description a feature solely of Courtade's treatment of the establishment and right-wing extremists. The group responsible for the organization of the concert represents a narrow range of political opinion fundamentally linked by a common belief in the rights of the individual and freedom of speech. With the exceptions of Bielinsky and the trade-unionist Ward, both Communists, and already fully committed, they gradually move towards a position of hardened determination. Ehrlich, an Austrian Jew who receives an anonymous threatening letter, shows himself at the concert to be 'un homme littéralement transformé' (p. 137, 8). He is savagely beaten by the police.[39] Stewart, a biologist forced out of his university post on account of his left-wing sympathies, gradually changes as well. He is imprisoned for a year. In this kind of company Jimmy and Lucy are ill at ease.

From the opening of the novel Jimmy is presented as a privileged and protected member of society. Cocooned in his powerful car ('comme un tank' (p. 9)) he returns home to the stereotypical security of his house and standard family. Not by chance is the insurance company for which he works called 'La Prudence', and the post he is offered in Albany is a guarantee of middle-class stability and security. But, as Bielinsky remarks of him, he is at the same time 'un type qui cherche' (p. 40), and from the beginning there is a nagging doubt in his mind that everything he does or says is really only a pretence. He is in danger of becoming another James White (Jimmy is, after all, the diminutive form of James). Like Hans in *Elseneur*, he lacks will-power; and only when he is part of a system (like the insurance company) or a social ritual does he feel safe. When he attempts to seduce White's secretary, Clara Boyles, he fails miserably, and she will subsequently accuse him of assault. When he and Lucy invite White and his wife for dinner he is incapable of raising any objections to the racist and anti-communist remarks that punctuate White's conversation.

He agrees to go to the concert more out of an inability to refuse than from conviction, and the prospect of meeting White there as a member of the declared opposition causes his world to collapse into 'un décor mou, de panique et de désastre' (p. 79). When Bielinsky explains to him why Stewart had been dismissed, 'Jimmy éprouvait un sentiment de gêne très étrange d'avoir en face de lui un de ces hommes qui n'hésitaient pas à sacrifier à leurs idées tout ce qui lui paraissait à lui si important, si nécessaire' (p. 128). When Ehrlich is attacked he wants to leave. Afraid of how he will seem to Bielinsky and the others, he justifies his action as being in the interest of his wife's safety

(p. 145). But the concert and its brutal aftermath do bring him to a decision: 'Je partirai, c'est fini avec ce pays. [...] je ne sais pas ce que je veux faire, mais il faut que je cherche' (pp. 153–4).

Benefiting therefore from a GI scholarship Jimmy goes to France, where not only will he be cut off from the rituals and patterns of his everyday life in the States, but he will be subjected to a number of 'lessons': he reads *L'Humanité* ('le marchand de journaux ne vous regardait pas comme si vous lui avez demandé une publication pornographique' (p. 189)); he meets a number of people (Françoise, Roger Craux and Bill Williams) who have a vital role in the formative process of these few weeks; and he is eventually accused by the American authorities of active complicity with Communist-inspired demonstrations. When he initially arrives in Paris he is in danger of being 'enveloppé par la société américaine' (p. 214) but he rents a room at the aptly named hotel 'L'Univers' as his horizons widen, and, even though his French is poor, when he does try to speak it he feels that the language turns him into another person (p. 215).

The three persons who came into his life have clearly defined roles, and it would have been easy for Courtade turn them into simple embodiments of qualities that Jimmy was to assimilate or benefit from. This is most apparent in the case of Françoise; but Courtade avoids the trap of having Jimmy embark on a romantic adventure with an attractive, politically active, articulate and independent Parisian girl, who would have been the exact opposite of Lucy. Françoise is not conventionally attractive; and, while she mixes and even dances with black men in a Parisian night-club (p. 290), we learn that she is quite content to be employed by the American press agency, which pays her three times more than any French employer could, and she dreams of the States as a paradise (p. 219) where 'les maisons lépreuses seraient remplacées par des buildings de marbre' (p. 219). She is accused by one friend of being a 'collabo' (p. 219).

On separate occasions each makes tentative sexual advances towards the other, but fundamentally Jimmy is incapable of understanding her. Furthermore his sense of guilt when he is with Françoise (p. 222) is a clear indicator of the way in which he remains trapped by the conventional morality of the American middle classes, and his later reaction, albeit a drunken one – 'ce fumier de nègre' (p. 290) – as she dances reveals even more forcefully how deeply engrained in him certain feelings are. It could of course be that in his portrayal of Françoise, Courtade once more betrays what seems to have been a deep prejudice of his own: namely that, even if they hold political views of which he approves, women are somehow incapable of becoming significantly engaged. Claire in 'Deux douzaines d'huîtres' was an exception; Justine-Laurence in *La Place rouge* will be even more so. But in general political action seems to have been viewed by Courtade as a masculine prerogative. In *Jimmy* even the wives of the likes of Bielinsky (Part I Chapter 4) lack sufficient commitment and are too easily sidetracked by superficial and irrelevant preoccupations. The only woman from that group who it is claimed is totally free to act as she will is Ethel Ehrlich; but she remains significantly absent from the action.

Despite Françoise and his dim awareness that he is still only half-glimpsing a world of different values, Jimmy remains fundamentally 'un touriste, un fuyard [...] un acteur' (p. 221).[40] For this awareness to begin to stiffen into resolve also requires his involvement with Roger Craux and Bill Williams. Jimmy first meets Roger when he refuses to add his name to a petition protesting against the use of the atomic bomb. Later, however, he agrees to testify on his behalf when Roger is wrongly accused of attacking a policeman and is arrested at a Communist demonstration held in the Champs Elysées against a newspaper *Le Journal* (in reality *Le Figaro*) for carrying contributions from a former Nazi colonel. Here Jimmy had watched the same policeman beat a defenceless young woman and had not had the courage to intervene. To testify gives him the opportunity to make some amends and it is also instrumental in finally persuading him to sign the petition.[41] Again it would have been easy for Courtade to have made of Roger Craux the model of the politically-engaged worker; but although he is used to underscore the parallel Courtade wishes to draw between the American presence in France and the Nazi occupation, and although we witness a conversation Roger has with an exemplary *ancien résistant*, he is not idealized.[42] Indeed, he is shown to have doubts about his own commitment, and even lies to a colleague (saying he has persuaded Jimmy to sign his petition) in order to gain prestige. But he is instrumental in causing Jimmy to act politically for the first time. So too is the journalist Bill Williams.

Employed by the American press agency, Williams initially covers events in France, and at one point is given the job of reporting on industrial unrest in the west-coast docks. His investigation reveals that the Americans are deeply resented, hated even 'autant que l'avaient été les Nazis' (p. 200). Williams is part of an organization whose task is to report events in such a manner as to persuade the rest of the world of the need for American presence in Western Europe in order to combat the threat of Communism. The propaganda is simplistic; but Williams, like Jimmy, is a man with some doubts. Eventually he is sent to Korea, where he learns the (Communist) truth about the war, and in his articles is increasingly critical of American involvement and practice. A visiting American general, Erikson ('mélange de scout et de mécano' (p. 307)) accuses him of betraying the American cause.[43] But the damage has been done, and Jimmy is only one of those who will no longer adopt the unquestioning patriotic stance expected of them.

When Jimmy is summoned by the FBI to answer questions on his involvement with the communist Craux and with the demonstration he is therefore at last willing to take a stand. Inevitably MacClure, the investigator, is caricatured, and is unable to cope with Jimmy's refusal to answer his questions in the way he expects. On technical grounds alone, however – Jimmy has not regularly attended the study courses for which his scholarship was granted – he will be able to recommend that his funding should be discontinued, and Jimmy is obliged to return to the States – but not before he has experienced his moment of revelation: 'il était calme [...]. D'un calme éblouissant, qu'il ne s'était jamais connu, absolument jamais. Mieux que calme: il sentait qu'il pouvait indéfiniment coincer cette mécanique absurde qui s'était déclenchée contre lui, bêtement, comme une farce-attrape mue par un ressort.' (p. 297)

On his return to America, therefore, it would again have been relatively easy for Courtade to have described a Jimmy full of new political conviction and ready to enter the struggle against an oppressive regime. Our first glimpse of him in the opening lines of Part III is with the Bielinskys 'au huitième étage d'une *haute* maison *isolée* sur la *crête* qui *domine* la baie' (p. 317).[44] Whether Courtade (like Camus in *La Peste* with his description of Tarrou's balcony) is here offering a comment about the gap between theory and action or about the self-ordained superiority of intellectuals is unclear. Jimmy, however, still does not belong. He leaves the Bielinsky apartment and travels in the New York underground, where he witnesses the brutal beating of a drunken negro by police. As in Paris, he does nothing. He simply feels guilty, and recalls the feelings he had earlier when Françoise had danced with the negro in the night-club; racism runs deep.

Nonetheless, the die has been cast, and Jimmy will gradually discover his way. Mistakenly, he tries to find employment with his former insurance company; when he arrives for an interview the black lift attendant is the only member of staff to show any real pleasure at seeing him again (p. 332). He has to sell his car, and, obliged now to travel by public transport, he discovers a town hitherto unknown to him (p. 338). He also finds that Lucy, who on account of her maiden name Goldman is suspected of being part-Jewish, has changed, though inevitably her evolution as a woman is slower than his: 'Il ne trouvait pas les mots pour les nouvelles pensées qu'il avait. Il était comme après une longue maladie lorsqu'on trouve aux aliments les plus ordinaires un goût nouveau. Et elle ne pouvait pas l'aider parce qu'elle était encore beaucoup plus loin que lui, en arrière sur ce chemin' (p. 346). Eventually he is summoned by the tribunal investigating the Rockfield incident. As in Paris, he is both amused and appalled by the form his questioning takes – 'cette comédie lui était apparue intolérable' (p. 350) – and he refuses to play the part expected of him. The battle has been joined, and the novel ends with Jimmy about to embark upon his new life. He has become part of the group around Bielinsky, and is potentially ready to go beyond them.

As with so many novels which advocate political action, whether as blatantly as *Le Cheval de Troie* or in as muted a way as *Bon Pied Bon Oeil*, for example, *Jimmy* closes at that point where exemplary behaviour is about to begin, where the decision has been taken and the direction has been clearly anticipated. To go beyond this runs the risk of schematization or a form of hagiolatry, of the kind we find in, say, Aragon's *Les Communistes* or Stil's *Le Premier Choc*. In *La Rivière noire* Courtade will make his point in a rather different way, and in *La Place rouge* will trace the evolution of his autobiographical protagonist Simon Bordes from political neutrality to total commitment to Communism and the Soviet Union. It can be argued, of course, that Courtade is less interested in Jimmy as an individual case than as a representative or type. He does, it is true, show some similarities with Karl in *Elseneur*, in that they are both creatures who glimpse a truth but are too inhibited, too fearful and too constrained by background and circumstances to embrace it unequivocally. But whereas Karl is killed before he can show sustained evidence of any new conviction, leaving Hans Peter's reflection 'Je ne sais pas ce qu'il cherchait'[45] unanswered, Jimmy is able to anticipate a future in which, we are to believe, commitment and action will be the norm. It is also true that, as the portrayal of Karl owed much to Courtade's own indecision, so that of Jimmy must reflect his evolution to political conviction. But Courtade's concern in this novel is less with individual behaviour than with issues – of which the principal ones are racism and the American driven crusade against Communism – and the threat that they pose in France.

At one point in the novel, as preparations are being made for the Robeson concert, Ehrlich reflects (Part I, Chapter 10) on the current anti-black and anti-Semitic climate in America, and compares it directly with that of Nazi Germany in the 1930s. David Caute has objected with justification that such a parallel was 'quite false'.[46] But strict accuracy is no more relevant here than it was in articles carried in the pages of *L'Humanité* or *Les Lettres françaises*. And in any case there is no doubt that for many on the extreme Left the comparison was valid, and was used in an attempt to shock people out of their complacency. In *Jimmy*, in line with standard Communist propaganda, America is shown to be at the mercy of a wave of hysteria or religious fervour encouraged in the interests of combatting communism and of preserving white America from all contamination. The governor of Albany, Thomas Dewey, for example, 'devenait le verbe incarné [il] avait avalé les Tables de la Loi et les recrachait par courtes sentences' (p. 84). Investigations and trials are inquisitorial, and any signs of rebelliousness or questioning are suppressed by whatever means available, however brutal. The true voice of America, that of the people (pp. 102, 126), is threatened with being stifled.

In writing *Jimmy* Courtade could have limited himself quite easily to an indictment of American society. He could have depicted the United States in this way in order to issue a warning of the potential dangers of increased American presence and influence in France and the Western world, and could have turned Jimmy's French experience into a form of parable. But his concern, like Stil's or even Vailland's in *Beau Masque*, is that American influence already enjoys too strong a hold in France. As we have noticed, Françoise, though in part a deliberate contrast with Lucy and therefore instrumental in Jimmy's education, has already been seduced by the American dream, and sees nothing wrong in working for the press agency.

The dockers on the west coast may express deep resentment about the American presence in their ports, but have not succeeded in translating anger into action; the demonstration against *Le Journal* is brutally suppressed; bottles of Pepsi-Cola fill the shelves in bars; the brightness of the *métro* from Châtelet to Etoile (elsewhere *blafard* and *puant* (p. 230)) recalls the 'serpent nickelé' (p. 11) of the freeway in New York; the hotel requisitioned by the Americans in which Jimmy is interrogated by the FBI is in that part of the *16ᵉ arrondissement* in which the Nazis had their interrogation centres less than a decade earlier. Shortly before the demonstration the streets in this same area are described quite unequivocally:

> Réservées à de longues voitures-crapaud, au nickel, à l'aluminium, aux fleurs, aux chiens lavés, tondus, à des cafés [...] où des femmes habillées tous les jours comme les dimanches, mangeaient des gâteaux, sans faim, à quatre heures de l'après-midi pour tuer le temps. Des rues où les officiers américains se promenaient tranquillement au bras des femmes parfumées, tout heureux de jouir de l'amitié des gens de bien, comme quelques années auparavant leurs prédécesseurs, jeunes gens gris-fer remontant dans les Opels découvertes vers le Bois et l'avenue Foch, où les attendaient, dans des salons à lambris, de mystérieux dîners fins, du champagne, dans le bruit assourdi des coups sur les reins d'un type effondré dans la cave. (p. 236)

But even more crushing than sustained observations of this kind is the general indictment of France's national leaders. Not only is the government conspicuously silent, but intellectuals are shown to have abdicated all critical responsibility. Even when, like Bernard (Aron?), they are seen to be in sympathy with American policy they cannot commit themselves by actions. As Bernard remarks to the ex-Communist Slaugherty: 'Je suis un intellectuel, vous savez, et pis est, un intellectuel français. Vous imaginez tout ce que cela signifie? Vous me voyez rédiger le texte d'affiches de dix mètres de haut, en couleurs peut-être? (p. 242)

All in all, therefore, *Jimmy* is already as much a sharply critical book as a warning. This is not to say that Courtade has nothing positive to offer. Jimmy himself is clearly exemplary; but his lesson is learned only slowly and painfully. Craux in Paris and Bielinsky and Ward in New York illustrate individual commitment, and Ehrlich is moved to act, while Tom White and

Bill Williams finally see through the brainwashing about the Korean war, but only when it is too late. But for Courtade hope rests with the people, the mass of working-class men and women in whom true national interest and sense of identity are vested. The same point will emerge in *La Rivière noire*, and it was, of course, as fundamental to the PCF's policies and commentaries on events in the early 1950s as it would be at the time of the Algerian war. And yet in *Jimmy* the voice of the masses remains distant or muted. There is no successful collective presence, as there had been in, say, Zola's *Germinal* or Barbusse's *Le Feu*, both of which seem to underpin *Elseneur*, or even in Courtade's next novel; rather it is by allusion or by representation that the point is made, and this is where the weakness of the book lies.

There is no doubt of Courtade's conviction in *Jimmy*. When an anonymous reviewer in *Europe* wrote of the 'unité profonde de son art et de son action' and of the 'expression totale d'un esprit et d'un coeur' he (or she) spoke for the Left as a whole.[47] Friends recall the intensity with which he set about writing the novel,[48] but there is no doubt that it could have benefited from a degree of reflection. For all *Elseneur*'s weaknesses, we leave that novel with the sense of there having been a strategy and a design. The dramatic infrastructure and the use made of light and water and of the elemental world in general and of Shakespeare's play suggest considerable thought on Courtade's part. In *La Rivière noire* a dramatic structure once again and a sustained series of contrasts between the Vietnamese and the French create a dynamic that despite certain excesses and moments of proselytizing, carries the novel forward to its conclusion, albeit the anticipated one. In *Jimmy* Courtade attempts too much. Almost as though he felt the structure of the *Bildungsroman* to be too narrow, if not too obvious, he shifts sideways to take in details of other people's lives or of other events that need only have impinged as external factors on Jimmy's development.

The most glaring example of this is the account at the end of Part II of Williams' visit to the American forces in Korea, which for all its impact could have been cut altogether; and Stewart's chance meeting with White (Part I Chapter 13) and the conversations of Craux and Lachaume (Part II Chapter 5) are equally dispensable. More usually we find that characters begin to take shape, only to disappear once our interest has been aroused (the militant Lachaume, Stewart or Ward for example),

With Génia in China, 1952.

and Courtade is not always certain whether his focus should be on Jimmy or on Jimmy as part of a group. We also find (as in *Elseneur* and *La Rivière noire*) that instead of allowing Jimmy's experience to be self-explanatory Courtade intervenes; he 'explains' Dewey's present role (p. 84), he interprets Jimmy's thoughts for him ('Jimmy sentait tout cela confusément. Il ne l'exprimait pas ainsi' (p. 183)); he pontificates on jealousy (pp. 226–7); and he never hesitates to impose his authorial and authoritative analysis of any situation. He also allows his political sympathies to colour his descriptions. On a fine spring day the Robeson concert has an air of joyous festivity that is gradually stifled by the slowly encircling forces of public order (Robeson himself, with his 'corps immense, cette puissance' (p. 131) becomes almost Messiah-like), while the hotel in which Jimmy is cross-examined is sinisterly silent, like 'une montre montée sur rubis et parfaitement huilée' (p. 294).

For all the evidence that it was written in a hurry, however, *Jimmy* remains a powerful book. Behind it there lies an indignation and an anger that drive the narrative forward in spite of its unevenness and moments of self-indulgence. Read it alongside Courtade's reports from the United States and it is frequently possible to go from one to the other with the changes of register barely noticeable, so central are these matters to his preoccupations. It is not difficult to imagine what his feelings must have been if he ever recalled or re-read the youthful speech he had given in Washington in 1931, with its approving acknowledgement of 'l'homme de couleur frère, mais frère inférieur'.[49]

With *La Rivière noire* there will be a change. Less directly involved as a journalist – though no less convinced of the correctness of the Communist cause in the Vietnam war – it is as though Courtade viewed events from a distance. The result is that the novel is tighter, more sharply focused and less frenetic. But it is no less angry. Taken together, *Jimmy* and *La Rivière noire* are two of the most politically engaged, albeit partisan, novels of this period.

La Rivière noire (1953)

The peace agreement signed in Geneva in July 1954 officially marked the end of what had become known as the 'sale guerre', eight years of bitter and bloody fighting in the forests, swamps and paddy-fields of Vietnam. It had not come too soon. Although the French army had already had the worst of earlier conflicts, notably at Cao Bang in 1950 and three years later at Lang Son, the defeat after fifty-six days of vicious fighting at Dieu Bien Phu was one of the most ignominious ever. This was worse than the Nazi invasion in 1940, when at least the military strength and supremacy of the enemy forces had been unquestionable and when they had been better equipped, disciplined and organized. Moreover, this whole campaign had been conducted at several thousands of miles' distance, and, as the French at home tried to piece together their lives in the early years of the Fourth Republic, talk of responsibilities to former colonies or French settlers abroad, or even of the need to struggle against the threat of Communism in the name of democracy aroused little general enthusiasm. Concerned, too, at what the public outcry would be, the government refused to insist on the mass drafting of French soldiers to Vietnam, with the result that the army was predominantly one made up of *légionnaires*, with a high percentage of ex-SS soldiers.[50] The effect on the soldiers, and especially on the regular officers in positions of responsibility, was inevitable. Trying to conduct a war in a part of the world which in terms of climate and terrain was completely alien to them, and for which they were largely without adequate preparation, and faced by very considerable indifference on a national scale at home, they became demoralized and often dehumanized.

Officially outside the government since 1947, the PCF from early on in the conflict voiced opposition, and, when Russia and China both recognized Ho Chi Minh's government in 1950, Party deputies and fellow-travelling intellectuals gave full rein to protest. The most celebrated pamphlet of all was undoubtedly *L'Affaire Henri Martin*, compiled by Sartre with the help of a group of liberal-minded intellectuals and writers including Vercors, Domenach, Prévert and Bazin. This focused on the affair of the young sailor who was sentenced to five years' imprisonment for inciting his fellow sailors at Toulon in 1950 to refuse to load armaments on to boats bound for Vietnam. The fact that the book was not published until 1953, and in fact shortly after Martin had been reprieved,[51] did not diminish its significance and impact. It was a statement of what had been an increasing campaign across the whole spectrum of the left-wing press, alongside the one vigorously sustained in the pages of *L'Humanité*.

But if the war prompted polemic and debate in newspapers and reviews, unlike the First World War or the Occupation it inspired relatively little imaginative writing of quality both at the time and subsequently. Michel Tauriac's *Le Trou* (1953), Laurent La Praye's *La Trompette des anges* (1956), and *La 317e Section* by Pierre Schoendoerffer (who also directed a film of the same name) all convey convincing impressions of the isolation, frustration, monotony and general feeling of alienation experienced by those who fought in Vietnam. There have been some documentaries too, notably Lucien Bodard's three-volume *La Guerre d'Indochine* (1963–7) and Jules Roy's *La Bataille de Dien Bien Phu* (1963), in which, with the advantage of hindsight, he is deeply critical of the government for ever having allowed the situation to develop to the point it had by 1954, of the French generals for their sheer incompetence and of the French public for their insensitivity and indifference. (Interestingly enough, in an early essay *La Bataille dans la rizière* (1953) Roy is more positive, at least in his high praise for the French forces, whom he rather grandiosely refers to as 'l'armée de la croisade'. And in a play, *Le Fleuve rouge* (1947), he offers us the portrait of an officer genuinely torn by doubts and increasingly disillusioned by French attitudes.)[52]

Courtade's *La Rivière noire* is one of very few novels of clear Communist inspiration. Two others, both post-dating the conflict, are Georges-Henri Guiraud's *Aux frontières de l'enfer* (1956) and Raymond Barkan's *Les Nauvragés de l'occident* (1958). All three bear some of the hallmarks of ideologically-driven literature; but after the barely-relieved propaganda of *Jimmy*, Courtade's third novel contains some of the qualities that made *Elseneur* such a promising début and saw it admired by more than just the Party faithful. David Caute has written that, for all its sincerity, the novel was 'opportunistic and utilitarian in both its subject matter and its timing',[53] and that it could have been written at any time during the previous four years. The point is fair; but, apart from Courtade's other professional commitments, the timing was opportune rather than opportunistic. The defeat of the French at Cao Bang had been the first significant indication both that this was a war that would not be won by continuing in the existing policies and by pouring in more and more weaponry, and that there was a spirit and an indomitability about the Vietnamese people that had not been fully recognized.

La Rivière noire tells the story of a successful Vietnamese offensive against a French military post at Minh Khai under the command of a young Saint Cyr-trained officer, Lieutenant Larillère. The location is 'real', and hovering on the edge of the action are some of the key military and political figures of the time – Ho Chi Minh, President of the Vietnamese republic since 1945 and leader of the opposition to French presence; General Vo Nguyen Giap, the Communist military commander; and De Lattre, who was sent out to Vietnam to head the French forces in 1950 and whose death from cancer two years later ensured that he did not have to witness the débâcle of 1954. The time of the conflict is indicated precisely in the opening sentence ('au début de décembre 1951' (p. 1)) and on several subsequent occasions; the entire action lasts for about forty-eight hours. As in *Elseneur*, there is in these features the basis for a fundamental dramatic structure. The whole action is seen from both sides, and Courtade is constantly recapitulating and switching his narrative in order to have a French and a Vietnamese perception of events. The thirty-two sections of the novel are unnumbered, but they can be divided quite neatly into five 'acts': 1–6 describe early evening and nightfall, and introduce most of the principal characters; 7–16 take the action to the following day, describe various incidents which serve to characterize the two sides, and introduce extra players; 17–20 give an account of the final preparation for the attack; 21 describes the assault on the French blockhouse and its destruction; 22–32 deal initially with events in Hanoï during the last day and then return to the aftermath of the battle, the death of Larillère and the recovery of the Vietnamese hero Van Tran Dan, and a statement of hope for the future.

In terms of its overall shape and movement (and indeed in its descriptive power) *La Rivière noire* is largely successful, and bears comparison with many 'war novels'; and, as we shall see later, there are also certain stylistic features that create important points of focus. But we also find the inevitable consequences of the need to ensure that the novel is ideologically 'correct'. The Vietnamese success in destroying the blockhouse spells out clearly enough the book's sympathies; but all too frequently Courtade allows himself to slip into some of the techniques which seem to be the penalty of so much politically motivated fiction.

The most blatant of these are undoubtedly the ways in which characters relate episodes from their experiences or in which

Courtade's role as an omniscient narrator allows him to select, shape and comment on particular events. Thus early on during the Vietnamese preparation for the attack an elderly stretcher-bearer gives an account of his life's exemplary struggle against colonizers, thereby encouraging Van Tran Dan and the small group whose responsibility it is to blow up the blockhouse (pp. 63–8). The general gathering of the Vietnam attack force is like a religious service, addressed by a leader whose voice 'montait de la profondeur du peuple' (p. 49). At the very centre of the novel (pp. 97–101) is a scene of the most violent atrocities (torture, rape and mutilation) committed by a band of commandos – French and Vietnamese – under the control of one Rustine, who clearly pays no heed to the platitudinous remarks about correct behaviour in war issued from time to time by the French government. There is, of course, no comparable scene of Vietnamese violence, and rumours of the sadistic treatment of prisoners are grudgingly acknowledged by the French to be without foundation. Peasants from the north tell of complicity between the Catholic church and the occupying French forces, and of a missionary priest who turned a blind eye to the atrocities committed in the name of anti-Communism (pp. 155–7).

In the last fifty pages of the novel we are given a glimpse of French colonial society in Hanoï. Prejudice, deviousness, superficiality and hypocrisy are everywhere apparent, and we have accounts of how peasants are cynically exploited and forced into selling their rice fields for absurdly low prices. Whereas the placing of some of the earlier episodes appears almost gratuitous, in this instance their relation to the structure of the novel as a whole is important. As we have already noted, the scenes in Hanoï take place at the same time as the successful assault is being made on the blockhouse, and Courtade is clearly saying, therefore, that even as the representatives of this society pursue their normal life-style their defeat has already begun.

If this is indeed the conclusion it is intended we should draw from this section of the novel, elsewhere Courtade leaves little to chance. As in his earlier fiction, he allows his authorial voice full rein; within a matter of a few lines he can be both inside and outside his characters, observing and interpreting at the same time. As the attack on the French defences begins Van Tran Dan and his fellow soldiers are met by gunfire. Two of them are killed.

Une fusée éclairante tirée par le poste éclata, *il leur sembla*, très haut dans la nuit au-dessus d'eux. *Tran Dan s'était retourné* et avait vu le corps de Nguyen Van Bach. C'était une chose molle, *qu'on distinguait* à peine des hautes herbes. *Ils ne savait plus* comment ils pouvaient marcher et respirer. [...] *A ce moment, ils comprirent* que les mitrailleuses de la compagnie d'assaut tiraient trop court [...] (pp. 142–3).[54]

In an early description of the French soldiers who have hoped that in the war they would find escape from their past lives, the narrator's voice reminds us that such hopes are in vain: 'Ceux qui avaient cru s'être détachés de la bêtise et de la tristesse de leur passé s'apercevaient que le passé continuait et les poursuivait [...]' (p. 25). This superiority is apparent again in the outcry against the exploitation and victimization of working-class people, who are thereby reduced to a state of total confusion: 'Les contradictions et les conflits n'étaient pas seulement dans leur crâne. C'était la réalité de ce monde cruel' (p. 180). It permits extra information as well. When Savel describes his own practices and those of this fellow business men, the narrator's voice tells us in an authorial aside: 'Il ne disait pas que lui-même, en deux ans, avait plus gagné dans la limonade et la piastre que pendant ses trente ans d'escroquerie légale' (pp. 169, 70). Fortunately, Courtade's interventions of this kind are not as frequent or as blatant as those by Nizan in *Le Cheval de Troie*, by Aragon in *Les Communistes* or by André Stil in *Le Premier Choc*, but they do impose one reading of the text only. Moreover, in view of the circumstances of the war in 1953 and of the kind of climate in which *L'Affaire Henri Martin* could achieve such success, it was a reading which readily appealed to a very large number of people.

Courtade has other means of persuasion at his disposal as well, of which the most obvious is his portrayal of individual characters. As in *Jimmy*, a number are quite simply stereotypes. Elizabeth Savel with her 'joliesse un peu facile' (p. 165); Li Ki To, the governor of the province, married to a French wife and who despite a 'machiavélisme naïf' (p. 75) is a natural collaborator; Griffith the opportunist, cynical representative of the American government; Bouvreuil, Larillère's senior officer from Hanoï, who is 'jovial et facile' (p. 16), but terrified once the attack begins, and concerned only with his own safety. Nor are such stereotypes to be found solely amongst or with the French. The elderly peasant, the Vietnamese army officer (whose name means 'Parfaitement jeune' (p. 49)), or the mayor Ta Van Lam, who realized the importance of and joined the resistance only late in life, are all little more than ciphers, albeit positive ones.

Others are rather more developed. Hans Werner is a former Nazi soldier now fighting for the French legionary forces, and his love of violence for its own sake and his continuing belief in an eternal Germany have an importance for the text which outweigh his fleeting appearance. François Jacquiot '(qui) ne s'était jamais occupé de la politique' (p. 31) has been persuaded to join the army during a drunken evening spent with soldiers from the Vincennes barracks, and becomes a mindless 'tueur de Viets' who only momentarily pauses to reflect on their reckless courage. There is also in the portrayal of Jacquiot the slightest possible suggestion of an autobiographical dimension, as there is in that of Pommardier, the supposed radical politician with a reputation for being a liberal. But this in fact is due less to conviction than to his readiness to find grounds for agreement with anyone he speaks to.[55] He arrives, ironically, with his 'rosette de la Résistance' (p. 71) in his lapel, and drifts through Minh Khai and on to Hanoï, where he is immersed in the social life of the Savels. He thinks in clichés. He imagines being ambushed and killed (p. 80) and wonders whether Ta Van Lam smokes opium (p. 83). His hypocrisy is completely exposed during his visit with Mme Savel to the Hanoï military hospital, where he is confronted by a young Vietnamese intellectual whom he had had deported from France on suspicion of communist activities (p. 80). Torture at the hands of the French police in Hanoï has left this man deeply psychologically disturbed, but he recognizes Pommardier, who can only withdraw in confusion.

On the Vietnamese side we have Nguyen Hung Hoe, the local Communist Resistance leader. Like the elderly peasant, he too has led an exemplary life, drawing his strength from the message of the Communist Manifesto, much of which he has learned by heart. As Rustine carries out his vicious attack on Suoi Bac he is in hiding beneath the floor of the blacksmith's workshop. Here he reflects on the social and economic progress achieved in China or Estonia, and imagines a future Vietnam with 'fermes modèles, et des automobiles sur les grandes routes qui remplaceraient les misérables routes coloniales' (p. 97). Later, with the complicity of one of the commandos, he kills Rustine, but is captured, tortured and thrown into the river for dead. He is found and taken to the Vietnamese camp, where he gradually recovers, and where the account he gives of his torture is overheard by Larillère, for whom just before he dies it is a final, potent illustration of the injustice and brutality of French policy.[56]

Larillère, of course, is the one character on the French side who is developed to any degree. He is a professional soldier. His training at Saint Cyr has given him a taste for discipline and order ('une vie réglée et claire' (p. 117)), he is acknowledged by the Vietnamese as being 'un officier consciencieux' (p. 43) and he speaks their language (p. 190). Too young to have participated in the French Resistance, he has come to Vietnam without experience, and his ideals or his belief in the rightness of the French cause gradually falter. Bearded, blue-eyed and with a young face, he is on several occasions likened to a missionary. (We may note as well that, like Christ, at his death he is thirty-three years old.) Even though he becomes increasingly aware of the fragility of the French position and of some of the horrors committed for the cause of democracy, he stubbornly refuses to modify his position and bravely defends Minh Khai to the last. Mortally wounded, he is taken prisoner. In the Vietnamese camp he is treated as well as their own injured soldiers, and an attempt is made to arrange for a hospital plane to airlift him away. (We learn from conversations Pommardier has in Hanoï that French bureaucracy alone will render this impossible.) Here through the narrator's voice he finally reflects that his earlier life has been empty ('Tout ce qu'il avait pu imaginer […] était tout juste bon à remplir les temps morts d'une solitude' (p. 196)) and that the comradeship and warmth he now sees around him is what he has missed. When the nurse, to encourage him, tells him that he will recover his reply is significant: 'Je ne veux pas, dit-il' (p. 197). And when, minutes later, she discovers that he has died the narrator's recording of her thoughts sums up one element of the book's message: 'Elle le considéra un instant. Elle pensait qu'il était venu ici plein de mépris et d'orgueil, persuadé que la cause pour laquelle il avait donné sa vie était une cause juste. Peut-être à la fin avait-il commencé à entrevoir la vérité? Mais c'était trop tard' (p. 204). Like Paneloux – and indeed like Tarrou – in *La Peste*, Larillère is 'un cas douteux'.

His opposite number, Tran Van Dan, comes of poor peasant stock, is self-taught and has learned Chinese and Vietnamese in roman script (pp. 39–40). Devoted to the cause of the liberation of his country, he has been given the task of leading the bomb squad in the assault on the blockhouse, and appears to be the only one who is a member of the Communist Party (p. 127). Although his age is not given, he is clearly young – younger than Larillère probably by ten years – and is portrayed as a kind of folk hero for his generation. With his responsibilities he becomes wise, disciplined, careful in his pronouncements and instantly respected. To him, for example, falls the task of explaining to another member of the group that, while French working-class people may have been responsible for making the bullets and shells that will soon rip through their ranks, this has to be seen as a necessary part of the revolution that is taking place, and that the true feelings of 'le peuple français' cannot be questioned (p. 56). In the course of the attack he is badly wounded: his right arm is smashed, and is eventually cut off by a fellow soldier. Somehow he manages to reach the blockhouse (where the equally determined Jacquiot is spraying the oncoming Vietnamese with machine-gun fire) and forces the bomb through a gun slit. Miraculously he escapes. He is stretchered to the Vietnamese camp, where Larillère also is, and within hours is beginning to recover and make plans for the future. No longer able to consider working in a factory, he determines to become a military instructor, and looks forward to sharing his life with the nurse Li Thanh Binh, whose name, we learn on the closing page, means 'Paix Sereine'.

While these two principal characters are self-evidently required to carry the ultimate significance of the novel, to summarize their roles in this way is reductive and detracts from Courtade's overall strategy. While both reflect privately on their respective positions a good deal, it is noticeable that Tan Van Dan belongs much more to his immediate companions and, by extension, to his people as a whole. There is nothing unusual in this. The French – and indeed their Vietnamese collaborators – are portrayed as a group of individuals, each motivated by personal gain or reputation. For those who make it to the temporary safety of Hanoï the fate of Larillère, Jacquiot or Bouvreuil is of no more interest or importance than the wishes of local peasants. And even at Minh Khai there is little impression of true comradeship, or even of unity other than that imposed by army discipline. Larillère's predecessor Fourcade was driven mad, not simply by the alien nature of the country but by his total isolation. At times Larillère feels himself to be breaking under the strain as well. By contrast the Vietnamese from the highest authority to the most humble peasant, strive together (p. 48). Hierarchy produces organizational benefits only; rank reflects experience and wisdom, and is not imposed. It comes as no surprise, therefore, that the officers should be willing to dig trenches during the night. Larillère has his dinner brought to him, drinks burgundy, and shares a glass of cognac with any visitor who finds himself at Minh Khai.

This use of contrast is perhaps best illustrated by the descriptions of the two military posts. The French headquarters and blockhouse have no place here. The former is a temporary structure made of bamboo; the latter an ill-ventilated concrete construction that will ultimately be the tomb of most of its occupants. The Vietnamese use a natural cave. Its primary function may be as a munitions store, but it also acts as a workshop and a hospital. Whereas the blockhouse has been crudely imposed on the Vietnamese countryside – it is in fact 'dans une île' (p. 19), and like the castle in *Elseneur*, separate and alien, the *grotte* is part of it, and at night it and the tracks leading to it are camouflaged with bamboo and banana leaves, 'cachée par l'avalanche de verdure des longues lianes' (p. 38). Inside, the light filtering through the foliage is tinged with green, and 'en levant les yeux on apercevait les arbres et le ciel' (p. 60).[57] The symbolic resonance of the two camps quickly becomes apparent. The former is sterile and a place of death; the latter, with its 'galeries souterraines qui prolongeaient très loin' (p. 60) and its damp atmosphere, is not only a place of hope and recovery but of rebirth. Thus it is made clear that Tran Van Dan will recover, as will Ngyen Hung Hoe, and leave and continue their struggle; Larillère spends the last day of his life at the entrance to the *grotte,* where 'depuis l'aube un calme merveilleux l'avait envahi' (p. 190), and even though hours later he will die here, he does so having experienced a kind of spiritual rebirth.

The resistant qualities of the cave itself are also important. Like Giono's *Le Grand Troupeau, La Rivière noire* shows us the destructive effects of war on the local natural world – rivers are polluted, forests smashed and burned, paddy-fields destroyed or illegally acquired by the occupying French. But the cave (and there are hundreds of similar ones across the country) will remain. In so doing it also underlines the unbreakable bond of the Vietnamese fighters not just with their land, but by extension with a whole culture, centuries old, of which they are both the expression and the defenders. At one point Tran Van Dan and his group listen to a husking machine that is beating rice 'inlassablement comme la pulsation d'un coeur' (p. 58).

Throughout the novel, and necessarily linked as well to this hint of lifeblood, is the near continuous presence of water, the 'crachin perpétuel': 'On ne savait pas d'où venait l'eau. Pas seulement du ciel, mais de partout à la fois, du sol et de la route grasse, de la masse vernissée et dégoulinante des arbres et des lianes. Une espèce de couverture étouffante, lourde et mouillée était tombée sur la forêt' (p. 81). Whether of the river or of the irrigation channels or in the form of this mist-like rain, water like the soil, is an elemental force to be harnessed once victory has been achieved (p. 55). Outraged by war, it can be hostile, and Larillère not surprisingly finds this aspect of the 'démence tropicale' (p. 14) unbearable. But no sooner have the bombings stopped than nature reasserts itself, and signs of life and growth are everywhere apparent.

In all of these ways Courtade leaves his readers in no doubt as to the novel's political direction. But there is more. Like André Stil in *Le Premier Choc* or to a lesser extent Vailland in *Beau Masque*, Courtade plays on echoes of the Nazi occupation of France a decade earlier to give his text greater resonance and force. In the figure of Werner the brutal SS officer is unambiguous; in those of Rustine and his 'Panthères Grises' are members of Darlan's 'milice'. But throughout the references to the Vietnamese troops as 'résistants', 'partisans' and 'terroristes',[58] the facts that they are forced to hold clandestine meetings in their own country, that there are some who side readily with French government policy, that the Catholic Church is shown to be complicit with atrocities and that the media is in the control of government combine to create a frame of reference that French readers would have no difficulty in identifying. And in addition Courtade appears to rely to some extent as well on allusions to three novels from an earlier period, all of which dealt with the issue of an emerging and increasingly militant working class. In the descriptions of the subterranean activities of the Vietnamese are echoes of Zola's miners in *Germinal*; in the character of the military commander whose voice 'montait de la profondeur du peuple' (p. 49) and in the thoughts of Nguyen Hung Hoe are clear suggestions of Barbusse's two First World War novels *Le Feu* and *Clarté*. Courtade is not unusual in this, of course. Whatever their degree of militancy, left-wing novelists, certainly since the 1920s, could rely on a network of references and associations that would either automatically strengthen the immediate texture of their own work or broaden it by providing it with a form of *sous-texte*. Moreover, they would themselves then have contributed to this reservoir of material, which would itself constantly need to be reconsidered whenever a new work was added to it.

With *La Rivière noire* Courtade was in this way not only dealing specifically with the immediate circumstances of Vietnam in the early 1950s, but moving beyond them to embrace issues with which the Left, and especially the Communist Left, had long been concerned. The result is not without considerable merit, and because of its relatively limited context and particular focus *La Rivière noire* is a less obvious and more resonant novel than *Jimmy*. And while each of them contains elements that have an echo of his personal circumstances and preoccupations, neither has the introspective dimension of *Elseneur*. But neither was personally satisfying. Just as Vailland nurtured the ambition to write a novel centred on the life of a truly revolutionary hero, so Courtade had hopes of one day producing a novel charting the political evolution of an ideal militant. He would approach this with *La Place rouge*; but meanwhile militancy was not his main concern. His domestic problems and his ill-health caused him, as we have seen, to withdraw, if only temporarily from the public arena. But once recovery was under way he was not idle, and during his convalescence turned his hand again in earnest to the short story.

Les Animaux supérieurs (1956)

For Courtade to publish a volume of this kind in 1956 was altogether a different matter from having done so a decade earlier. Then the approval, virtually the *imprimatur*, of Aragon and to a lesser extent of Tavernier had been significant if not crucial, and while Courtade had already begun to make his mark as a journalist of very considerable talent in the pages of *Action* he was far from being a major public figure. Now circumstances had changed. His commentaries on foreign affairs were widely recognized as being authoritative, and while *Jimmy* and *La Rivière noire* may bear some of the hallmarks of ideologically-driven imaginative writing their impact had been considerable, and with them Courtade had reaffirmed his claims to be considered a novelist as well as a journalist of talent. Moreover, with the wider range of quality newspapers and reviews now available than there had been in 1946, it was inevitable that the public reception of *Les Animaux supérieurs* would be more extensive. On the whole reviews were favourable. Predictably, the left-wing press praised the stories for their perceptive sociological dimension, for their realism ('nourries de dialogues enregistrés dans la rue')[59] or for their exposure of 'la décheance bourgeoise', 'faux semblants' and 'le confort sentimental'.[60] Several reviewers, including once again Claude Roy, commented on Courtade's tone of bitterness, mockery and even cruelty. Some found his handling of the short story form skilful, others self-conscious and at times over-elaborate.

Apart from the occasional reference to an individual title or to a potential subject his diaries for 1954 and 1955 make no mention of the collection, though in March 1956 we do find him considering calling it 'D'une part ... d'autre part'. He appears to have hit upon the eventual title by chance; but this first possibility indicates clearly enough the return to the related themes of hesitation, alternatives, choice and responsibility. The idea of using the phrase 'les animaux supérieurs' came to Courtade upon reading the work of the zoologist Léon Bertin, and he takes the relevant quotation as an epigraph for his volume in 'Les animaux supérieurs – oiseaux et mammifères – ont une indépendance plus grande à l'égard de la température extérieure et ne s'endorment généralement pas au cours de la mauvaise saison. L'homme par exemple ...'. In an interview published by *L'Ecole et la Nation* in October 1956 Courtade glossed this quotation by explaining that such creatures 'ne s'endorment pas pendant la guerre, l'amour, le mariage ... ils luttent contre le sommeil de l'habitude et de l'inconscience'.

It is indeed precisely this awareness and consequent attempt to refuse to submit to an imposed régime or system of values, with more than a hint of lucid Camusian acceptance and revolt, that constitute a good deal of the interest and significance of *Les Animaux supérieurs*. But there is rather more. In his review of the collection for *La Parisienne*, Michel Zeraffa substantially echoed what Courtade had said when he wrote: 'Chaque personnage [...] pressent ou découvre qu'il ment à lui-même'; but more pertinently he continued: 'le monde réel lui présente ce mensonge comme un miroir.'[61] Now it is clear that in several of the stories Courtade sets out to demonstrate that only when an individual recognizes this reflection is he brought to realize that he is part of it and alerted to the need to take action. And this may be all that Zeraffa intended. But he was also aware, perhaps, that in other stories Courtade appears to be saying that a refusal to accept any imposed system of values is precisely what is expected; that such a refusal is therefore itself reflected as well; and that by becoming in this way part of that system it is itself in danger of being rendered impotent. If this is the case then a large part of the overall meaning of *Les Animaux supérieurs* is a long way from the fundamentally positive intent of *Jimmy* and *La Rivière noire*.

As with *Les Circonstances*, there is no indication beyond the texts themselves of any order in which they should appear. That 'Une affaire de coeur', with its double focus on illness and love, should come last is appropriate enough given the circumstances of Courtade's life, even if the bitter irony of the last sentence ('Le coeur tient' (p. 252)) could not be appreciated at the time. It is also possible that the sixth story, 'L'utilité des miroirs' is intended to have a pivotal role. In it a corporal is separated from his soldiers during a German attack at the outbreak of the Second World War. Exhausted, his immediate attitude is to dismiss the whole affair as idiotic and beyond his understanding or concern. To avoid death is certainly important, but only in order that he should be able to return to the kind of life he had known before: 'La guerre était fini pour lui. Il pouvait revenir en arrière, revenir à la source de ce murmure d'eau tranquille que n'interromprait plus le tonnerre des événements' (p. 143).

As he waits for the German troops to arrive he reads a notebook that he has kept from the past, which he hopes will one day provide him with material for a novel. Family life in the 'Banlieue de L... entre 1930 et 1939' is described; once again it is Courtade's own in Sceaux: 'il ne s'y passait rien. Dans ce décor incertain les passions étaient un perpétuel compromis. [...] La vie était une oscillation perpétuelle qui précipitait le jeunes gens des folies romanesques à l'application raisonnable en vue de l'obtention de places stables à l'extérieur' (p. 149). Nantua emerges through recollections of a period that the corporal has spent teaching in the Institut Lamnenais; Génia, Nicole and possibly Jacqueline Dyard become surreally amalgamated in the figure of a mermaid (in the style of some of Courtade's early attempts at fiction), only to lose all exoticism and become 'une femme ordinaire dépouillée de toutes les imaginations, de tous les artifices de la passion' (p. 155). As night falls the narrator realizes that however great his capacity to dream and imagine might be, nothing in his past life had helped him to become aware of the momentous events that were about to occur, and he hurls his notebook away in disgust.

A short while after he comes upon another soldier who, like himself earlier, is waiting for the Germans to arrive. The explanation he gives is almost identical: 'Je veux qu'on me foute la paix. [...] Je n'ai besoin de personne. Il n'y a qu'à attendre qu'ils viennent' (p. 160). Not surprisingly, the narrator persuades him otherwise, acknowledging his own change in attitude ('il n'y a pas une heure je pensais comme toi' (p. 163)), and the story closes as they set off in search of their fellow soldiers. The moral is clear, facile even; but even here the closing words hint at an element of doubt: 'Il se répétait qu'il n'était plus le même homme. *Qui sait?*' (p. 163).[62] This last sentence suggests quite clearly that, while in response to specific circumstances the corporal has realized that an alternative, more purposeful attitude is necessary, there is no guarantee of sustained commitment thereafter. Most of the stories in *Les Animaux supérieurs* illustrate this problem; several of them also examine that of the individual confronted by a system or organization that absorbs and manipulates him and to which he finally surrenders. And permeating the whole collection is an awareness of time passing and of death.

The first of the stories, 'Le Sang-froid professionnel', at once addresses the problem of the individual and the group. Four journalists have gathered somewhere on the Normandy coast to cover the shipwreck of a pleasure boat that had clearly been carrying more than its legal number of passengers. The range of papers represented varies from the major regional publication *Phare de l'Ouest* (based probably on *Ouest-France*) to the agency *Presse Union* (*Agence France Presse*) and two Parisian daily papers *L'Echo du soir* (*France-Soir*) and *L'Univers* (*Le Monde*). Each of the journalists is compromised and constrained by circumstances or style. Parent of the *Phare de l'Ouest* is sufficiently aware of local politics and pressure groups to be cautious about attributing blame for the disaster too directly; Arnauld has a strict deadline to work to for his agency and is ready to be less than precise in his facts in order to meet it; July is concerned that an item of international news will be given priority over his sensational front-page article for *L'Echo du soir*; Boudier ('le plus intellectuel des quatre avec une moitié de licence d'histoire' (p. 19)) anticipates the reflective piece he will be expected to write for *L'Univers*, but is concerned that in spite of its tragic impact on a number of individual families the accident as an event of national importance will be as quickly forgotten as the traces of it on the beach will be washed away by the incoming tide.

When Jean Fréville reviewed *Les Animaux supérieurs* for *L'Humanité* he interpreted this opening story predictably enough as 'une critique de la presse bourgeoise'.[63] There is some truth in this. None of the papers represented in it is politically engaged, still less based on the Communist press. But Courtade's concern is surely wider. As in *Elseneur*, he is once again raising questions about the role and efficacy of journalism and about the relationship of individual reporters to their profession. Of the four only Boudier (in whom there are allusions to Courtade himself) shows any real concern, but that is short-lived. Like that of the others, his 'sang-froid professionnel' has turned into a tired cynicism and he is as ready as they are to enjoy dining on lobster and shellfish from the very same sea in which twenty people or more have just been drowned. Courtade is not necessarily accusing Boudier and his colleagues of failing in their duty as journalists, though he is strongly implying that they have allowed themselves to become part of a system and to be conditioned by it. Beyond them the real target of 'Le Sang-froid professionnel' is a press – of whatever political hue – that erodes and eventually smothers individual consciences and is content to report events in precisely the way its public expects. How this might be changed is a question that is not addressed. At the end of the story Boudier goes to check on what is happening on the beach. He returns to the hotel:

> Alors? dit July, rien de neuf?
> Rien.
> C'est toujours comme ça, dit Parent. (p. 28)

Journalism, or more precisely the journalist's responsibility, is also one of the issues to be dealt with in the second and third stories of the volume. In the first of these, 'L'enfant que tu auras de Marie-Madeleine', the narrator, a Communist and a war correspondent, is giving information to a resistance fighter, Paco, whose job is to blow up a generator. They discuss whether the narrator should go with him; but Paco argues that were he to do so and be killed, any account he might write would be lost: 'Si tu ne t'en tires pas tu ne peux rien raconter. Ton travail c'est de voir, et ensuite d'écrire, de raconter. C'est ça ton travail. Ça aide les autres' (p. 33). Their conversation turns on the question of writing, honesty and truth, and the narrator admits that before the war he had published an account of a shipwreck (possibly an intratextual echo of 'Le Sang-froid professionel') without ever having seen one:

> Avant la guerre je n'écrivais pas d'une façon absolument honnête. Je ne cherchais même pas à écrire d'une façon absolument honnête. Je n'étais pas malhonnête [...] mais je croyais qu'on avait le droit d'inventer, que ça n'avait pas d'importance. Je croyais qu'on avait le droit d'arranger les événements réels de la vie et d'en faire pratiquement ce qu'on voulait. Maintenant je ne le crois plus de la même façon. Je crois qu'il faut tendre à écrire la vérité, même si la vérité n'est pas très intéressante. (pp. 34–5)

At the same time he admits that, while there are particular moments such as war when truth is necessary, public preference will ultimately always be for 'des livres sur l'amour, sur le mariage' (p. 35). The story then develops around the relationship both men have had with Marie-Madeleine, thereby bringing love and war together. At once the narrator, who has known her well during his youth, modifies his account of their relationship in order that Paco's expectations in the present circumstances will not be affected by jealousy. By this example, which provides a kind of mirror image of the issue being discussed, Courtade keeps the debate open and underlines the difficulty, if not the impossibility, of arriving at a conclusive position.

In contrast, the third story 'Les Idées et les tanks', seems to be quite unambiguous. This is the remarkable account of the last hours of a collaborationist writer – generally held to be Drieu la Rochelle – who recognizes that his fate has been decided by the positions he has publicly adopted in his articles. Courtade's exploration of his anguish and attempted self-justification is subtle, and all the more persuasive because much of it could be made to apply equally as well to a writer of the Left as to one of the Right. While admittedly it is lifted from its immediate context, a sentence, for example, such as 'J'étais un acteur [...] dans cette comédie nécessaire' (p. 73) would have a distinctly hollow ring to it in January 1956, and there seems to be something of the same, as well as a hint of sympathy for the narrator's decision not to have written about fashion, love and women's tastes (as he accuses others of having done), but of having been consistent with himself to the end:

> J'ai été conséquent avec moi-même. J'ai été jusqu'au bout de ce que ces larves n'osaient dire que du bout des lèvres. Et maintenant je dois payer pour leur lâcheté, pour les millions de collaborateurs de fait et de consentement qui à cette heure sont en train de coudre des drapeaux à la croix de Lorraine, dans la cuisine, ou plus probablement de les faire coudre par la bonne ... (p. 72).

But throughout the story runs a damning thread of bad faith. As events turn against the collaborationist position, so he thinks of ways of justifying what he has written: 'Il pouvait prouver qu'il était nécessaire d'écrire ces articles pour se maintenir à un poste d'où il avait pu aider les gens' (p. 77). An article written before the rounding up of Jews in the Drancy camp, for example, could be turned, he tries to convince himself, in such a way that his name will not be associated with anti-Semitic policies despite its having contained phrases such as: 'Est-ce que nous allons nous apitoyer sur le sort des gens qu'en somme on ne fait que renvoyer chez eux?' (p. 77). Now, he reflects, 'il dirait qu'il avait écrit ce qu'il avait écrit pour rassurer les gens, puisque de toutes façons on ne pouvait rien faire pour empêcher ces rafles, ni rien dire contre, est-ce qu'il ne valait pas mieux donner aux familles l'illusion que ça n'était pas si terrible? Donc c'est par humanité qu'il avait agi ainsi' (p. 78). The logical conclusion of such a portrayal would seem to be either suicide (as eventually in the case of Drieu) or surrender or capture and execution (as in that, say, of Brasillach). But we have neither. The writer leaves his flat to make for the centre of the Nazi administration across the river, and at the southern end of the Rue des Pyramides is picked off by a German sniper. The irony, like the moral at the end of 'L'utilité des miroirs', is evident. But there is also a twist. Whatever judgement posterity will make ultimately, he dies convinced both of the inevitability of a German victory and of the rightness of his own position.

Although they differ quite considerably, then, in both content and style these three opening stories of *Les Animaux supérieurs* deal in one way or another with the relationship between a writer and his work (in this case articles in newspapers or reviews), his responsibility and his freedom. In all three there is compromise, and certainly in 'Le Sang-froid professionnel' and 'L'enfant que tu auras de Marie-Madeleine' an acknowledgement that journalism is limited, necessarily circumstantial, often inaccurate, and produced less to convince than to confirm. And no matter how aware any individual writer might be of this, it is evident, too, that 'Le sommeil de l'habitude' of which Courtade speaks in his interview in *L'Ecole et la Nation* has too powerful a hold for them to break away. Only in 'L'enfant que tu auras de Marie-Madeleine' is it suggested that action might be an alternative; but the point is not pursued.

If, as seems likely, these opening stories owe something to Courtade's own circumstances as a Party journalist, the next two seem in all probability to be inspired by his personal relationships. The first, 'La Fin de l'Italie', describes the honeymoon of a young couple, Armand and Laure, spent in Italy, and in particular in Rome and Capri. At first Courtade appears to be making a contrast between the mystery, romanticism and glamour of Italy and a marriage that has already begun to show signs of being threatened by habit and convention. The entire episode is recorded by Armand, and Laure, despite her equal educational training ('Licenciée ès lettres comme lui' (p. 84)) is presented as self-deprecating and unsure both of herself and of his feelings for her. Moreover, she discovers herself to be pregnant, suffers from bouts of sickness, and develops a spot on her nose that becomes an emblem of the irritation Armand feels and of potential discontent, whatever protestations he may make to the contrary.

Already they know they will return to Caen, where 'avec un poste double, ils étaient assurés d'une vie paisible' (p. 84); it is hardly surprising that they should have passively chosen a package holiday organized by L'Agence Universal, whose guides speak in clichés (p. 83), that they read their tour books attentively and visit Rome conscientiously. There are occasions, especially in Rome, when they succeed in escaping from the Italy prepared for tourists, and when, as during an evening spent in Trastevere, they have a real sense of the past. But such moments are short-lived; and, while that is in part due to the fact that Armand and Laure are incapable of sustaining them, it is also because modern Italy has allowed itself to become glossy and superficial. Canova's statue of Pauline Bonaparte in the Borghese gardens only has a modern equivalent in the sculpted form of the actress Maria Pasqua perched on a bar-stool and surrounded by admirers (p. 108); the hills around Rome have been scarred by mammoth hoardings advertising 'la consommation de l'apéritif Branca et de l'huile Esso' (p. 85); the 'chars antiques' which once plied the Via Agrippa have been replaced by the scooters of young Italian lovers (p. 95); the atmosphere of 'sensualité' once associated with Naples has given way to one of cheap bartering, as children try to sell the young couple pens and watches that they have bought from American sailors. Descriptions slip into the stereotypes of tourist brochures. Thus, for example, their hotel in Capri selected for them by the Agence Universal:

> on les conduisait avec d'autres de la troupe de l'Universal jusqu'à leur hôtel, par un chemin profond entre les jardins en terrasse débordants de fleurs rouges. La fenêtre de leur chambre s'ouvrait sur la baie et sur les coupoles de la chartreuse mauresque. Un silence parfait y régnait, troublé seulement de temps à autre par le crissement d'une cigale, par le claquement d'un parasol, par le frémissement des petites feuilles sèches des oliviers dans le vent marin. Les jardins descendaient abruptement jusqu'au golfe. L'eau comme le reste était parfaite: bleue, limpide, jusque dans les grandes profondeurs. Un canot à moteur y traçait un long sillage blanc. (p. 100)

In this passage virtually every phrase is a cliché, and the dominant colours of red, white and blue underline here as elsewhere a brashness that has completely obliterated all that Italy once represented. We are of course prepared for this from the beginning of the story in two other ways as well. One is by the references to and quotations from Stendhal's *Pages d'Italie*, with its moments of irritation and disillusion, though the amusing and ironic sexual commentary contained in the nineteenth-century writer's description of the 'tristes pins' is something of which Armand is totally unaware. And the second is by their names. Armand has no more of a Stendhalian hero about him than has Laure of the Italian Renaissance beauty whose praises were sung by Petrarch.

Eventually, just as Boudier in 'Le Sang-froid professionnel' comes to realize the inadequacy of any article he might write about the boat disaster, so, shortly before they leave Italy, Armand senses the shallowness of life around them. The reappearance of the statuesque Maria Pasqua underlines this, but alongside Laure, with her red face, hair like 'une perruque de baguettes noires' (p. 105) and the enflamed spot on her nose, she still attracts Armand's attention. At this point Laure reveals that she might be pregnant, and Armand's irritation with her and evident interest in the actress turns instantly into a protective concern. Laure is characteristically apologetic: 'Ça m'ennuie [...] que ça me soit arrivé pendant ce voyage. Mais nous reviendrons.' Armand's response is heavy with bitterness 'Ah! non, dit Armand, pas en Italie' (p. 108). Ostensibly this is due to his realization that the kind of life he had hoped would be represented by Italy has now escaped him for good; that family responsibility and parenthood are about to close in upon him. To a large degree this is indeed the case. But, as we have seen, Italy is no longer what it was; Rome's reputation as 'la ville éternelle' has been cheapened, even if its monuments remain. The past in any form cannot be recreated, and the ease with which Armand has slipped into his new role is an acknowledgement that once again the system – or at least a fresh one – has proved too strong.

The past is also the starting-point for the last of the stories in the first half of *Les Animaux superieurs*. 'Vingt ans après' describes a chance meeting between a couple who have not seen one another for twenty years, and whose relationship had come to an abrupt end when Catherine, prompted by friends, realised that Fred had nothing to offer her and refused to have any more to do with him. She agrees to have dinner with him, and they decide to go to the restaurant at the local airport. The point of what Courtade himself acknowledged to be 'la plus artificielle de mes nouvelles'[64] is obvious.

Approaching middle age and trapped by the circumstances of their lives, the airport represents for the couple a kind of oasis, a moment of timelessness when they can reflect on their earlier brief romance and dream of escape ('On voyage sur place' (p. 113)) from an existence described as 'une succession de jours et de semaines et de mois et d'années monotones' (p. 133) during which 'on commence à vieillir sans s'en apercevoir' (p. 134). Throughout are verbs denoting travel and movement (*s'en aller, partir, voyager, dépayser*) and there is both a real journey (from town to airport in Fred's grey car) and, once there, a series of imagined ones to Italy or India or unnamed exotic places. All are false. Clichés and stereotypes abound. At the airport the restaurant is cut off from the world outside by a huge window, they appear to be the only people dining and their sun-tanned waiter has the aura and glamour popularly associated with his having been formerly an air steward (p. 117); the aircrew and passengers emerge uncrumpled from the plane as though from another world (p. 127); the description of Catherine's imagined visit to Paris is as artificial as that of Armand's and Laure's hotel in Capri:

> Elle se réveillait le matin dans le lit capitonné de soie crème d'une chambre de grand hôtel. Une chambre qui faisait partie d'une 'suite', avec une série de numéros. Quand elle sonnait on lui apportait exactement ce qu'il fallait sans qu'elle ait rien demandé, c'est-à-dire une demi-pamplemousse, un café très fort à l'italienne et des toasts merveilleusement grillés, dorés. La lumière d'été illuminait les marbres et l'émail de la salle de bains voisine [...] vers onze heures elle se rendait en cabriolet décapotable à Paris quelque part du côté de la place Vendôme où sont photographiés les modèles de *Pour Elle*, exactement habillée comme il le fallait en cette saison, à cette heure de la journée, obligée de se hâter tout de même, vers une heure, pour le déjeuner à propos duquel elle avait donné des instructions pour qu'il soit servi dans la salle à manger de la 'suite', disposé si joliment, si artistiquement sur une table de marbre noir lisse, servi dans des assiettes rouges, si jolies qu'on ne savait plus très bien si c'était pour manger ou pour regarder. (pp. 119–20)

Her mental picture of India, in which tigers roam the streets (p. 122), owes even more to the travel brochure, and Fred has to remind her that it is in fact cows that are allowed to do this. His superiority is significant. While Courtade attempts to preserve a neutrality in the narrative point of view, recording the whole episode alternately through characters and an omniscient voice, it is Fred's which ultimately dominates, as does Armand's in 'La Fin d'Italie'. Throughout the story there is a barely hidden subtext of intended seduction and sexual revenge. Never having understood why he had been so abruptly rejected by Catherine twenty years earlier Fred gradually tries to insinuate himself into her confidence, to break down her defences. As they leave the airport to drive to a lakeside bar she finally reveals that it had been his dullness and lack of initiative which had prompted her to act as she had done. As her friends had said of Fred, he was 'un brave type mais il n'a pas inventé la poudre' (p. 112). Hurt, he reacts strongly and refuses to prolong their evening. But Catherine responds by not accepting his offer to drive her back to town, opting instead for the local bus. As it moves away, bumping across a road under repair she watches the plane for Milan take off and dreams once more of eventual escape.

By having the end of the story focused on Catherine in this way Fred is forgotten, rejected a second time and obliged to return to his life as an *impresario*. For her part Catherine will continue to make clothes. The two professions are surely significant and will find echoes in subsequent stories. Both deal with superficialities; neither has any element of originality. Like the varieties of journalism in 'Le Sang-froid professionnel', they depend on the demands and tastes of the consumer, and while both characters may be relatively successful in what they do, their roles in society are essentially anonymous and easily forgotten. Meanwhile the stones around them, like the ruins in Rome or the trees and the paving slabs in the grounds of the hotel in 'La Chasse' remain (p. 110), ironic reminders of the inconsequence and transitory nature of human life.

The disillusion and bitterness evident not far below the surface in this story re-emerge with even greater force in 'La Chasse'. In it a former actress approaches the end of her life, is possibly terminally ill and lives alone with her dog in a hotel. While her body and bearing are still those of a younger woman, her face reveals her age all too quickly, despite her heavy make-up ('un masque pour la scène' (p. 168)). As she takes a pre-lunch walk through the grounds she reflects on her former glory and recalls one of her early, elderly loves, Ferral, a kind of Balzacian or Zolaesque figure grotesquely forcing himself to resist his physical decline: 'cassé sur sa selle, se laissant conduire par sa bête, l'oeil vague, la lèvre molle, mais culotté de blanc, botté de noir, sanglé, coiffé de la bombe, jouant le jeu jusqu'au bout' (p. 170). Women from the past haunt her as well, their faces 'marqués par le souci effroyable de ne pas se laisser aller' (p. 171). As she walks through the trees – dying with the approach of winter but guaranteed rebirth in the spring – she is noticed by a passing motorist. At once she imagines a romantic pursuit of the kind she enjoyed in her youth, only suddenly to realize with terror that a single glimpse of her face will ruin everything. This is precisely what happens, and the driver accelerates away in frustrated irritation, leaving her alone with her dog. The story closes with the premonitory sentence: 'Elle eut un frisson et murmura: 'Allons, c'est fini, viens Bobby' (p. 177).

While every bit as clear in its intention as 'Vingt ans après', 'La Chasse' is more effective because it is more tightly controlled. Everything is registered through the narrator's experience, and the sense of bitterness or resignation is sharpened by the constant awareness of death. Trees are autumnal ('feuilles mortes' (p. 171), 'branches dépouillées' (p. 175)), the grass has yellowed, the riding path gives way to 'un terreau noir labouré' (p. 171), the hotel owner advises her to take advantage of 'les derniers beaux jours' (p. 169). The passing of time is stressed by a constant use of *jadis* and *jusqu'au bout*, which adds a sense of inevitability further sustained by the motif of travelling – through the grounds, through time, through life – and by the idea of pursuit and hunting, not only of animals and by lovers but also by death. And no matter what subterfuges, lies, pretences or masks are resorted to, escape from the last is impossible.

If Courtade did give any thought to the internal organization of *Les Animaux supérieurs* it is possible that he placed the next two stories, 'L'esprit Gacom' and 'Le Piano', immediately after 'La Chasse' because each deals in its own way with the same problem of the individual confronted by systems (in these cases political, social and commercial) which threaten to destroy him. In the first Babin, who has been without employment for some time, attends a residential selective training programme with the American Gas Company (hence Gacom) in the hope of being invited to join their sales staff. During this candidates are scrutinized to see whether they can develop the required collective mentality, the 'esprit Gacom', and they are subjected to a series of ceremonies and rituals under the critical eye of a senior company employee, Merril. From the beginning it is clear that the regime is a mixture of school, officers' mess and religious order. Before undertaking it each *stagiaire* is obliged as well to talk in detail about his previous experience, in other words to confess. Babin has been dismissed from his last employment for having acknowledged that workers who had struck over inadequate security were justified, and for arguing that from a technical point of view alone safety-guards should have been installed on their machines. While Merril initially gives the appearance of approving Babin's action, it will be this which ultimately stands against him and results in his not being appointed.

'L'esprit Gacom' is not simply a satire on American recruitment methods or on commercial practice, however; nor is it about people's gullibility or their willingness to sell themselves to this kind of capitalist enterprise. The story surely also contains a barely disguised critique of the PCF (Ga-com) with its discipline, methods of indoctrination, pretence of collective decision-making and 'police extraordinaire' (p. 190);[65] and in Merril with his 'lunettes d'écaille', 'petites mains grasses' and near-permanent smile it is tempting to see the figure of Jacques Duclos. Certainly such an interpretation can be supported by Courtade's disenchantment, recorded in his diary, with the attitudes and policies of the PCF. Curiously, none of the reviews of *Les Animaux supérieurs*, including those in the bourgeois press, read the story in this way, and, however unlikely it appears, Courtade himself may not have been aware of this possibility. His concern seems rather to expose one aspect of Americanization, and in this he was entirely in line with Party orthodoxy and propaganda.

Such a view is supported by the penultimate and arguably most political story, 'Le Piano', first published in *L'Humanité-Dimanche* (30 September 1960), which deals with the American exploitation of a Caribbean sugar-producing island, San Juan. The head of Taft Sugar Inc., Harvey H. Taft,[66] is portrayed as the archetypal uncultured opportunist American business man in a manner which, like the portrait of Colonel White in *Jimmy*, becomes caricatural. Taft's grotesque house is full of tributes to his achievements (including a fresco of his life). He has had a replica of the Trianon palace built in the grounds, and he engages Régnier ('décorateur–ensemblier' (p. 205)) to complete the decorations, instructing him to incorporate a piano ('Liszt ou un autre comme ça, très connu, a joué dessus' (p. 208)) that his wife has had imported from Germany. And just as the Taft household is full of incongruous and distorted images of European and even exotic eastern culture, so the island and its native population have been forced to assimilate American values and life-style. There is even an exact copy of the Washington Capitol in the island's main city, built, Régnier is reminded, from imported marble and at great expense.

All of this and more is a transparent commentary on the worst aspects of colonialism, and while the target may be specifically American we should not forget that France had already been engaged in the Algerian War for two years. But it is not such superficial features (albeit significant in their very superficiality) that really matter. American influence in San Juan is so strong that most of the local population have either been cowed into submission or won over by bribes and promises of positions of influence. Taft in fact is more than a pawn of the American government; he is a petty tyrant in his own right, whose economic leverage can and does shape government policy: 'San Juan est comme un grand navire qui marcherait au sucre au lieu de marcher au mazout. Et le sucre, c'est moi. Si je décide que le sucre baisse de deux cents, le navire ralentit et l'équipage vient se rouler à mes pieds. L'équipage je veux dire le gouvernement' (p. 213). He organizes 'revolutions' in order to settle them and thereby demonstrate his liberal views and political common sense. Even though there remains amongst the negro population a small minority of 'contre-révolutionnaires et même des communistes purs' (p. 215), they present no overt threat to the Taft regime. But the potential for the overthrow of American capitalism is there, and is reflected through Régnier's thoughts (recorded in italicized passages) and in Courtade's use of colour. White (Taft 'cravaté de blanc' (p. 210); 'la terrasse blanche' (p. 204); 'le rhum blanc' (p. 202) is opposed to red ('mer rouge' (p. 202); 'terre rouge' (p. 203); ' ... *suppose que l'incendie s'étende, s'étende et que le cercle de l'enfer se referme et que la terrasse blanche roussisse* ...' (p. 204) – a simple but effective way of conveying political significance.

Yet while the anti-Americanism of the story and its implied political statement may well have found favour with the readers of the PCF's Sunday newspaper, the ending is inconclusive. After an arranged military coup, Taft instantly ingratiates himself with the new regime and quite without irony, remarks 'à régime nouveau architecture nouvelle' (p. 226). Régnier is dismissed with a return ticket to Paris and a hundred dollars, but Taft remains, and we are left at the end of the story with the feeling that while 'une poignée de communistes' (p. 224) may still be present in San Juan they are politically impotent, and that the present régime with its superficiality and gloss and its belief in capitalism and market forces, will continue. This is strikingly similar to the end of 'L'esprit Gacom'. Although he is turned down by the company as unsuitable, Babin realizes how misguided he has been and responds accordingly: 'En somme, dit-il, je n'ai pas l'esprit Gacom? ... Il ne reconnaissait plus sa voix. Il n'avait jamais eu cette voix. C'était comme s'il venait de muer pour la seconde fois' (p. 198). And the endings of both stories recall that of 'L'utilité des miroirs'. All three focus on a moment of realization and decision, but with the exception of the corporal's success in persuading the soldier not to surrender there is no promise of an extended, positive alternative. In 'L'esprit Gacom' the company will continue to operate in its usual (successful) way; in 'Le Piano' Régnier may privately despise what he encounters in San Juan, but at no point does he raise political or social objections to it even in private conversations, and we can assume that it too will continue. In a sense the resignation and even despair registered in personal terms in 'La Fin d'Italie', 'Vingt ans après' or 'La Chasse', or in professional ones in 'Le Sang-froid professionnel' ('c'est toujours comme ça' (p. 28)), in 'L'esprit Gacom' and 'Le Piano', are broadened.

The real thrust of these stories seems to be that not only is the individual virtually powerless to challenge the dynamic and organization of the group – here of a capitalist, entrepreneurial kind, but by implication of any nature – but that the group and its collective thinking is the only way forward. There is also something significant about the professions of the protagonists in these stories – teacher, journalist, actress, fixer, interior designer – which are all essentially passive, directed or even purchased by others. As a result virtually the whole volume resonates with a tone of resignation and bitterness, and quite clearly is a projection of Courtade's current private reflections. And yet in spite of everything, and as is the case in all his published fiction, the ultimate message is clearly intended to be one of hope. In the final story, 'Une affaire de coeur', Charles Petrel's determination to recover from a heart attack is directly linked to his faith in a new and better world to come, and the story closes with the lines: 'Il pense à l'amour. Il pense à l'amour dans un monde mirobolant. Le sang cogne dans l'aorte. Le coeur tient' (p. 252). However, at the same time, the thinly disguised autobiographical nature of this story, the facile play on words of the title, and the self-evident meaning of the text as a whole render it the least successful of the collection. The imagined reconstruction of Courtade's illness reads too much like a personal footnote, and he will return to his near-constant preoccupation with the heart condition with more success in his final and unpublished novel *Le Jeu de paume*.

Given the circumstances of their composition it is hardly surprising that Courtade's past should resurface with regularity in these stories. Although it was there, as we have seen, in *Les Circonstances* and in different ways in *Elseneur*, the overall focus of both these earlier books was sharper. In *Les Animaux supérieurs* it is too apparent, and as a result tends to diffuse much of the book's socio-political impact. 'Une affaire de coeur' is the most blatant, but each story makes a general reference to his earlier years, whether it be to his adolescence in Sceaux (the 'banlieue de L ...' in 'L'utilité des miroirs'), his experience as a correspondent for *L'Humanité* in America, the first years of his marriage or the Resistance, for example. There are also precise details: Petrel's mother was '(une) employée de téléphone' (p. 245); Fred (p. 28) and Petrel (p. 251) are exactly the same age as Courtade; Babin and Gisèle have a room in the Hôtel Manchester (p. 187); and, with a minor modification, Fred's father has been 'un petit employé des douanes françaises' (p. 116).

At the same time it is hardly surprising, given the circumstances, that a constant theme of this collection should be the threat or inevitability of death. While this is sometimes linked rather too closely to an individual character's personal experience (in 'Les Idées ou les tanks' or 'La Chasse' for example) it is the ultimate expression of a general fear of being trapped within any system – political, social, economic, intellectual and so on. This gives rise to a network of images reflecting frustration or impotence, which in turn then modify those of water and light, which, as in *Les Circonstances*, otherwise provide *Les Animaux supérieurs*, like the earlier collection, with a degree of stylistic coherence.

The first of these images appears with much the same wide range of association. The sea, for example, may suggest release and freedom. In 'La Fin d'Italie' it signals a life Armand imagines could have existed before Laure announced that she was pregnant (p. 107) and for Régnier it offers escape from the cloying, sexually frustrated Cecilia Taft (p. 222). In 'Le Sang-froid professionnel', however, the sea is associated with death. In 'L'utilité des miroirs' water is linked to peace – 'ce murmure d'eau tranquille que n'interromprait plus le tonnerre des événements' (p. 141), in 'L'esprit Gacom' the port at Confluens-Sainte-Honorine is a divide between freedom and imprisonment; in 'L'enfant que tu auras de Marie-Madeleine' the damp atmosphere and the 'flaque d'eau noire' (p. 30) anticipate danger, and not surprisingly in 'Une affaire de coeur' it appears in the indirect recording of Petrel's awareness of death: 'Charles Petrel écrasé par la morphine et d'autres somnifères efficaces avait coulé dans un sommeil fiévreux, sans autre rêve que celui des battements de son coeur devenus soudain énormes, répercutés sous des voûtes, mêlés aux clapotis de rivières souterraines' (p. 241).

Images related to light may also at first appear to function much as those in the earlier collection did: for example in 'Le Sang-froid professionnel' the beach scene takes place in 'un violent rond de lumière' (pp. 14; 27); the conversation in 'L'enfant que tu auras de Marie-Madeleine' is lit by 'la mauvaise lumière de la lampe à pétrole' (p. 29), and in the same story Paco 's'était remis à marcher, les mains dans les poches, silencieusement d'un bout à l'autre de la pièce assez grande pour qu'il pût surgir puis disparaître dans une obscurité presque totale' (p. 46); in 'Vingt ans après', Catherine and Fred sit in 'un coin secret de la salle. Une petite lampe à abat-jour éclairait deux oeillets dans un vase de cristal à long col' (p. 117) and the runway outside is brilliantly flood-lit (pp. 118; 131). Having celebrated his being accepted for the Gacom recruitment programme Babin and Gisèle return to their hotel room, passing through the pools of light cast by street lamps (p. 196). In *Les Circonstances* such images, with their strong suggestion of theatrical scenes, tended, appropriately, to highlight moments of drama and tension; in *Les Animaux supérieurs* they are used rather differently, underlining an experience or situation that is false (or falsified) and cut off from normal life. When Catherine describes the airport as 'féerique' (p. 117) and 'mystérieux' (p. 118) the adjectives could apply equally well to any number of scenes culminating, in different ways, in the overall artificiality of 'L'esprit Gacom' or 'La Chasse'.

A further reflection of this can be seen in the use of related images suggesting frontiers or barriers. Again in 'Vingt ans après' the 'coin secret de la salle' is separated from the arriving passengers by 'une grande vitre' (p. 126); only when or because they are cut off from the outside world in this way can Catherine and Fred reminisce about the past or speculate on the future. In 'Le Sang-froid professionnel' the journalists readily retreat from the brightly-lit scene of the tragedy to the restaurant in the 'Hôtel de la *Digue*' (p. 10),[67] where, behind windows, glazed doors and even 'un rideau de brume' (p. 9), they will prepare their particular versions of the accident for their various papers. Beyond the 'baie de la salle à manger' (p. 190) there is also a permanent mist through which Babin will have to pass if he is to escape the clutches of Gacom and discover the real world. Régnier leaves the island of San Juan, but the actress in 'La Chasse' is trapped within the grounds of her hotel. In 'Les

Idées et les tanks', in which images of this kind occur most frequently – the Seine, bridges, windows and curtains, for example – the collaborationist writer leaves the upholstered comfort of his study only, ironically, to find death.

Clearly there are marginal differences in the ways this image functions across the stories; but fundamental to it is a sense of enclosure, which may be either protective or restrictive. In the first case, it is usually an excuse for not accepting responsibility. Fred, the journalists, Régnier or the narrator in 'L'enfant que tu auras de Marie-Madeleine' are all in their own ways guilty of bad faith, in that while they recognize the falseness of their situations they do little to challenge them. Elsewhere, in the case of Babin or the corporal, there is a realization that escape is possible even though there may be little or no indication of a long-term alternative. But beyond any of these considerations – political, social or professional – remains the one barrier that can be neither crossed nor avoided, namely that of death. Whatever weaknesses it may have as a *nouvelle* this alone justifies the place of 'Une affaire de coeur' in the collection. Here the image of the barrier (for example 'une porte-fenêtre [qui] ouvre sur le jardin' (p. 242)) is strengthened by a number of references to Petrel's sense of being stifled: 'Charles, allongé avait passé plusieurs heures à essayer d'écarter ce fardeau qui l'étouffait. Il rêvait d'air frais' (p. 234). As we have already noted, the story closes on a note of optimism or at least on a reaffirmation of the need to struggle, and is the most positive statement in the whole collection. At the same time we – with Petrel and with Courtade (CP:PC) – are aware that death, like chance in *Les Circonstances*, can strike when least expected.

In an article in a series entitled 'Le travail d'écrire', published by *Les Lettres françaises* (2 – 8 April 1958), Courtade confirmed that his preference as an imaginative writer was for the *nouvelle* 'composée rigoureusement comme un poème ou comme une pièce de théâtre [...] elle fournit au lecteur des indications, un canevas, et ensuite c'est à lui d'inventer, à lui d'imaginer'. When we consider the best of the stories in *Les Circonstances* this assessment is difficult to challenge; but those in *Les Animaux supérieurs* are less convincing. That there are certain similarities between the two collections is hardly surprising. In addition to the use of recurrent images we find the same preference for a shifting narrative voice and for a flexible use of tenses. Even if characters often remain underdeveloped, Courtade's handling of dialogue is good. While we may not find the same willingness to experiment with language as in 'Occupations' or 'La Salamandre', our attention is drawn to a number of striking images: an aeroplane is '[une] grosse mouette stupide' (p. 123), 'son nez depuis longtemps buté dans la terre, les ailes brisées' (p. 126); one of the actress's tears in 'La Chasse' 'glissa lourdement puis se perdit dans le fard comme une rivière ensablée' (p. 167); Petrel's heart beats like 'le battant de bronze d'une cloche folle' (p. 234); the setting sun seen from San Juan is 'l'astre en forme de poire [...] aspiré par la mer rouge et or loin derrière les immenses champs de cannes' (p. 202).

But the problem remains that, unlike the stories in the first volume, which grew *out* of specific incidents or experiences, most of those in *Les Animaux supérieurs* have not been given the chance to be modified or transformed through the creative process. There are exceptions: 'L'esprit Gacom', with its satirical verve (and possible alternative meaning); 'Les Idées et les tanks', for its psychological exploration and irony; or 'La Chasse', for its control and tone of despair. But in general we have the impression that this collection turns in upon itself, and fails to escape from the author's current personal and political preoccupations. In the same article in *Les Lettres françaises* Courtade acknowledged that he had embarked on another novel. This would be *La Place rouge*. After *Jimmy*, *La Rivière noire* and *Les Animaux supérieurs*, from the most militant, tortured and frenetic period of his life he would produce a work which, while still deeply rooted in autobiography, offers a fascinating panorama of left-wing intellectual development and debate through the inter-war years and beyond to the late 1950s.

NOTES

1. *Marxism and the French Left*, Oxford University Press, London, 1986, pp. 207–8.

2. See in particular George Ross, *Workers and Communists in France*, University of California Press, Los Angeles and London 1982, Chapter 3.

3. Courtade's first article in *L'Humanité*, 'L'âme du sénateur Vandenberg' appeared on 18 July. He was given the front page for his coverage of the talks in Paris on the adoption of the Marshall Plan on 28 and 29 July. His first contribution to *L'Humanité-Dimanche* was a *grand reportage* on life in the United Stages ('L'Amérique a peur') on 12 June 1949.

4. Courtade's principal assignments for *L'Humanité* took him to the following countries, sometimes more than once in the same year. USA (1947, 1949, 1950, 1954, 1956, 1959, 1960); United Kingdom (1947, 1954, 1956, 1958); USSR (1947, 1952, 1953, 1957, 1959); Siberia (1962); Italy (1953); Germany (1954); Austria (1955); Hungary and Yugoslavia (1949); Albania (1949); Switzerland (1954); Cuba and Mexico (1950); Egypt (1951, 1952); China (1952).

5. Courtade also wrote regularly for the weekly *Parallèle 50* between 1950 and 1952. Substantially the articles were the same as those in the daily press. His contributions to other PCF publications were irregular. During the same years he wrote in *La Nouvelle Critique* on four occasions (Nos. 18, 20, 25 and 33) and in *La Pensée* twice (Sept. – Oct. 1952 and Sept. – Oct. 1956) on the American presidential campaign and on the Suez crisis respectively. There are no articles signed by him in the weekly *France Nouvelle*. Many of the contributions in this paper are anonymous, but several on American affairs in particular bear marks of Courtade's style. No one I have spoken to has any recollection of Courtade writing for *France Nouvelle*, but it is possible that some of his articles for *Démocratie nouvelle* were

syndicated.   Courtade broadcast quite frequently.   In particular he appeared regularly on the programme *Ce soir en France*, directed by André Carrel and Francis Crémieux, providing a round-up of international events, 'Les grands événements internationaux de la semaine'.

6.   Editeurs Français réunis, Paris, 1949, p. 2. See too Rolland, *Un dimanche inoubliable près des casernes*, pp. 228–9.

7.   In *Paris–Montpellier, PC–PSU 1945–1963*, Paris, 1982, Emmanuel Le Roy Ladurie recalls listening to Courtade lecture on the Rajk affair at the Ecole Normale. He was struck, he says, by a 'pseudo-sincérité' which hid 'un doute absolu et désespéré'. Le Roy Ladurie is writing, of course, with the benefit of thirty years' hindsight.

8.   See in particular Courrière, *Roger Vailland ou un libertin au regard froid*, pp. 438–40 and Rolland, *Un dimanche inoubliable près des casernes*, Chapter 15.

9.   La Table ronde, Paris, 1956, p. 19.

10.   Ibid., p. 115.

11.   Ibid., p. 175.

12.   In his diary in 1955 Courtade records the women with whom he had had affairs. The tone is boastful; the list acknowledged to be incomplete.

13.   René Cazaux was a journalist for foreign affairs employed by *L'Humanité*.

14.   Roy, *Nous*, p. 410.

15.   Not all agree. Andrieu and Génia Courtade claim that these novels were entirely spontaneous.

16.   On 26 February the paper carried an announcement that Courtade had recovered from 'une longue maladie' and that his contributions to both daily and Sunday paper would begin again. Already on 1 January *L'Humanité-Dimanche* had carried a piece critical of Mendès-France's policy, 'Assurez-vous contre la guerre'.

17.   That Génia's jealousy was ferocious and that Courtade was physically afraid has been confirmed by both Génia

herself and Nicole Chatel. Génia has also expressed the view that Courtade had become envious of her own political commitment and activity.

18. See in particular 23–28 April.

19. Like many, it would take Courtade several years before he began to understand that by issuing this report Khrushchev was merely making the first major move in the power game that would eventually allow him to enjoy the same supreme power as Stalin had had.

20. References are to articles in *L'Humanité* and *L'Humanité-Dimanche* unless otherwise stated.

21. See Pierre Daix, *Une vie à changer*, Editions du Seuil Paris, 1975.

22. The cultivation of this image had been begun by the launching of Thorez's complete works in 1950.

23. Irving Wall has a happy phrase for this: 'elements of Catholic tradition were secularized in PCF propaganda', *French Communism in the Era of Stalin*, Greenwood Press, Westport and London, 1983, p. 99. See too Chapter 6 of this book and, for a well-documented if not very analytical account of this phenomenon, Bernard Legendre, *Le Stalinisme français. Qui a dit quoi? (1944–1956)*, Seuil, Paris, 1980.

24. See Courrière, *Roger Vailland*, pp. 694–5. The publication of the letter was acknowledged in *L'Humanité* on 2 November; two days later the paper published an open letter from a number of Soviet writers in which they justified the report and appealed for understanding.

25. The title of Pierre Daix's review of the same work in *Les Lettres françaises* (12–18 November 1959) was precisely 'Du culte de la personnalité': 'La Personnalité s'approprie, catalyse, réalise. La notion même d'un programme issu de la lutte des Français et l'application de ce programme [...] lui est parfaitement étrangère.'

26. See in particular 'Les Fruits de Satiet' (21 February 1958): 'Les "médiateurs" américains continuent à se comporter en Tunisie comme s'il s'agissait d'un protectorat.'

27. For some interesting observations on the stylistic features of 'Stalinist' journalism see Legendre, *Le Stalinisme français*, pp. 47–53.

28. *Commune*, May–June 1934, p. 1028. See too Flower, *Literature and the Left*, Chapter 5.

29. Editions de la Nouvelle Critique, Paris, 1948, p. 36 quoted in Flower, *Literature and the Left*, p. 140.

30. 25 August 1949.

31. See Flower, *Literature and the Left*, p. 147.

32. See as well Vailland's essay *Expérience du drame*, Buchet-Chastel, Paris, 1953, for an original and pertinent contribution to this debate.

33. *Entretiens: Roger Vailland*, ed. Max Chaleil, Editions Subervié, Rodez, 1970, p. 92.

34. The typescript of this novel has survived and was generously lent to me by Max Léon. There are a few alterations in manuscript but nothing significant.

35. The three volumes are: *Au Château d'eau* (1951); *Le Coup du canon* (1952); and *Paris avec nous* (1953). These incidents are described successively in I, 16; II, 27; II, 200.

36. *L'Humanité*, 16 October 1950.

37. She is described by the militant Bielinsky later in the novel as 'une vraie petite bourgeoise'.

38. Her language is studded with words like *épatant* and *formidable*.

39. The local sheriff is named Ruscoe. In *La Rivière noire* the sadistic leader of a mercenary group will be called Rustine.

40. He refuses to admit having been a witness to the demonstration in the Champs-Elysées: 'Quand il aperçut

Bill, il résolut de jouer l'abruti, le bon garçon hurluberlu'
(p. 248).

41. He does so in the spring ...

42. A similar use is made of an ancient sage, the *aïeul*, in *La Rivière noire.*

43. Interestingly, the question of censorship in the press is not raised. In *La Rivière noire* articles in American papers give a positive description of life in Vietnam.

44. My italics.

45. *Elseneur*, p. 263.

46. *Communism and the French Intellectuals*, Deutsch, London, 1964, p. 193.

47. October 1951.

48. The typescript is dated 'septembre 1950 – mai 1951'.

49. See above, pp. 22–24.

50. For a discussion of the reception and reporting of events in some reviews and newspapers in France see Robert Hudson, 'Et Bourreaux et victimes! Eye-witness accounts of the French war of decolonization in Indo-China, *Les Temps modernes* 1946–50', *Journal of European Studies*, September 1989, pp. 191–204.

51. Martin was released from prison 16 February 1953.

52. See too Vailland's play *Le Colonel Foster plaidera coupable*, Editeurs Français réunis, Paris, 1951.

53. *Communism and the French Intellectuals*, p. 210.

54. My italics.

55. See pp. 28 and 70.

56. Throughout the Nguyen Hung Hoe episode Courtade plays on the image of death and rebirth to reinforce the strength of his message.

57. The light in the hospital in Hanoï is *triste* (p. 174).

58. References to the native population as 'Vietminh' are made by the occupying French only. In all other cases they are the 'Vietnam' – a single, united people.

59. Gabriel Venaissin, *Combat*, 29 November 1956.

60. P. Bertrand, *Avant-Garde*, 5 November 1956.

61. *La Parisienne*, November 1956.

62. My italics.

63. 4 October 1956.

64. Diary entry, 29 January 1956.

65. There is a suggestion of similar criticism in 'Les idées et les tanks' (p. 62).

66. The portrait of Taft is possibly based on the Republican Robert A. Taft, a devoted supporter of Eisenhower and a staunch conservative. He is described by William O'Neill in *American High*, New York, 1986, pp. 93–4, as 'no-one's idea of a popular politician. Wealthy and aristocratic, he remained aloof even from his colleagues, some of whom he treated with open contempt.'

67. My italics.

– 4 –

The Promised Land

Whatever his misgivings in private were, as we have noted, there seems to have been little or no public reaction from Courtade to the kinds of internal debates that developed within the PCF in the wake of the Twentieth Congress and the Khrushchev disclosures. As all political commentators have agreed, the Party was obliged during the next few years to face up to a new climate. The emergence of De Gaulle and the birth of the Fifth Republic could continue to give rise to warning noises about the threat of dictatorship and of fascism, but the demonstration of massive popular support in the referendum for the new regime in September 1958 would necessitate a new approach if the PCF was not going to find itself even more isolated. Thorez had anticipated this already. In a speech 'Union et action pour le "non" au référendum-plébiscite' (17 July 1958) he nonetheless managed to suggest that while a Gaullist government might be a 'classic bourgeois regime which would directly precede a transition to socialism'[1] it would in the immediate term allow the working class to reassess its position, focus on broad democratic principles and look for opportunities of co-operation with the Socialists and Radicals. Such an argument became even more necessary when the extreme Right moved into hostile opposition to De Gaulle's Algerian policy.

Behind the scenes, however, dissent was considerable. Just as Hervé's *La Révolution et les Fétiches* had touched on a sensitive nerve in 1956, so in 1960 did Jean Baby's *Critique de base*. In this essay Baby approved neither those who were now challenging the Party and moving to the kinds of revisionist positions that would become the norm within a few years, nor the old guard clinging to past values and dismissive of all dissent.[2] Baby, a Party member for thirty-six years was, like Hervé, expelled, but around him the debate was engaged, and a new climate slowly taking shape.[3] Courtade did not participate, at least in public.

He remained a member of the Party's Central Committee, but was fully occupied with a workload which threatened to assume the proportions of the one he had carried in the years before his heart attack. While his sympathies, according to those close to him, were broadly for those of the 'new style', his faith in Communism ('la vérité' to which he refers in his diary) remained, and he continued to admire Thorez. All of this, together with his personal circumstances, argued that a complete change and an opportunity to reassess his position would be nothing but beneficial. By mid 1959 the possibility of his being sent to Moscow by *L'Humanité* arose, and having requested a move Courtade made a preliminary visit in September before leaving with an open-ended contract in July 1960 as the paper's 'envoyé permanent'.[4] His posting was announced on the front page on 11 July: 'Nul doute que, connaissant le grand talent de journaliste et d'écrivain de Pierre Courtade, nos lecteurs se féliciteront qu'il ait été désigné pour suivre à leur intention l'actualité la plus exaltante, celle du grand pays qui est en marche vers le communisme.'

During these three years Courade's articles can be grouped under three broad heads. His principal responsibility was to continue to cover developments in world events, but in addition he produced regular reports on the domestic progress of the Soviet Union in a post-Stalin world under the guidance of Khrushchev, and a handful of articles on life there as he saw it.[5]

The first event of major international significance that he wrote about in *L'Humanité* was the United Nations' Conference in New York in September 1960. Attended by Khrushchev (but boycotted by De Gaulle, who sent Couve de Murville as his delegate) the conference marked a noteworthy step forward in the thawing of relations between the superpowers. The line in Courtade's articles is predictable. The initiative for world peace clearly comes from the Soviet Union. Khrushchev speaks not simply as a politician but on behalf of workers and peasants throughout the world who clamour for peace: 'personne n'oubliera le combat infatigable de Nikita Khrouchtchev qui a fait retentir ici la voix des paysans et des ouvriers qui exigent la paix' (14 October). The election of Kennedy to the presidency of the United States on 8 November is greeted by Courtade as a sign for optimism, though within months doubts reappear; American foreign policy is really no different under Kennedy who, it is claimed, is manipulated by politicians behind the scenes still intent on pursuing the tactic of imperialist expansion

(8 and 11 March 1961). Khrushchev, in contrast, is presented as a leader of wisdom and patience. When the two men meet in Vienna in June 1961 the contrast is apparent: 'à des manoeuvres dont l'inexpérience de John Kennedy souligne la maladresse, le chef du gouvernement soviétique opposera une politique de paix dont une des caractéristiques les plus remarquables est d'être absolument sans préjugés' (3 June). Within this general context, and with Moscow labelled elsewhere as the 'véritable capitale de l'anticolonialisme mondial' (29 December 1960), any direct interventions using military force or statements of support for rebel factions – in Hungary,[6] Vietnam, Cuba, Algeria for example – can be justified as necessary in the face of counter-revolutionary factions and developments.

During Courtade's last years most of the articles in *L'Humanité* dealing with foreign policy were written by Max Léon, and when Courtade did contribute any their tone and argument, as the few examples quoted above show, remained strictly orthodox.

This is equally true of his numerous pieces on life in the Soviet Union, but here we have the impression that his was an authoritative voice whose responsibility is not simply to extol Soviet virtues but to show in particular how open and conciliatory government policy had become. Nowhere is this better illustrated than by his commentaries on destalinization. When in late October 1961 the decision was taken to remove Stalin's body from the mausoleum in Red Square Courtade approved – but only because it was a reminder of the way in which a policy could become distorted. Stalinism, as he would write in February of the following year had, whatever its weaknesses, made a vital contribution to the evolution of the Communist Party and to the Soviet Union: 'la question n'est pas de rayer Staline de l'histoire du Parti et de la Révolution, mais de lui donner sa juste place en soumettant tout ce qui a été écrit à son sujet à une analyse critique fondée sur les documents et les témoignages vérifiés' (8 February 1962). However difficult it may be, the willingness to examine objectively, to be scrutinized and above all to subject oneself to *autocritique* is both normal and typical, Courtade argued.

Whether the issue was agricultural policy (21 January 1961), the new statutes of the Party (5 August 1961) or intellectual and artistic developments, what the world was witnessing was the emergence of a new, dynamic Soviet society. His report on the various delegations who spoke at the twenty-second Congress

With Max Léon in Moscow, 1962.

of the Party in October 1961 captures the tone of all his articles that return to this theme: 'Ils n'hésitent pas à rendre public tout ce qui ne va pas et c'est pourquoi la critique et l'autocritique sont dans les meilleures interventions que nous avons entendues étroitement associées au bilan des succès et des victoires' (23 October).[7] Already, earlier in the same year, Yuri Gagarin's successful space flight had provided the Soviet Union with precisely the kind of spectacular achievement that its politicians and spokesmen were not slow to take advantage of. On 13 April, in his article 'La preuve de la toute-puissance de l'homme', Courtade was no exception:

> Comme toute science, la science de la conquête de l'espace est née de la nécessité de satisfaire les besoins matériels de la société humaine. Et ce n'est pas par hasard si les pionniers de l'espace ont été des Soviétiques, c'est-à-dire des hommes appartenant à une société dégagée du préjugé religieux et fondée non sur le profit individuel, mais sur le dévouement et la collectivité.

In August, in a series of six articles, 'Le projet de programme du communisme', he traced the progress made by the Soviet Union in all aspects of life there during the previous forty years. This was a nation which had progressed from being amongst the most backward in the civilized world to one of the technologically most advanced. Moreover, this had been achieved not for the benefit of just a privileged few, but for all Soviet citizens, and a vision of the future is offered in which free travel, free hospital care and free holidays would be available to everyone irrespective of age, sex or position in society. Courtade reminded his readers that most Soviet tourists already possessed expensive cameras and that other normal features of urban life in particular included 'l'usage du téléphone (les communications urbaines sont gratuites pour les abonnés), l'avion dont on peut dire sans hésiter qu'il est ici un moyen de transport démocratique, le livre (y compris le livre de luxe), le disque (quatre ou cinq fois moins cher qu'en France), etc.' (18 August).

In April of the following year Courtade visited a new steel-production centre at Lipetsk, 400 kilometres south of Moscow. In October, together with Max Léon, he went even further afield, to Krasnoïarsk in Siberia, to report on the construction of a new hydro-electric station. In each case there is nothing but praise and admiration. This indeed was a brave new world in which everywhere evidence of '[une] attention soutenue qui est celle du travail humain intelligent, responsable' (16 October) was to be seen, in which the best of Western art (Picasso, Léger, Pignon, ...) and culture generally was made accessible to all workers and in which cafés and restaurants served to bring people together democratically where they read newspapers and discussed matters of importance, and were not merely places, as in France, for relaxation and self-indulgence.

But nowhere was Courtade's utopian reading of Soviet society more evident than in some articles he wrote shortly after his return to Moscow from New York in October 1960. In these American and Soviet life are compared. Eleven years before Courtade had written that such were the provision and level of information in America that 'il est extrêmement difficile au bout d'un certain temps de ne pas devenir idiot.'[8] The point is here made again. Four-fifths of all American newspapers can be thrown away, and the rest read in only a few minutes. Debate and discussion are discouraged and virtually non-existent, with the result that people speak 'par de petits bouts de phrases, comme celles qu'on voit sortir de la bouche des personnages des *Comics*, dans une poire' (25 October). Racial discrimination abounds, privilege is encouraged and social difference the accepted norm.

By contrast the life he reported as seeing around him and sharing on his arrival in Moscow is, not surprisingly, described in an utterly flat, unemotional way as an idyll of reasonableness, good sense and balance in an atmosphere of peaceful coexistence and modest seriousness:

A Moscou, j'habite une rue large et tranquille où poussent des arbres et, en été, un gazon d'herbes folles émaillé de fleurs de champs. Je vois par ma fenêtre entrer et sortir les ouvriers d'une usine qui, après avoir longtemps fabriqué des mitrailleuses, fabriquent maintenant des aspirateurs.

A 11 heures, le travail s'arrête; les ouvriers écoutent des concerts ou des orateurs, ou bien ils jouent aux dominos dans le parc. Un peu plus loin, sur la gauche, on aperçoit le combinat où s'imprime *la Pravda*. En face du combinat il y a un magasin d'alimentation, un *Gastronom*. On peut y boire du champagne sucré dans des flûtes en respirant l'odeur du poisson fumé.

Strategically placed in the streets are newspaper hoardings:

> des gens [...] s'arrêtent pour lire de bout en bout un article de 5 ou 6
> colonnes sur les question idéologiques ou la culture des blés de
> printemps et je ne sais pas ce qui est plus extraordinaire: qu'on puisse
> publier des articles tellement sérieux dans un journal quotidien, ou qu'il
> y ait des gens pour lire ces articles. Mais c'est ainsi.[9]

But no more than in his articles on international affairs did
Courtade allow such descriptions to develop into simple eulogy.
To reach the present position had only been possible because of
the Soviet leaders' (and Khrushchev is exemplary, of course)
wisdom and common sense. And if progress is to continue
vigilance and a willingness to learn from earlier errors must be
sustained: 'ils n'hésitent pas à rendre public tout ce qui ne va
pas' (21 October). As long as this was the case a prosperous and
peaceful future, *L'Humanité*'s readers were assured, was
inevitable and the lesson is there for all of France to learn.

With the benefit of hindsight most of the claims which
Courtade made – and especially those concerning conditions in
the Soviet Union – seem either naive or wilfully self-deluding.
On the evidence of friends and colleagues, in particular of
Nicole Chatel and Max Léon,[10] however, the opposite was true.
Certainly Courtade enjoyed certain privileges. A three-roomed
flat was made available, and a woman who came every day to
clean and to go shopping; he had a car; he was allowed to take
holidays at little cost in country houses reserved for government
officials. While he was not well paid, a supplement to his salary
sent to him in French francs gave him (and Léon) access to shops
not open to the average Soviet citizen, there were no restrictions
on his travel, his journeys, including any to France, and hotel
accommodation were free, and his status as head of *L'Humanité*
gave him access to Khrushchev's immediate entourage and to
the embassies. Arguably, with such benefits as these,
admiration and enthusiasm could be readily expressed; but, if
his contemporaries and colleagues are to be believed, Courtade
was utterly sincere. Moreover he would always take visitors to
the poorest parts of Moscow in order to see precisely how much
progress there was to be made – and indeed how much had
already been accomplished.

However painful at times it unquestionably was, what was
taking place in the Soviet Union was a true revolution, heading

unerringly for the 'société absolument nouvelle' of which Sacha and his family are part in *La Place rouge*.[11] The years of faith, waiting and argument that would be recounted in this novel in an only thinly disguised autobiographical form had finally been justified. At the same time, for all the public display of conviction, doubts about potential corruption or the problem of sustaining belief remained. Already they had surfaced – albeit in a rather different context and climate – in *Les Animaux supérieurs* and could be found expressed more directly in his diaries. Now too they were compounded by anxiety over his fragile health. All of this was brought together in his unpublished novel *Le Jeu de paume*, and while its precise dates of composition are not known it has to be read alongside *La Place rouge* as a cautionary statement, a reminder that behind the public persona the uncertain and anxious individual was still very much in evidence.

La Place rouge (1961)

Courtade began his last major work on 27 June 1956 in the immediate aftermath of the Khrushchev revelations; he would not finish it until mid-1961 at the earliest.[12] While Stalinism and its potentially distorting influence on Communism was an important stimulus it is evident, from what working notes remain, that Courtade was intent on dealing with the general issues of authenticity and truth and the quest for self-fulfilment that all should undertake on both a personal and a political level. Not all will be successful: a lack of vision or determination, an acceptance of immediate, short-term values or a willingness to compromise or to bend before external pressures all present threats:

> l'idée philosophique du livre est la suivante: le problème de la vérité est au centre de tout – sur le plan politique et social des hommes découvrent que 'la vérité est révolutionnaire'.
>
> Sur le plan humain (la vie personnelle, l'amour) ils découvrent que c'est seulement par la recherche de la vérité (des passions *vraies* etc. ...) que l'on peut parvenir à la plénitude.
>
> Mais sur le plan de la vie sociale comme dans la vie privée [...] la recherche de la vérité est une recherche dramatique. Elle peut conduire à la catastrophe – elle peut être inefficace et finalement ceux qui étaient partis à sa recherche peuvent être conduits à accepter un compromis.

Red Square, 1961. (Photo Pic.)

When the novel appeared in the cheap 10:18 series in 1970 its front cover carried the reproduction of a Russian poster with the words for 'yesterday' and 'today' in Cyrillic script at the top and bottom. The illustration in the upper half shows three darkly clad, stooped figures: an old lady carrying an oil-lamp, a cleaner with two buckets on a kind of yoke across his shoulders and a clerk complete with ledger, pen and ink. Beneath are their modern equivalents, head high and striding purposefully forward: an electrician and a plumber in smart, light-coloured overalls carrying their tools and a young female office-worker holding a typewriter.[13] The blurb on the rear cover informs us that the novel describes 'l'itinéraire spirituel, politique et sentimental' of its protagonist, whose life is shaped and given meaning by 'la Révolution': 'le jeune homme idéaliste et passionné du début [...] est devenu adulte.' Our expectancy therefore is of a standard *Bildungsroman*, in many ways the natural extension of what Courtade had set out to achieve in *Jimmy*.

This was a theme commonly adopted by the book's reviewers when it was first published in the autumn of 1961. Some, like Jean Spangaro in *L'Education nationale*,[14] saw it less as the account of an individual's development than as that of a whole generation. André Stil, in a predictably fulsome article in *L'Humanité* (9 November 1961), suggested that the true subject of *La Place rouge* was the forward march of history itself. Elsewhere, others focused on the mixture of private and public issues, predictably (and correctly) seeing the novel as an 'autobiographie (romancée par pudeur)', to quote Claude Roy,[15] and being more concerned for what it revealed of a man still wracked by uncertainty. For Bernard Frank Courtade was a 'communiste fragile',[16] who needed the protective support of the Party, however much he may have wanted to write 'independently'; Maurice Nadeau, anticipating his obituary of Courtade, simply saw in him two characters – novelist and journalist, of whom the former was immensely the more talented and attractive.[17]

More than any of these public assessments, however, it was a personal letter from Vailland that drew from Courtade some interesting reflections on his novel. On 4 January 1962 Vailland basically accused his friend of having failed to raise the level of debate in *La Place rouge* high enough. If he had found the first half of the book successful, it thereafter remained at the level of 'une confession sentimentale et un plaidoyer d'universitaire', which, Vailland said, was both disappointing and irritating.[18] He suggested that Courtade had already glimpsed a means of raising personal issues to the level of important public debate when he wrote *Elseneur*. Shakespeare, Vailland claimed, had used historical figures as actors for ordinary emotions, thereby giving them tragic status. Racine had done the same. Given Courtade's position within the Communist Party he had a ready-made context, Vailland suggested, and he went on to develop an analogy between the Party and the Catholic church to which he would return in the pages of his diary, as it was relevant to his own work. Courtade's reply four months later was honest, and focused very precisely on the dilemma which he and all other politically committed writers faced:

J'aurais à choisir entre la possibilité d'écrire un livre plus brillant [...] et une certaine idée que je me fais de ma responsabilité politique comme homme de Parti, ou si tu veux comme homme d'Eglise. Courir le risque de l'excommunication pour cela? Quitter l'Eglise? le fait est que je ne le puis ni le veux. [...] le personnage que je suis *ne pouvait* pas écrire un autre livre [...]

Par contre, je me demande si un romancier communiste peut écrire des romans sur le communisme? Là était mon erreur sans doute. Dans le meilleur des cas je ne pourrai jamais être qu'une espèce de Bernanos dans mon Eglise. Ça ne va pas très loin ... Je vois bien que comme romancier je me suis engagé dans une voie sans issue, et en même temps je *n'en puis pas sortir*, car au fond le seul sujet qui m'intéresse c'est la politique et, très précisément, le communisme. Mais le seul sujet que je connaisse, un peu, est le seul sur lequel je ne puisse dire toute la vérité, de crainte de porter atteinte à une cause qui m'est oui, plus chère que mon oeuvre ... La solution que tu me proposes (la solution Elseneur) m'apparaît comme une manière de fuite. Je m'y résignerai peut-être un jour ... Mais à vrai dire, *pour moi* peut-être vaudrait-il mieux renoncer à écrire que d'écrire des Semaines Saintes ...[19]

Courtade's death just over a year later precluded this option, but the typescript of *Le Jeu de paume* is evidence that he was at least willing to experiment with the kind of introspective, psychological novel about which, in public at least, he was usually less than enthusiastic. But given his sense of political responsibility and his wish to demonstrate the correctness of Simon Bordes' evolution, it is arguable that he had forced himself into an *impasse*. If that is so, then one of the reasons why

La Place rouge would appeal at least initially to more than the Party faithful (his immediate congregation) must lie in the naturalness with which conflict and tension in Bordes or between him and others is established. Its appeal will also depend to some extent on its historical authenticity and on Courtade's success in offering his readers a coherent interpretation of events over a period of more than two decades.

Given the circumstances of his private life in the mid to late 1950s it is hardly surprising that the composition of *La Place rouge* should have taken so long. Working papers and random notes also suggest that it was difficult. From the beginning it is clear that Courtade intended the novel to be in the form of a series of episodes, each one significant for the development of the Left in France as a whole and of his own (or his protagonist's) political maturity within that context. Not surprisingly, the earlier periods appear to have created the greater problems, and Courtade appears to have spent considerable time documenting himself as fully as possible on the 1930s. There are scribbled references to and notes taken from a range of texts by Malraux, Aragon, Ehrenburg and Thorez, and pages torn from a copy of *La Correspondance internationale* (27 June 1936) containing tributes to Gorki, who had died nine days earlier, from a group of writers invited especially to Moscow, of whom one was Gide.[20] Gide's praise of Gorki was fulsome, though it would only be a few months later that his reservations about the direction the Soviet Union was taking would be made public in the *Retour de l'URSS*. This essay, together with Gide's diary for 1936 and Eugène Dabit's *Journal intime* (1939), are the texts to which Courtade appears to have turned most frequently during the early stages of preparing *La Place rouge,* and from what we know about the development of his attitude towards the Party in the late 1950s it is tempting to speculate that the doubts and caution expressed by both writers were not without appeal.

An outline of *La Place rouge* indicates that Courtade at first envisaged it should have at least seventeen sections. Despite his concern, recorded in his diary, to maintain '[une] description réaliste de l'extérieur qui enlève le caractère autobiographique', the personal dimension is instantly evident. The first section, for example, 'Origines de mon adhésion au communisme', contains notes clearly referring to his early years in Sceaux; the second, 'L'expérience soviétique', is based on the visit he and Génia made in 1935; the twelfth, 'Le procès Rajk', examines his behaviour at the time ('pourquoi je prends ce parti, sincérité de ma conviction'); the fourteenth is devoted to Thorez ('ce que je pense de lui, comment je l'imagine – aspects positifs de cette personnalité'): and the last, dealing with the investigations about Communist intellectuals at Ivry in 1953, reflects the doubts recorded in his diary: '*Mars 1953* l'apothéose du Stalinisme intellectuel – commencement chez moi d'une gêne profonde.' From more detailed notes still, made on a section entitled 'Le Cuirassé Potemkine', which would ultimately develop into the first part of the novel, it is also clear that several of the characters were to be modelled on Génia, Boris, Hervé, Altmann, Francis Cohen, Guéhenno and Charles Plisnier. Gide, too, was to feature in his own right. And running through the notes like a leitmotif – though we should not forget that these are written from the vantage point of the late 1950s – are references to a fundamental belief in the Soviet Union and in the Communist revolution. Trotskyism, acknowledged as a temptation in the third section (though there appears to be no evidence for this in Courtade's life), is rejected 'au nom de l'efficacité'. In the sixth part, dealing with the defeat in 1940, we read: 'sentiments à l'égard du communisme et des communistes au moment de la défaite – dans l'écoulement général des valeurs cette seule valeur demeure'; and with the Liberation is a realization that 'après la victoire la Révolution est nécessaire et inévitable.'

While deviating little from the plan outlined in Courtade's notes, the final version of *La Place rouge* is much more tightly controlled. There are only eight parts designated by specific years. Each is subdivided into smaller, ones though often without precise continuity between them, creating the overall impression of a series of discrete episodes and even short stories. The first four sections in the notes dealing with the early years have gone, and are replaced by a single part, '1935' , in which the main characters and key themes are introduced. Elements originally to have appeared here have either been eliminated altogether – the journey to the Soviet Union in 1935 – or worked into the novel elsewhere. Thus descriptions of Simon's early years or his political evolution during the 1930s are picked up in conversations or reflections on later occasions, thereby bridging the individual episodes and helping to draw the novel together in spite of it episodic structure.

The opening part of the novel begins with a screening of Eisenstein's film *Battleship Potemkin*, at which Simon Bordes,

Camille, Cazaux, Prévôt, Grange and his wife Paulette are present. André Gide is also there.[21] When the film has finished they gather to discuss it in a café somewhat obviously called 'L'Avenir', where they are joined by Sacha Bernstein, a Russian Jew, who is about to return to the Soviet Union. (Simon will meet him again in Moscow in the last section of the novel.) The conversation turns on the need for revolution, the interpretation of art, the problems faced by young working-class couples, life in the Soviet Union, anti-Semitism and in general the future: 'L'episode du *Potemkine* avait été un lever de rideau sur leur propre vie' (pp. 24, 5).

While it becomes apparent almost at once that Bordes is not only the principal character but a thinly disguised version of the author, by adopting an almost omniscient narratorial voice throughout the opening section Courtade allows himself to comment at will on all the characters and to adopt their particular perception of events when necessary. Thus while he simply provides information about Simon (p. 9) or Cazaux (p. 10), he also interprets Grange's reaction to the words of the *Internationale*:

> Pourquoi lui qui n'aime pas les phrases et qui effectivement n'en fait pas, est-il pris et secoué par certaines phrases: 'Debout les damnés de la terre', par exemple ... Des phrases qui le feraient rigoler s'il ne s'agissait pas de *l'Internationale*? Pourquoi? La réponse que Grange ne formule pas, mais qu'il connaît est que, depuis qu'il a senti et compris tout cela, il n'est plus seul. Il ne marche plus seul entre les murailles grises vers une fin obscure, vers un trou: il avance sur une immense avenue avec une foule qui veut comme lui changer le monde. (p. 22, 3)

Later he comments on the group as they are about to discuss the film they have just seen:

> C'était le moment où, comme Eisenstein l'avait un jour expressément souhaité, les images déjà transformées en émotions allaient se transformer en idées puis en thèses politiques. Cette transformation serait d'autant plus rapide qu'il n'y avait pas encore dans leur tête ces expériences mortes, ces épaisseurs de vie qui, plus tard, joueront le rôle d'un filtre ralentisseur. (p. 47)

He registers Cazaux's perception of Simon ('un sympathisant qu'il fallait aider, qu'il fallait prendre par la main' (p. 45)); he interprets Camille's private thoughts (p. 55); and he even knows what Gide is thinking as he waits for the film to begin (p. 24).

Gide's presence is important. On the one hand, he is the archetypal bourgeois artist, whose financial circumstances allow him complete autonomy. On the other, he is an example of the wavering intellectual of the early 1930s, sympathetic to certain aspects of left-wing thinking, but incapable of committing himself fully to a political position. Gide will disappear from the novel; but his appearance in this opening section is a reminder of his significance for a whole generation of young people whose sense of purpose and political awareness have been blunted as a result of his influence. In a later conversation with Cazaux Simon remarks: 'ce que nous n'avons pas compris c'est que Gide était un homme du passé' (p. 191). By the time he says this (1944) Simon is well on the way to becoming 'un homme de l'avenir'.

If the opening section of the novel serves, conventionally enough, as an introduction to the principal themes and characters, the next two focus on Simon's personal evolution. The first ('1939') describes his period of military training, and contains a number of asides on the nature of war and on military (and social) hierarchy. But through a series of conversations with Prévôt (based possibly on the philosopher Jean Desanti, who had also attended the Lycée Lakanal with Courtade) we have a summary of Simon's political evolution – his reasons for not having joined the Communist Party, his attitude to the Nazi–Soviet Pact and to the trials in the Soviet Union. In Prévôt's eyes Simon is a 'romantic' (p. 105), he is too easily swayed by the present or by events as they affect him as an individual and incapable of taking a dispassionate overview. In contrast Prévôt represents the ideologue, the purist for whom the end is all and whose faith will subsequently be seen by historians to have been justified. In the short following section, '1940', covering the German advance, the *exode* and the preparation of defensive positions near the Loire, Prévôt is killed accidentally – and ironically – by a lorry. It is Simon's first experience of violent death; but the removal of Prévôt also means that he is now alone and obliged to think and act politically in his own right. The entry of the Soviet Union into the war has been announced, Prévôt's faith has been justified: the lesson is there to be learned.

That it has been is clear from the following, fourth section of the novel, '1944'. Although not yet a member of the Communist Party, Simon is now active in the Resistance. The section '1944' describes his experience of journeying by train from Lyons to Paris and of being stopped and searched by the police. Although he is carrying no incriminating papers or messages, he is challenged over some books, and especially over Malraux's *La Lutte avec l'ange*. As we have already seen the conversation he has with the Nazi officer is significant: acts, not words, are what cause people to change their attitudes. And on a personal level this is what happens in this section as well. On the train Simon discovers Justine, whom he has met briefly before in Toulouse; they spend the night together and plan a shared future. Furthermore, in the fifth section of this part, 'Le rendez-vous du Palais-Royal', Simon meets Cazaux, whose hardline commitment to the Communist Party allows him to be critical of what he sees as Simon's continuing hesitation. When Simon reports their conversation to Justine and describes Cazaux his words are defensive: 'c'est un homme très honnête. Je l'ai beaucoup admiré ... Il a tout ce qui me manque, mais il est ... comment dirais-je ... c'est un homme abstrait, systématique ...' (p. 200). The past tense is significant. Politically and personally Simon is on the threshold of a new phase in his life, even though he will not embrace Communism in the same way as Cazaux.

Structurally, almost to a page as well as thematically, '1944' is therefore pivotal in *La Place rouge*, with the journey from Lyons to Paris reflecting the metaphorical one of Simon's evolution. By the sixth section, '1954', we learn that he took the decision to join the Party in 1945 (p. 237). There is, however, no direct account of this, and it is clearly intended that we should see it as a natural progression and one that is wholly compatible with Simon's changing personal circumstances. These are explored in '1946', the fifth section, which describes the atmosphere in Paris on 14 July and Simon's sense of guilt as he is forced to break free from Camille in order to join Justine, who by now has dropped her resistance name for her real one, Laurence. The sixth and seventh ('1957') are increasingly monopolized by discussion and debate. Not surprisingly, given their dates, they strongly reflect Courtade's own progress through the late 1950s and in particular his attitude to Hervé. The final section, '1958', finds Simon alone in Moscow, where he visits Sacha. Here the spirit of Lenin continues, the momentary aberration of Stalinist excesses has been accommodated and even turned to advantage, and a new era and 'une société absolument nouvelle' (p. 316) in which all are equal are already much in evidence.

Where the novel is reduced to its essentials in this way, it is not difficult to agree with Vailland's criticism of *La Place rouge*. The opening of '1935' is atmospheric, sets up the principal characters in the roles they are to play and, even if it anticipates the eventual outcome in the fashion of many a *roman à thèse*, gives few hints of how it will be reached. Similarly '1944' significantly moves the plot forward, and is excellent in its descriptions of the train journey and of Simon's being stopped and searched. Elsewhere, however, there is indeed a tendency for the book to slip into what Vailland called 'un plaidoyer d'universitaire'. But Courtade's response is surely justified. *La Place rouge* is as much a novel about an individual's progress (albeit his own) as it is about the much larger and grander stage occupied by Party politicians. They exist only in so far as their actions and pronouncements are perceived to be relevant by Simon for his personal evolution. If the novel is to be the kind of book Courtade wishes it to be, then the focus must be inwards and not outwards. Certainly Simon's perspectives and awareness change, but Courtade is determined that at no stage should he utter the Party's line unthinkingly or without conviction; nor should he act out a role for the sake of expediency or because he felt it was required of him. By the close Communism should be seen to have become (to quote Nizan's character Carré in *La Conspiration*) 'un style de vie', embracing public and personal matters alike and providing the political and philosophical basis for the creation of a new world order for which evidence can already be found in the Soviet Union. As Sacha remarks about the young of his own child's generation: 'le communisme pour eux c'est l'avenir' (p. 310).

Nonetheless, while they are less obtrusive than they were in *Elseneur*, the reflections of Courtade's own background to be found in *La Place Rouge* remain frequent. Roy's description of the book as 'une autobiographie (romancée par pudeur)' is accurate enough, though it is less for reasons of modesty than from a desire to shape his material in a particular way that Courtade stresses some elements while inventing, omitting or altering others. Sceaux reappears as Saint-Rémy, with its 'vies prudentes, monotones, secrètes' (p. 12), the new 'banlieue pourvue d'un lycée [où] le décor est celui des trains biquotidiens, entraînant vers la vieillesse et la mort, année après année, des troupes somnolentes de travailleurs levés une heure plus tôt, couchés une heure plus tard qu'à Paris' (p. 9). The Lycée Lakanal, remembered as a convent (p. 28) is completely out of touch with society in 1935. Simon has become a teacher (p. 79). His father has worked for the post office (p. 32), his mother for the telephone services (pp. 290–1). Home life is a series of patterns and rituals, and while his father was 'plutôt gauche' (p. 32), he has never been politically engaged.

Within these recollections two incidents in particular demand our attention. The first relates to the demonstrations against fascism in 1934. In the first part of the novel we learn that Simon and Cazaux secretly regret not having participated: 'chacun d'eux se reprochait secrètement de n'avoir pas saisi l'occasion de courir le seul risque qui pût à leurs yeux conférer à leurs convictions une valeur indiscutable' (p. 13). The second is the matter of Simon's membership of the Communist Party. He joins in 1945, the normal practice for many a young militant emerging from the Resistance. In the first case, the failure to be on the Place de la Concorde in the early days of February 1934 is biographically correct, of course; but Courtade's expression of regret more than twenty years later is significant. In the second case, by having his protagonist join the Party in 1945 Courtade has suppressed, even if only subconsciously, the months of his own uncertainty following the Liberation, and through Simon has restructured a political evolution that is more acceptable.

If such matters as these are familiar and grounded in fact, a new and, in biographical terms, anticipatory element is introduced with the description of Simon's father's death and his reaction to it (pp. 285–92). Having been close to his father as a child, Simon reflects that subsequently 'je m'étais délivré de lui presque complètement' (p. 289), and that now in death he can rediscover him, love him and rescue him from 'cette banlieue triste où il avait somnolé' (p. 289). Within the context of the novel there is nothing amiss here; moreover, M. Bordes' death is surely intended to signal the breaking of Simon's last remaining tie with a past that has always threatened to erupt into the present and inhibit his newly discovered freedom. In biographical terms, however, the incident is rather more revealing. Courtade's father would not die until 1959. By anticipating his death by two years, and by situating it in the novel in the immediate aftermath of the exposure of Stalin and alongside Simon's dispute with Cazaux it clearly symbolizes a wish to break with authority in the most fundamental way. It also suggests that Simon's claim that he had *already freed* himself almost completely from his father's influence is false, and, more significantly, that by writing it into *La Place rouge* in this way Courtade recognized, if only subconsciously, that his problems with authority and decision-making were still there.

Whatever conclusions we reach by the end of the novel, it is evident that through Simon Courtade wishes not simply to describe the progress of an *alter ego* from political naivety to enlightenment, but to show how such progress is inevitable. Punctuating the text at regular intervals are statements – both authorial and by Simon himself – about growing awareness. Looking back on the period five years earlier Simon remarks to Prévôt in 1939: 'c'était du temps où je n'existais pas [...]. J'étais fantastiquement romantique. Romanesque même si tu veux' (pp. 88–94). He acknowledges that on his visit to the Soviet Union with Camille he had been blind, 'J'avais du coton dans la tête' (p. 102), and that he had believed in instant transformation ('un coup de baguette magique' (p. 113)). Others pick up the same refrain. Prévôt accuses him of being 'romantique' (p. 105), Cazaux of being 'romanesque'. 'Il croit qu'il y a des moments où les choses changent brusquement' (p. 244). But while others may continue to see him like this, Simon argues that in fact it is they whose views are blinkered. Although he acknowledges that he comes to decisions only with difficulty (p. 277), he claims that fundamentally he has always adhered to a conviction – the 'truth' about which Courtade writes in his notes, however unclearly it may have been formulated. In the course of his last conversation with Cazaux Simon reflects that 'à aucun moment je n'avais senti vaciller une certitude que j'avais établie sur une longue réflexion' (p. 279), and that his present position is one that has evolved quite naturally and now fully equips him to take his place in society: 'il ne doutait pas qu'un changement s'était produit en lui qui se préparait depuis des années. Il y avait de l'allégresse là-dedans, et comme une lumière qu'il se proposa de diriger désormais sur les hommes et sur les choses et non plus seulement sur lui-même' (p. 284).

If Simon's evolution were charted solely through his political stances and utterances *La Place rouge* would be less successful than it is. The selective nature of the account would be too disjointed and the 'announcement' of Simon's 'conversion' to the Party faith would lack conviction. However unidimensional the experiences of Larillière or Jimmy were, and whatever other weaknesses the books may have had, *La Rivière noire* and *Jimmy* did at least have a kind of continuity, allowing the protagonists to move forward to their new positions in a logical manner. *La Place rouge*, however, treats a much wider spectrum of events and a much longer time-span than these earlier books, and, as we have noted, Courtade is also concerned to describe Simon's personal development as a necessary adjunct to his political one. This he does in two ways: first, as in *Elseneur*, by offering us a range of characters based on people he knew who had had a formative influence on him; second, by giving prominence to the affective dimension of Simon's life.

Not surprisingly, not all characters have clear models. As we have seen, Prévôt would seem by his political statements and unwavering belief in the Soviet Union to be modelled on Jean Desanti. In Part V Le Commandant, who makes a fleeting appearance and is younger than the others, is possibly based on Jacques-Francis Rolland, Marco on Jean Pronteau. Paul Grange, the young working-class militant of the opening scenes who is killed in the wake of a Resistance ambush on a German tank, has elements of Gabriel Péri, Aragon and Vailland, especially the last, with his 'visage maigre taillé à la serpe [...] des dents abîmées' (p. 8). More precisely, Vailland is the model for Busard (the name of the principal character of *325.000 francs)*. He carries out his Resistance activities of issuing and distributing false papers as though they were 'aventures galantes' (p. 143); he is elegant, believes in luck (pp. 170–1) and he is described as having 'des yeux qui lancent des éclairs, un nez coupant et des tendons. Il ressemble au Diable, et il le sait' (p. 214).

None of these, nor indeed most of the minor personages who pass across the scene, however, are shown to have had any major political influence on Simon. But two characters who have are singled out – Le Bras, his former teacher at the Lycée Saint-Rémy, who, like Herion in *Elseneur*, is a projection of Jean Guéhenno, and Cazaux, who, as has already been noted, one of Pierre Hervé (p. 7). The two are compared and contrasted. Cazaux succeeds Le Bras in his post at Saint-Rémy. Le Bras is presented as a romantic, tormented, vacillating creature whose teaching led his pupils away from action and decision and into a morass of generalities and aimless discussion ('Nous avons nagé dans les mots' (p. 188)); and, like Karl, Simon attributes much of his own failure to commit himself fully to his *lycée* experience.

If Le Bras with hindsight is seen to be responsible for adversely influencing a whole generation, Cazaux, at least initially, is projected as a model of positive behaviour. At the screening of the Eisenstein film he is the most sure of himself and of his interpretation of it, and he criticizes those too easily moved by its artistic merits at the expense of its political message. To Simon, Cazaux, who 'donnait l'impression d'appartenir à une secte d'initiés' (p. 12), who is a militant member of the 'jeunesses communistes', reads the works of Lenin and prefers Vallès to Malraux, is to be admired. For Cazaux Simon is 'un sympathisant qu'il fallait aider, qu'il fallait prendre par la main' (p. 45). But as the various episodes in the novel pass we are made to realize that not only does Cazaux not evolve, but he is shown to become even more firmly entrenched in views that are inappropriate or outmoded. When Simon reports the conversation he has with him to Justine at the end of Part IV he describes Cazaux as 'un homme abstrait ... systématique' (p. 200). He has lost his original passion, and has become arid: 'je voyais la passion, la foi toujours vivantes sans doute, se transformer insensiblement en un mécanisme trop parfait' (p. 241).[22]

This last remark is made in the section of the novel dated 1954. If at this point we remind ourselves that Cazaux 'is' Hervé, and of the fact that Courtade did not begin to write *La Place rouge* until 1956, the year of the 'affaire Hervé', the accusation is both unjust and ironic. Unjust in that Hervé objected most precisely to the imposition of inflexible Party guidelines on art and literature and to the intolerance of Party intellectuals; ironic in that from what we know from Courtade's private diary at this time he secretly admired Hervé for his courage. Only at one point in the novel is there a suggestion that this is acknowledged. Commenting on certain kinds of Communist activists, Cazaux claims: 'ils veulent bien coller des affiches et ramasser des signatures et c'est très bien, je ne dis pas, mais si on leur demande d'écrire un roman utile ... un roman qui les engage ... et moi je n'ai pas peur des mots, un livre de militant ... ils crient comme des écorchés' (p. 263). While it is not a novel, this is exactly what Hervé would do (we are still in 1954 in *La Place rouge*) in 1956 with *La Révolution et les fétiches*, and what Courtade perhaps recognizes he had been incapable of achieving himself.

But more important still is the fact that by the end of Part VII Cazaux is written out of *La Place rouge*, and Simon is seen now to have a more acute perception of revolutionary progress than his original mentor. It is surely no coincidence that in the same section of the novel the two principal embodiments of authority – Simon's father and Cazaux – are conveniently removed, thereby completing the process already set in motion when Simon meets Justine.

Simon's parallel affective development is fashioned by two women: Camille, in whom we discover Génia, and Justine/Laurence, who derives largely from the wife of Jean Pronteau. In the opening section of the novel Camille is depicted as being essentially sentimental, passive (p. 46) and as feeling herself incapable of participating in the debate about the film (p. 72). Of the discussion in L'Avenir she remarks 'vous êtes entre vous' (p. 72), to which Simon can only reply: 'Tu es tellement secrète. Quelquefois j'ai l'impression que je ne te connaîtrai pas' (p. 73). The problem of communication is fundamental to their relationship and, even more significantly, after less than a year of being together (they first meet on 14 July 1934) Simon already feels that habit and the constraints imposed by the kind of life they are obliged to share (pp. 17–18) are potentially destructive. It is no surprise that during the night they spend in the Hôtel des Rois Mages he should dream (and not for the first time) of being stifled (p. 81). Already in a story like 'La Fin de l'Italie' we find the theme of disillusionment within marriage, a theme quite unequivocally stemming from Courtade's personal circumstances.

In *La Place rouge* hindsight and the need to develop a particular perspective and have his protagonist's affective development brought into line with his political one are obviously important, but this portrait of Camille does more than reflect a particular perception of his life with Génia, even in the light of his relationship with Nicole Chatel. It is vital that politically as well as personally Camille should be incapable of offering the kind of support and understanding that Simon requires if he is to move forward. Certainly the guilt Simon experiences when he meets Justine and eventually leaves Camille, is as we know, an exact echo of Courtade's own; so too is his sense of still being held by Camille in such a way that part of him can never escape: 'elle est ma vie, jamais il ne pourra y avoir entre une autre femme et moi ces liens qui parfois me font mal, qui parfois m'étouffent' (p. 179). And when, during the 14 July celebrations in Paris, she shows signs of a life quite independent of him in her relationship with Marco (p. 218), Simon is tormented by jealousy. He does, to be sure, inwardly acknowledge that such a response is quite unjustified; but it is Busard who sees to the centre of his problem. His advice that Simon should simply leave Camille to get on with her own life in the heady atmosphere of the Liberation ('Laisse-la tranquille. Joue le jeu' (p. 220)) is pragmatic, but, he claims more pertinently, it will help Simon 'couper un cordon ombilical' (p. 221), a phrase that Simon uses later in a conversation with Laurence (p. 226) and that also prompts the comment: 'Je n'arrive pas à me débarasser de mon enfance ... enfin je veux dire de l'idée enfantine que je me faisais de la vie' (p. 225).

The words could, of course, have been taken directly from Courtade's diary, and are crucial. Moreover, Laurence's role and attitude are intended to be instrumental in helping him achieve this. On all counts she is different from Camille. She has been married, but her husband Probus has been killed in the Resistance, leaving her with a young daughter (p. 240); she is from a middle-class background ('une enfant des beaux quartiers' (p. 201)) and of Jewish extraction (p. 172). But critically her experiences have taught her independence and decisiveness, and her comments to Simon on this same 14 July are tinged with impatience and irritation that he cannot free himself from the past. Clearly her role in the novel is pivotal; but it may not be quite as schematic as Courtade seems to have wished it to be.

We first see them together in Part IV on the train from Lyons to Paris, in their capacities as resistance workers. The description of Laurence is important: 'La lumière bleue du couloir lui fait un visage de théâtre et l'on peut par conséquent lui parler comme à un personnage de théâtre. Elle est à l'abri derrière son masque sur la scène où Simon et elle jouent leur rôle dans le décor planté par la guerre' (pp. 152, 3).[23]

At once scenes from *Les Circonstances* and *Elseneur* come to mind, with their emphasis on the enforced artificiality of the circumstances of the Occuption and on the roles played by those resisting. But in *La Place rouge* what is important is the personal dimension. The false identities necessarily assumed in these specific circumstances will ultimately be discarded; they may even be momentarily so, as people withdraw into their private world. When Simon and Justine return to her flat after Simon has been released by the police ('personne ne sait où nous sommes' (p. 174)) her face is the one 'qu'elle devait avoir lorsqu'elle était seule, sans fard, et regardait brûler un feu de bois' (p. 174). After they have made love 'Justine était hors du temps. Elle n'avait ni passé ni avenir' (p. 178) and she reveals her true identity: 'La Justine que tu a rencontrée dans le train, c'est du chiqué ... C'est Justine. Moi je ne suis pas Justine. Je m'appelle Laurence' (p. 181). When later they meet outside, however, the role returns: 'elle reprit tout d'un coup le masque de théâtre qu'elle avait eu dans le train' (p. 196).

For Simon it is vital, of course, that his relationship should be with *Laurence*; and when in the closing lines of this section of the novel he affirms 'Je t'appelerai Laurence maintenant [...] c'est important. Justine c'était une autre période de ma vie' (p. 229) the first but crucial element in his break with the past would seem to have been made. The dream world or allegory (p. 227) in which he senses he has lived hitherto will be replaced by a new reality, certainty and self-belief to be confirmed and completed by the removal of political and parental authority. Yet, despite what appears to be her vital role in this process, Laurence then virtually disappears from the scene. In Part VI she is fleetingly present as she discusses – and criticizes – an article Simon attempts to write in memory of Grange (p. 256); thereafter, she exists only as someone to whom Simon telephones or writes. Significantly, she does not accompany him to Moscow. The point of this may be to underline her independence, and certainly her readiness to criticize the article is echoed in her Camille-like rebuke of Simon's discussions with Cazaux: 'Vous avez un côté curé quand vous êtes ensemble' (p. 237). But it is also possible that with her role as a form of catalyst now over she returns to a state of neutrality and even of anonymity: 'Depuis qu'elle a retiré le masque qu'elle portait dans le train de Lyon, elle a eu presque toujours le même masque' (p. 212), and within the context of the novel it is surely arguable that having set the process of freeing Simon from his past in motion she too can now be discarded.

There is something strikingly familiar about this state of affairs. In *Les Circonstances* only Claire ('Une demi-douzaine d'huîtres') of all the women depicted in that volume is, as we know, politically active and independent. In *Jimmy* Ethel dies before her convictions find expression in action; Nancy Reed is only on the point of political awareness when the novel ends, and in any case both women are subordinate to their husbands' roles. The failure to develop the portrayal of Laurence more fully is disconcerting, however, and one to which we shall return.

It is equally true, of course, that, like Jimmy, Simon has himself still to turn political conviction into action; he merely states his belief and reports what he sees. At one point he remarks to Laurence that only with hindsight will it be possible to measure the true role of the Resistance and of their parts in it (pp. 204–5); the same is true of what he considers to be the achievements of revolutionary socialism. *La Place rouge* certainly goes beyond *Jimmy* and *La Rivière noire* in that in the closing pages we have a description of *what* has been accomplished; we do not know *how* it has been, nor how it can be sustained. Early in the novel Prévot suggests: 'ce que les gens ont été ... ça ne compte pas beaucoup ... c'est ce qu'ils deviennent' (p. 99). The use of the future tense would have been even more pertinent. However unwavering his political conviction may be, at best Simon is only on the threshold of a new life.

When, in his letter to Vailland, Courtade acknowledged that a novel about Communism was perhaps not possible (at least for him) and that it amounted to writing for the converted, he clearly was aware of the problem. His idea of producing a survey of key episodes in the development of the Left and of Communism in particular, against which his principal character would evolve, does not materialize as he hoped it would. Only in Part I ('1935') and Part IV ('1944') can Courtade be said to have fully demonstrated his capacity for vivid, atmospheric description and to have succeeded in pointing up his protagonist's significant experiences. Elsewhere there tends to be overmuch dialogue, and the recording of Simon's reflections somehow separately from the material and historic circumstances from which they should grow naturally.

Nor is this helped by a constantly shifting narrative viewpoint. As an omniscient voice Courtade is once again both inside and outside his characters at will, and, as in his earlier novels and especially in *Elseneur*, he is not afraid to offer an authorial interpretative or corrective gloss. There is also the matter of the overlap between Courtade and Simon, which goes beyond the use of biographical material. The first person pronoun is used as early as the eighth episode in Part I ('La faucille et le marteau'), when Sacha joins the group in the café with his visa for the Soviet Union: 'Cazaux se tourna vers nous. ... Nous nous penchions sur les caractères cyrilliques ... Je me souviens d'avoir eu entre les mains un papier officiel de la Commune de Paris ...' (pp. 56–57). We also find inverted commas used in a strange and irregular manner. Sometimes they signal Simon's private thoughts, and function as an alternative to the more normal indirect style, even though such thoughts may then be recorded in that very style! Sometimes they introduce an authorial comment or reflection (p. 150), or they may indicate the inner thoughts of another character. It is difficult not to conclude that a firm editorial hand would have been of some value here, and that Courtade would have been well advised to write *La Place rouge* quite unambiguously as a first person or even an autobiographical novel. This would undoubtedly have given it more stylistic coherence; but it would also have been more appropriate to the kind of work that it is. Yet even if this had been achieved it is still probable that a number of recurrent images or motifs would have moved the novel in a direction that Courtade had not fully seen (if indeed at all), in the way that the treatment of Laurence does.

Largely on account of the amount of dialogue, there is far less opportunity for Courtade than in any of his three earlier pieces of long fiction to concentrate on descriptive writing and through metaphor to develop it in a supportive or meaningful way. Occasionally there are typical examples of sharp, striking observations: a derailed train engine is 'touchée en pleine course comme une bête qui fuit, éventrée, morte' (p. 155), for example. Elsewhere, however, the need to reflect or underline a political or ideological point can result in exaggeration. After the announcement of the Soviet Union's involvement in the war Simon and Prévôt look at the Loire: 'A un tournant la Loire leur apparut non plus dorée mais argentée. Des poissons sautaient à la surface en accrochant à la lumière' (p. 139); when Simon arrives in Moscow: 'une grue géante dressée au-dessus d'un chantier bien loin de choquer s'harmonisait naturellement à ce décor de la Sainte Russie auquel elle conférait une étrange modernité' (p. 305); the Nazi officer who checks passports in the train to Paris 'était sous l'uniforme d'aujourd'hui, le cavalier-reître des guerres de religion. Glabre et froid la Mort l'accompagne' (p. 144).

At the same time there are three motifs that run, albeit irregularly, across the text, helping to draw the different episodes together. Allusions to the theatre and role-playing reappear in the scenes relating in a specific way to Resistance activities, but throughout they remind us of the artificiality of Simon's position. Only in the last section has he discarded (or so he believes) the inhibiting influences from his past and is free to express himself naturally. The journey too is central. In *Jimmy* and *La Rivière noire* the protagonists have to travel to another country in order to learn and mature. So too does Simon; but more significant is his journey through life. The battleship of Eisenstein's film, which Simon imagines 'ouvrant la mer longuement, tout droit, comme la charrue ouvre la terre pour la semence ...' (p. 42) heralds this journey, and the closing word of the film – 'Frères' (p. 42) – will be the last of the novel as well, as he looks back at what he has achieved. The Potemkin is also used as an image for Simon's life with Camille (p. 82) – even though in this case it will be wrecked (p. 246); the train taking Simon from Lyons to Paris is what propels him forward to his new life; and the section describing his father's death is called, though not without some irony, 'Le dernier train'.

Each of these motifs admirably suits the retrospective nature of Courtade's technique in charting the 'itinéraire spirituel, politique et sentimental' of his protagonist. But perhaps the most successful of all is that of death. In Part I Simon's dreams of being stifled are symptomatic of a generation marked by 'la fascination de la mort' (p. 27) (again the echoes of Nizan's work are strong), a generation that has lost its sense of direction and purpose. At the time Malraux's *La Condition humaine* is held up as a work illustrating the kind of alternative attitude that the young should adopt; but when, a decade later, Simon is interrogated by the police he dismisses Malraux's *La Lutte avec l'ange* as 'une longue et parfois ennuyeuse dissertation sur la mort' (p. 164). Death has to be turned into life. The climate necessary for regeneration will be discovered only in Moscow, where in this 'société absolument nouvelle' (p. 316) the May Day celebrations create an atmosphere outside time ('le temps est arrêté (p. 316)) and eternally young.[24]

Despite its occasional over-long passages of dialogue, the undisguised presence of Courtade's authorial voice and (in biographical as well as historical terms) the careful selection of critical episodes,[25] *La Place rouge* has considerable merit as a *Bildungsroman*. It goes beyond his two previous novels, and is far more complex both in its exploration of the central character and in the way it offers a spectrum of other positions and beliefs, even if only to discredit them, and all the while never loses sight of its principal aim. And with its closing tone of high optimism, which is certainly in line with that of Courtade's articles in *L'Humanité* and *L'Humanité-dimanche*; it would appear genuinely to reflect his feelings about life in the Soviet Union. Yet his diaries continue to suggest that this is a public profile. Alongside the confirmation of his belief in revolutionary socialism is the expression of a need to be part of a *collective* voice. Behind this surely lies his knowledge that he was seriously, if not terminally, ill. In the end he, like Simon, is alone, and we need to turn to the unpublished *Le Jeu de paume* for the exploration of the kind of anguish that had already surfaced in 'La Chasse' and 'Une Affaire de coeur', and also for a final expression of the conviction to which, in spite of everything, he continued to cling.

Le Jeu de paume

In a letter to Jean-Jacques de Meyenbourg (7 March 1957) Courtade refers to his having begun 'un roman assez court qui paraîtra au mois d'octobre "*Le Jeu de Paume*"'. No other information has come to light, and the bundle of papers and school exercise books which contain his working notes are without dates. Whether Courtade had some kind of agreement with a publisher, and whether he did indeed continue to work at the book throughout 1957 is not known.[26] When the review *Chorus* published some extracts in 1965 the editors claimed that Courtade had abandoned it in 1958 in order to devote himself entirely to *La Place rouge*, which, we know, he had begun two years earlier.[27] However, these extracts are taken from what is clearly a *second* extant typescript (153 pages long), based on the initial 79 pages of an earlier, more closely typed draft, heavily corrected in Courtade's own hand, which in total has 189 pages. Certainly substantial correction seems to have been abandoned at this point; but it is likely that, if only in its first draft, the novel had in fact been completed. A line drawn beneath the text would suggest so too.

The story of *Le Jeu de paume* is simple. It tells of a research scientist, Janse, whose work is primarily concerned with the irradiation of the seeds of cereal crops in order to induce genetic changes resulting in plants with more resistant stems, that will hence withstand, more readily, strong destructive winds. Having failed to take necessary safety precautions Janse has been exposed to radiation himself, has contracted leukaemia and has probably no more than three months to live. On holiday in September with his wife Laurence in the family château at Beyssac in the Lot he decides to return to Paris for a few days, on the pretext of having to discuss his experiments with a fellow scientist. In fact he intends to try to obtain a second opinion about his illness from Grangier, a friend and colleague who specializes in cancer, and to face up to the prospect of death alone. He spends much of the first night talking to a prostitute he meets in a bar, La Cabane in Montparnasse, that he and Laurence had frequented in earlier years. The following day he consults Grangier, who studiously, and infuriatingly for Janse, refuses to confirm the latter's own diagnosis of his illness. Janse returns to his flat and decides to commit suicide. He is planning to use the gas supply to the water heater in the bathroom when the *femme de ménage*, who was not due to come until the following day, arrives unexpectedly.[28]

From the evidence of Courtade's notes, and assuming that the novel does in fact end in this rather melodramatic way, *Le Jeu de paume* in its intended final form clearly underwent substantial pruning. The outline suggests that it was to have had episodes describing Janse seeking refuge, first, in a life of debauchery in Paris, and, secondly, in his work, when he has an affair with a new laboratory assistant, a young Italian woman called Antonetta. His own principal assistant Beaufils is to be portrayed as a militant communist (based on Joliot-Curie, who was so outspoken in his opposition to the proliferation of nuclear weapons in the early 1950s) who is also affected by radiation and has an arm amputated. In this version, provisionally entitled 'Un roman de l'énergie', Janse was to leave a diary of the last months of his life as 'un message de confiance', presumably in man's capacity to struggle for the future and for his general improvement. Elsewhere we find a suggestion that Beaufils should marry another laboratory assistant, thereby setting up a parallel couple to Janse and Laurence; Robichou (Robert), Janse's son, who in the final version has the threat of being sent to fight in Algeria hanging over him, was to have been drafted there already.

It seems possible, in fact, that the war, as well as the debate about nuclear weapons, would have been given much greater prominence than they eventually are. In one particular respect Courtade's notes contain an interesting document. This is the text of an address given by Sir Ernest Rock Carling of the British Home Office on the effects of radiation to the 'International Conference on the Peaceful Uses of Atomic Energy' held at Geneva in August 1955, which Courtade covered for *L'Humanité*. On it is scribbled: 'Très utilisable' and 'Janse dans son mémoire attaque violemment le type qu'il a connu à Genève où il représente le H.O.' Much of the paper is in semi-technical language. In general, it argues that experiments carried out on animals have not yet provided sufficiently consistent results for any reliable prognosis about the effects of radiation on humans to be made, and that in any case man has shown himself to be so adaptable and resilient in the past that his chances of survival are high. A number of exclamation marks, underlinings and marginal comments indicate clearly enough what Courtade's opinion of this document was – an opinion fully substantiated by his articles in *L'Humanité*; but one sentence in particular drew his anger and the accusation – not without some justification – of a form of Malthusianism: 'In a world contemplating a future in which the expansion of its population may outrange its food supply it is conceivable that diminished fertility and shortening of life-span might not be altogether to be deplored.'

Atomic warfare, radiation and the Algerian conflict could easily have led Courtade to write another heavily committed and quite sharply focused novel in the style of *La Rivière noire* and *Jimmy*. But his personal circumstances were too dominant. His heart attack and his continuing preoccupation with ill-health push these immediate concerns into the background. It is possible as well that the unease he would eventually confess to over *La Place rouge* was already worrying him. Whatever the reasons were, the result is a more general and meditative work than any he had written before, and one that acts as a kind of minor-key accompaniment to some of the themes in the last two sections in particular of *La Place rouge*.

From the opening scene of *Le Jeu de paume*, a meeting and conversation Janse has with the local postman Henri, we are in no doubt about the novel's tone. Both reflect on man's role and his place in history. For the latter there is a natural scheme; man forms part of a cycle of healthy life and equally healthy death. Certainly there are those who do strive, scientifically or politically, to change the conditions of existence for the better; but in Beyssac people are affected only marginally. Janse, of course, perceives matters differently. The prehistoric drawings in local caves may be a reminder that any individual life is short; but they are also evidence that man has been in existence for a long time, and is still only in the early stages of his evolution ('à peine au début de son histoire'). These two different attitudes lead in turn to a reflection by Janse on what the family property means to him. In his notes Courtade wrote that the château should signify 'l'idée de refuge, de fuite' and this is what we are told Janse (in his present state, with some guilt) feels:

La possession de grands biens comme le château de Beyssac avait
probablement interrompu chez un homme comme Janse une réflexion

sur les problèmes sociaux qui l'eût probablement conduit au-delà du vague radicalisme laïque auquel il s'était arrêté pour se fabriquer finalement une philosophie d'humaniste sceptique, indulgent, avec un tour libertin, philosophie qu'il avait récemment étendue à la science elle-même et à ses propres travaux. [...]

Le simple bonheur d'y vivre enlevait toute signification à la lutte, à l'activité, aux tentatives de changer le cours des choses.

And while to own it and live here, if only for two months of each year, affords him a certain prestige in the eyes of local people, it provides an escape, putting him 'indubitablement à l'abri des vicissitudes de l'existence.'

Prompted by his near-certain knowledge that he has little time to live Janse allows himself to become obsessed by the need to leave Beyssac and return to Paris. Laurence, in whom he is unable to bring himself to confide, is seen in terms that are now familiar to us as a negative presence – 'une mère couveuse' [qui] 'a gonflé ses ailes maternelles' – whose response to his announcement that he is leaving for a few days is a mixture of anger and incomprehension. When eventually Janse discusses his condition with Grangier he again claims that life with Laurence is over-protective, and that he needs to escape: 'J'aime mieux être un vieux chien seul qu'un poussin sous une aile et tu connais Laurence il faut absolument qu'elle étende ses ailes. J'en ai assez des ailes.'

But Janse is deluding himself. As in his conversation with the prostitute Paulette, when he lies about his occupation and plans to tell her that his wife is dead, he is looking for an excuse, for a reason not to face up to the reality of his situation. (And it is not merely by chance that he is unable to bring himself to sleep with her.) When later he learns that Grangier himself is seriously ill from a heart condition, he realizes that hidden behind anyone's public person are circumstances that may never be made known and indeed that it may be impossible for that person to disclose. The result is a sense of panic and disintegration: 'une partie de son être [...] soudain s'est mise à proliférer absolument entraînant le reste dans une folie d'anéantissement.' Faced with this predicament Janse decides to commit suicide, thereby intending to act positively and, more significantly, to affirm his freedom: 'la solution était [...] qu'il devait la [la mort] devancer, qu'il devait aller au devant d'elle pour affirmer sa liberté, pour vaincre la fatalité de la seule manière possible'. By arriving at the last moment Germaine frustrates his intentions; ironically he is not as free as he imagined, but neither, as a result, is his life as uncertain or as directionless as it was when he drove away from Beyssac two days earlier. The reprieve he has been given may not be the one he would have wished; but, as we shall see, it is significant for the novel's ultimate meaning, even if *Le Jeu de paume* is less wide-ranging than some of Courtade's working notes indicated it might have been.

Whether or not the composition of *Le Jeu de paume* coincided with or was interrupted by that of *La Place rouge* is of no great significance. In many ways where the latter is a public statement (whatever Courtade's misgivings) the former is a private one, more muted but ultimately no less optimistic. It echoes less the issues and debates with which *La Place rouge* deals than the preoccupations of several of the stories in *Les Animaux supérieurs*, especially 'Une affaire de coeur', 'La Chasse' and 'Le Sang-froid professionnel'. The recent circumstances of Courtade's ill-health explain this readily enough. The physical descriptions Janse gives of his condition are very similar to those of Charles. Fatigue 'remonte vers le haut du corps, brisant chaque fibre, chaque muscle au point que les zones déjà atteintes cessent de lui appartenir'; or with the same image of water as we find in the earlier volume, 'l'angoisse qui l'étouffait depuis plusieurs jours recommence à monter dans sa poitrine comme une eau sournoise.'

Rather more significantly, of course, Janse's illness may also be read as an expression of Courtade's growing disillusion with the contemporary political climate, barely hidden, as we have seen, in 'L'esprit Gacom'. Janse envies Grangier for having retained his professional contact with people: 'Janse n'ayant affaire qu'à des plantes dans la pratique quotidienne, s'est peu à peu privé de cette richesse.' But he is also becoming increasingly distant from his own research work, and finds it impossible to share the enthusiasm of Beaufils, who, we should not forget, is a Communist ('son optimisme de boy scout communiste'). This sense of resignation and withdrawal is emphasized too by the function of the château and by Janse's vague socio-political stance of 'humaniste sceptique'. Nor should we overlook the fact that these few hours of Janse's life are set in the early days of autumn, a season when 'tout crève et change' and when 'un nombre infini de créatures [...] ont accompli leur cycle'.

Alongside allusions to his health there are as well those to Courtade's personal circumstances. The accusations in his diaries of Génia's possessive, maternal attitudes and jealousy are echoed in those of Janse against Laurence when he prepares to leave for Paris or when he telephones her. And there is a general sense of her not being interested in his scientific work. While they have been married for more than twenty years, to see Laurence as a fictional projection of Génia even to the same degree as Camille is in *La Place rouge* is too neat. And while her naturalness and freshness, still evident despite her years, could owe something to Nicole Chatel, the parallel would be just as misleading. Rather, Courtade appears to be making a not very original statement about marriage and about the routine of domestic life. Resignation rather than acrimony or resentment is what emerges. And this is also true of Janse's recollections of his childhood and adolescence. Signs of the real bitterness of the kind we find in *Elseneur* or *La Place rouge* are briefly glimpsed – Janse recalls his father as a petty tyrant – 'il terrorise les siens autour de lui, pour leur bien' – with whom he had been engaged in a constant struggle:

un combat ténue, journalier et sordide contre la crainte de l'échec scolaire contre la peur de mal faire ceci ou cela. [...] l'apprentissage d'une rigueur dont il ne pourra jamais par la suite se débarasser ayant pour toute la vie apparemment enfermé son être dans le moule de métal où le vieux Janse a voulu couler la statue du fils parfait.

Moreover, it is surely not without interest that it should be the *postman* who brings confirmation of Janse's illness, effectively delivering his death sentence. And when he eventually falls asleep after his lunch he dreams of his father, 'son père qui lui parle, son père qui lui a donné la lettre [...] c'est le vieux Janse qui parle par la bouche du facteur.'

Despite this somewhat macabre echo of Courtade's continuing suppressed anguish over his relationship with his father (reflected as well, as we have seen, in the death of Simon's father in *La Place rouge*) the broader perspective which in the other novels and short stories embraces life in the Rue du Chemin de Fer in Sceaux and in the Lycée Lakanal is missing. Furthermore, there is a new and unexpected element of humour in *Le Jeu de paume*. Janse's father, a pharmacist by training, had made considerable wealth from his claims for having invented a hair-restorer, the basic ingredient of which was chicken-embryos![29]   There is also in the way Janse is portrayed a recognition of his own stubbornness, belief in will-power and regret that Robichou (Serge?) not only has no intention of following a scientific career, but is gradually drifting away from him and appears to enjoy a closer relationship with his mother.[30]

Resignation, fatigue and a sense of apparent purposelessness are then what give *Le Jeu de paume* its dominant tone; but it is surely not meant ultimately to be a pessimistic work. A note in the accompanying papers suggests that Courtade originally contemplated writing the novel in the first person. This would almost certainly have resulted in an unwarranted degree of self-indulgence and sentimentality, and his final choice of an indirect style allows just enough authorial control for him to develop a critical distance between the narrative voice and that of Janse, even if it also permits the kinds of occasional intrusion in the forms of reflections or explanations that are characteristic of his work as a whole. In the opening pages for example, we find the reflections on local history and the conclusions that can be drawn from it for the future development of society; a little later are several pages on social standing as revealed by material possessions. When Janse meets Paulette he learns that her sister has chosen to remain in their village in the Savoie, and for a while Courtade indulges in a discussion of the economic forces at work that can draw young women away from their natural country environment to a life of prostitution in the city. But this is no more developed than are references to France's attitude to the Algerian war or Janse's recollections of the Geneva conference. Occasionally, too, there are 'explanations' resulting from an omniscience which extends beyond the characters' awareness. Thus when Janse announces to Laurence that he intends to return to Paris and is met by her incomprehension and jealousy we read:

> Elle ne sait pas qu'il a besoin de mourir seul, après avoir coupé les amarres. Lui non plus d'ailleurs ne le sait pas. Il ne sait pas qu'il est en train obéir à l'instinct des bêtes qui s'en vont au plus loin des taillis, dans un endroit où on ne pourra pas les épier et assister à la transformation de l'animal qu'il était, soyeux, musclé, rapide en une chose qui va trembler puis se mêler complètement à la terre ...

In general, however, this kind of gloss is unnecessary. While the narrative of *Le Jeu de paume* is more reflective than that of any previous novel, Courtade succeeds on the whole in following in a fairly natural way the meanderings of his protagonist's mind as he tries to come to acknowledge his terminal condition. But if there is to be the possibility of a positive or optimistic reading of the novel that is not imposed precisely by authorial omniscience, some kind of adjustment is necessary. Were it not quite so melodramatic Janse's reprieve in the closing pages might be sufficient. Certainly it has the effect of drawing Janse back from the solitary act of suicide to society and to an awareness of collective responsibility however, temporarily, and in that it reflects the general direction that, according to Courtade's notes, the novel should take. Elsewhere in his papers there is an outline of the novel in a slightly different form. In this Janse discovers an article criticizing his research work (based on the Rock Carling speech), telephones Beaufils, and expresses his desire to live and his willingness to undergo treatment. Sometime later Beaufils returns his call and announces that their experiments have produced some of the results they had been hoping for; a number of the petals of the carnations grown from irradiated seeds have turned (with neat political significance) from white to red.[31] In the final version of the novel much of this has been either reworked or dropped altogether; but Beaufils does telephone to announce the news of 'une mutation positive', though he refuses to disclose the precise details until the following morning.

Even in this form the ending of *Le Jeu de paume* is fairly transparent; only if it is read alongside *La Place rouge* can its full significance been seen. At the end Janse knows he is doomed and that his death will bring *his* work to a close. But whether through the agency of chance or by his own reflection he has come to realize that he has a responsibility and commitment to others. Moreover, his action will serve as an example. While in *La Place rouge* Simon states his faith in a society which, despite Sacha's certainty and some evidence of material renewal, is yet to come, Janse is portrayed as being part of that process. Fundamentally the statement of faith is no different, but through Janse Courtade recognizes that the new, revolutionary society will not be realized without commitment, and may even demand sacrifice. That Madeleine Riffaud should say of Courtade that he came back from Moscow 'plus communiste que jamais' is therefore understandable. Whether he would have continued to have confidence in the Party's organization and in his colleagues' capacity to sustain the same conception, however, is not possible to say, though his disillusion over the reactions to the whole Stalin affair is enough to suggest that his was a faith which was becoming increasingly personal. Moreover, it seems likely that he would at long last have turned his attentions – and talents – wholly to imaginative writing. Even before finishing *La Place rouge* he had already begun to plan a new novel which had as its provisional title *Au souvenir de l'avenir*, to which there is an oblique reference in the earlier work. According to those close to him, this was to have been a political novel in which the true hero would be the working-class masses in their struggle for freedom. The title is as promising as it is intriguing.[32]

   None of this was to materialize. On a personal family level, Courtade's time in Moscow could hardly have been more testing. Not only did his father die on 30 August 1959, but on 17 April 1962 Serge was killed in a car accident in the south of France. When the news was phoned through to Moscow Soviet officials took it upon themselves to have all calls to Courtade's office blocked, fearing the harm that a blunt disclosure might do. Unquestionably, however, even though the news was released to him carefully, the shock was deeply felt and one from which he never fully recovered. Courtade was again taken ill at the very beginning of May 1963, but not so seriously that he could not return to Paris for treatment. He was admitted to the Clinique Rémy de Gourmont and underwent surgery, but died without regaining consciousness.

Notes

1. See R. Tierskey, *French Communism 1920–1972*, Columbia University Press, New York and London, 1974, p. 230 and Max Adereth, *The French Communist Party*, Manchester University Press, Manchester, 1984, Chapter 6.

2. Caute, *Communism and the French Intellectuals*, p. 234.

3. See in particular Philippe Robrieux, *Histoire intérieure du Parti Communiste*, Fayard, Paris, 1980–4 for a discussion of this.

4. Morin's comment in his obituary (*Arts*, 22 August 1963) is instructive: 'on vit alors un Courtade, Khrouchtchevien modéré et prudent, se réfugiant à Moscou pour ne pas être totalement asphyxié dans le parti français.'

5. There was no formal agreement between Courtade and Léon about responsibilities. The latter recalls that they wrote more or less according to interest, but that all issues whether foreign or domestic were thoroughly debated and that they often called on government representatives for assistance.

6. See in particular an interview with János Kádár, secretary of the Hungarian Socialist Workers' Party, 21 October 1960.

7. According to Léon articles that they telephoned directly to Paris were subject to censorship by *L'Humanité*'s editorial committee. This was particularly so when they wrote too enthusiastically about the liberal reforms taking place in the Soviet Union.

8. *L'Humanité*, 18 June 1949.

9. 'Vu de ma fenêtre', *L'Humanité*, 25 October 1960. See too the account given by Nicole Chatel in *Carnets russes*, Julliard, Paris, 1971.

10. Max Léon (6 July 1994) remarked that 'ce qu'on a écrit on l'a cru', but acknowledged that conditions did horrify them.

11. Page 316.

12. There are references to an unspecified 'roman' in papers dated Spring 1955 and in a letter to Jean-Jacques de Meyenbourg on 7 March 1957. On 6 March 1961 he writes in a letter to Serge: 'j'ai écrit 2/3 de mon livre.'

13. Letter to Serge, 16 January [1961]: 'Ici les choses vont bien, en dépit de quelques accrochages dans l'agriculture. Ce n'est pas commode de transformer en homme de notre temps des gens qu'il y a vingt ans avaient en guise de cheminée, un trou dans le chaume.'

14. No. 106, February 1962.

15. *Libération*, 14 November 1961.

16. *L'Observateur littéraire*, 16 November 1961.

17. *L'Express*, 9 November 1961.

18. *Ecrits intimes*, p. 669–70.

19. Ibid., pp. 679–80.

20. See *La Place rouge*, p. 191.

21. See as well *Les Cahiers de la petite dame*, 1929–1937, Cahiers André Gide, V, Gallimard, Paris, 1974, p. 428:

    > Ce soir, dans un cinéma populaire, un cercle fermé, nous allons voir *Le Potemkine* et *La Ligne générale*, qu'Elisabeth et moi ne connaissons pas encore. Très bon. (20 December 1934)

22. Cf. p. 245: 'C'est un type qui vit dans les mots [...] il les arrange jusqu'à ce qu'ils collent ensemble comme les pièces d'un puzzle et après il est content ... '

23. Cf. p. 156: 'Tout le monde porte un masque ici.'

24. He has the same feeling during the Resistance, when 'le temps n'avait plus de limites' (p. 204).

25. There is, for example, no mention of Hungary.

26. Julliard have no record. The archives of what used to be the Editions sociales are said to have been destroyed by fire.

27. In his notes is an unfinished short story called *Le Jeu de paume* with a different opening dated 19 August 1957. On 14 January 1959 an entry seems to point more directly to the novel: 'schéma sur l'individu et la société. Besoin de se situer dans une collectivité, ne pas s'isoler. Reconnaît que ses mots sont naïfs [...]. Biologie, plaisir, action politique pour le socialisme, activité artistique.'

28. As in 'Les Idées et les tanks' (*Les Animaux supérieurs*) there is possibly an allusion here to Drieu la Rochelle. Drieu's second attempt to commit suicide by an overdose of drugs was thwarted when he was discovered by his housekeeper, Gabrielle. Days later he succeeded in killing himself by gas. There is also a much earlier reference to the same idea. In October 1935, in the notes for a projected short story involving a character called Khral, Courtade wrote: 'Le suicide de Khral, le rêve du grand voyage – le gaz d'éclairage – le sauvetage – Essai de vie nouvelle.' All of this is crossed out in red ink, and has the comment 'voir la Conspiration (Nizan)'. This is another pointer to Nizan as an influence on Courtade, and also suggests that he returned to his notes (*La Conspiration* was published in 1938) for ideas.

29. Courtade's father was interested in science and was a regular reader of various magazines. In the notes for the novel both parents are *instituteurs*. The father of Janse's first wife, Jeanne, was a *receveur de postes*. Both his parents had died before the Second World War.

30. There is only one reference (a photograph) to Janse's own mother.

31. One of the titles Courtade appears to have considered was *Les oeillets rouges*.

32. In fact from what evidence we have the last novel had *Le Cénote* at least as its provisional title. See below: p. 230–231.

It is interesting that as in *Elseneur*, where Gertrude is absent, Janse's mother (who could be seen as a kind of double with his first wife in the way that Courtade links his own mother with Génia) is alluded to once only and, then in a photograph.

Conclusion

There remain from the last months of Courtade's life a few papers, amongst which, dated 27 August 1962, are three pages bearing the outline of the beginning of what was to have been his next novel, *Le Cénote*. Its setting is the United States, and the anonymous protagonist, married to a former American actress (M.), is negotiating the film rights for his last book. It opens in the early hours of the morning and he is beset by uncertainty and reflects that his life with M. (after the death of L., presumably his previous wife) has become one of habit, if not of failure. Later, in the post is a copy of a Mexican newspaper in which the assassination of a former friend and colleague, Juan, is announced. He is asked to write a tribute, but will not be able to bring himself to do so. Interviewed by a journalist later that day he is incapable at first of giving a truthful account of his life ('se fabrique une vie "arrangeé"' is Courtade's phrase). Their conversation is interrupted by another request from Mexico for an article and by a telephone call from Hollywood, during which he agrees to the film contract. Then, off the record, he produces for the journalist 'un portrait terrible, amer, désolé' of himself. On returning home M. tells him that yet again the Mexican paper has telephoned, but that she has made excuses on his behalf. He begins to drink, and remains alone on the terrace before taking a sleeping-pill and rejoining his wife, who is already asleep. He dreams of his youth with Juan.

Quite how this would have developed is impossible to say. The Mexican element may link it to his earlier plans for *Au souvenir de l'avenir*, and the theme of freedom could have been explored in two ways. First, as a political ideal, exemplified by the character of Juan; second, as a missed opportunity, through the life of the protagonist. The question of whether *Le Cénote* would have developed into the major political novel Courtade had hoped to write, however, must remain unanswered; but from these few pages a number of familiar features of his imaginative writing and personal preoccupations re-emerge: the death (or loss) of a former loved one and dissatisfaction with his new life (and partner); the temptation of suicide (by drowning); the recognition of a life in which pretence has played an increasingly large part; wealth as a means of escaping from the routine of daily life; solitude and an increasing sense of being an onlooker. There are also hints in these notes that once again it is the set-piece to which Courtade is naturally drawn – the night drive, the breakfast, the conversation with the journalist. As a novelist his way seems to have become established; but on a broader front a number of questions and issues remain which are relevant finally to how he must be judged.

In his perceptive and sympathetic obituary of Courtade, Pierre Hervé wrote: 'Pierre Courtade avait une vocation d'écrivain plutôt que de militant. Ce n'était pas un politique, mais la vie, les entraînements, les fatalités l'ont finalement placé dans un cadre politique dont il n'était pas dans son caractère de se dégager.'[1] This remark goes to the very core of Courtade as a public figure. Thirteen years earlier, in 1950, Roger Vailland had written to his friend making a similar observation: 'Peut-être paies-tu [...] d'avoir au lendemain de la Libération cédé au préjugé de la Carrière, en te spécialisant dans les questions diplomatiques, alors que le reportage ou (et, puis) le roman conviennent mieux à tes penchants.'[2] In the same letter he made the point as well that the currency of the language of political journalism (like that of surrealism or existentialism) is necessarily limited, and that 'le vrai écrivain n'écrit pas dans le langage type de son temps.'[3]

As we have seen on several occasions, however, and as Hervé observed, not only did Courtade not escape from the bind imposed by his responsibilities, but he appeared to lack the desire to do so, preferring to be seen to be at one with Party orthodoxy. The same accusation was made as well by several who knew or worked with Courtade, and especially, of course, by those among them whose own allegiance to the PCF was behind them. Thus Claude Roy, whose admiration and appreciation for and of Courtade were entirely genuine, could write in *Nous*: 'Je soupçonne aujourd'hui que la nécessité intérieure de Pierre était d'abord celle de *se* convaincre, de vaincre la part de scepticisme qui subsistait en lui';[4] and, even more critically: 'Pierre, d'échelon en échelon, escaladait l'échelle de Jacob de l'hystérie fidéiste et autopersuasive.'[5]

Emmanuel le Roy Ladurie, while of the opinion that Courtade had begun to perceive matters differently shortly before his death, saw him as 'un homme à talents momentanément perverti par le stalinisme.'[6] The point has already been made that in this Courtade was far from being alone. His case was typical of those who in the end forced themselves to accept a faith that could accommodate all doubts. Even if the system could eventually collapse, '[la] foi est le moyen de refouler [le] doute. Sur cette double assise de foi et de doute s'édifie une construction intellectuelle cohérente et équilibrée.'[7] Claude Roy, in a language more suited to Courtade's own case, referred to such acolytes as these who 'se laiss[ent] bercer et submerger par le *tous-ensemble*.'[8]

Certainly by the early 1960s Courtade was far from being blind to the situation in which he found himself. As he acknowledged in his reply to Vailland's letter about *La Place rouge*: 'Quitter l'Eglise? le fait est que je ne le puis ni le veux. C'est ainsi. C'est ma vérité [...] je suis membre du Parti Communiste. J'habite Moscou. Je sais à peu près tout ce qu'on peut savoir, et néanmoins je ne reviens pas sur le choix fondamental que j'ai fait il y a une vingtaine d'années.' And he recognized too that as a novelist he was wittingly trapped: 'je ne pourrai jamais être qu'une espèce de Bernanos dans mon Eglise [...] je me suis engagé dans une voie sans issue.'[9] This, then, was the paradoxical situation in which Courtade found himself as a writer who believed he had a specific political vocation, whose task it was to voice publicly his belief 'qu'il est plus important de changer le monde que d'enfiler des perles à l'usage des pseudo "intellectuels".'[10] Journalist and imaginative writer may share much common ground here, but the criteria and potential problems are different. One reason for this, as Vailland had commented, is to do with currency or *actualité*. Courtade acknowledged this. A political newspaper article, however successful, would be out of date and irrelevant within a week; a piece of imaginative writing 'tient compte d'une certaine permanence des choses et d'une actualité *relativement durable*.'[11] But more fundamental still is the coexistence and potential tension between a public front and a more complex personal reality. In Courtade's case the effect this had on his imaginative writing even at its most militant was beneficial. *Jimmy* and *La Rivière noire* both avoid the two-dimensional straitjacket in which the ideologically driven works of a writer like André Stil (or even Aragon and his rewritten *Les*

Communistes) are trapped. Elsewhere, however, the results are more complex, and in many respects remained unresolved.

At one moment in *Le Jeu de paume* Janse reflects on the futility of his existence, 'comme s'il y avait quelque chose à faire pour arranger la vie d'un homme ou d'une femme après qu'ils se sont formés dans le secret de l'enfance et pour toujours.'[12] The key to much of the interest of Courtade's work lies here, even if his own perception of it was never fully realized. His reaction in his journalism and imaginative writing alike to the formative years of his adolescence was usually to produce a satirical portrait of family life in Sceaux. Courtade was not alone amongst writers of the Left in responding like this. It was not uncommon for those who, in spite of themselves, had inherited or had benefited from features of the bourgeois milieu into which they had been born to try to exorcise them through their writing. Nizan with *Antoine Bloyé* is one example; Vailland with *Un Jeune Homme seul* or *Bon Pied Bon Oeil* is another. Furthermore, it is hardly surprising that for someone who sought so much of his inspiration in autobiographical detail the crises from which both his domestic life and his health suffered should be reworked with such persistence in his fiction. But beyond the mere content of his works it is the means of expression, certain features of style and organization, which make of them (and of their author) a subject deserving of more than passing interest.

Quite consciously Courtade turns for the subject of his fiction almost without exception to the real world. But it is less the recording of that world – of war, of commercial exploitation, of political intrigue and scandal, of journalism and so on – that is important as the manner in which it is explored. Exploration results in the protagonists' improved self-knowledge. In his Preface to the 1978 edition of *La Place rouge* Alain Poirson wrote: 'la question semble être: de quelle manière prend-on conscience de tel événement' and 'l'écriture est un moyen d'investigation. Tout individu est en quête de son identité.' In the novels Eric, Karl, Jimmy, Larillère, Simon and Janse all learn – about themselves and about the particular circumstances around them of which they are an integral part. In some of the short stories the same is true as well, though in others, as we have seen, Courtade, like any good short story writer merely describes and exposes, leaving his reader to draw his own conclusions. ('La nouvelle [...] exige la collaboration du lecteur parce qu'elle laisse à penser, parce qu'elle ne dit pas tout.')[13] Yet despite this unquestionable direction, there ultimately remains a sense either of futility or of despair or of incompleteness. Arguably this is inevitable. If Courtade's concern is to illustrate his faith in the ongoing improvement that revolutionary socialism would bring to society there can be no moment of satisfaction or complacency. In his journalism there are no illusions; the message is clear and repeated. And it is in much of the fiction too, though not always with results that are entirely satisfactory, as some of his heavy-handed authorial interventions demonstrate.

But in those episodes which with Courtade's use of images of light and their neat demarcations have a clear theatrical quality, there is the sense that characters learn from a discrete experience and are thereby better prepared for the next. In some ways such a pattern, on both a small and a large scale, would, as the imaginative illustration of a repeated argument, be sufficient. But what should surely emerge as a collective experience does so at the end only as a solitary one. Given Courtade's evolution, there is a sense in which an Eric or even a Karl has to remain alone; but Larillère dies, and Jimmy is left on the threshold of a new and, we are to understand, politically active life, though we see none of it. Perhaps in these two cases, given the militant nature of the novels as a whole and of the formative experiences which both protagonists undergo their isolation is again acceptable. But with Simon and Janse a more fundamental problem is raised. In these two novels it is not simply that the protagonists have in the one case evolved and in the other overcome despair before expressing their conviction of the way forward. It is that they do so alone. In both *La Place rouge* and *Le Jeu de paume* the *decision* to be alone at the end is theirs, and not the result merely of circumstances. And even from the little evidence we have it seems possible that the protagonist of *Le Cénote* would have found himself in the same position. As early as the mid-1940s the title of one of the short stories in *Les Circonstances*, 'Personnes seules' seems, with hindsight, to have been prophetic.

What can be made of this must inevitably remain highly speculative. Once he had become disenchanted with the PCF (as he would as well with the way in which life in the Soviet Union threatened to evolve under Khrushchev)[14] it is possible that such a development represented the internalization by Courtade of an ideal. There was, as we have seen, no loss of faith on his part, but perhaps – maybe even only subconsciously

– the recognition that in the end it could only remain intact if it were private.

But this withdrawal into himself was also the expression of something more intensely personal. Often in his papers and diaries this is expressed in statements directed against his immediate family, and later and by extension against Génia. At the height of his crisis in January 1956, for example, we read: 'Je n'ai pas besoin de quelqu'un plus de quelques heures dans ma vie personnelle. Si j'avais compris cela – *su* cela à vingt ans je ne me serais pas marié – j'aurais été plus heureux et ma vie incontestablement eût été plus réussie ... mais ---.' And there are fewer more transparent projections of this in his fiction than the way in which almost without exception the family unit, and in particular female characters (Irène, Camille, Clarissa, Laurence, for example) are either marginalized or rejected altogether.[15]

But the issue stems from something much wider than his relationships with family. Fundamental and buried in his early years is a fear of failure in the face of both external challenge and of self-imposed targets, and hence of disapproval, especially from his father. And it is for this reason that war and the Resistance, journalism and the experience of *Action*, and Thorez's *invitation* to join *L'Humanité* were so vital. What he saw as achievement on a personal scale was rewarded by his being absorbed (we should not forget Claude Roy's *bercer*) into a system with its own values and criteria, which would, whenever it might be necessary, provide him with protection and excuses. Whatever doubts or anxiety he may have privately felt over issues of importance – the Hervé affair or Yugoslavia, for example – they could be left unspoken, in the knowledge that it was the collective voice that mattered.

Courtade had become the successful son, and through success had found an approving and supportive family. But doubts there were compounded by an increasingly difficult domestic situation and ill health. Unwilling and indeed unable to deal with these in the public domain, Courtade allowed them – frequently in spite of himself – to filter through his imaginative writing. One result of this is a kind of ebb and flow between a desire to act decisively as an individual and a retreat, when the consequences of such an action become apparent, into a protective collectivity.[16] Furthermore, as political disenchantment increased during the late 1950s and early 1960s, alongside his personal anxieties he found, as he confessed to

Vailland, that he was engaged in an impasse, increasingly frustrated but unwilling to try to discover a way out.

When Vailland's *La Loi* was published in 1957 it heralded a change of political heart on the part of its author, even though it retained many thematic and stylistic links with the preceding political novels and Vailland himself continued to be a card-carrying member of the PCF for two further years. It is hardly conceivable that Courtade could (or dared) envisage taking a similar step.[17] But while his legacy remains therefore limited, his talent was unquestionable, as Roy, Hervé, Nadeau and others have acknowledged. That his strictly political journalism was widely respected even by opponents is not in doubt; and, as Vailland recognized in 1950, his *grands reportages* display an acuteness of perception and a gift for creating atmosphere not matched by many. But it is as an imaginative writer that Courtade had most promise. Despite their moments of *lourdeur* or self-indulgence his novels deal with key political and intellectual issues of mid twentieth-century France in a forceful, challenging manner that alone should remove them from the oblivion to which, with the exception of *La Place rouge*, they have largely been consigned. And, at his best, as a short story writer Courtade surely ranks alongside Aymé or Camus. Nonetheless, it has to be recognized that much of what remains promises more than it delivers. That there is not more is self-evidently due to a punishing work schedule as a journalist and an early death. But it also has a lot to do with the problem outlined above. Courtade allowed his talents to be bought. He willingly submitted himself and his pen to the discipline that made of him one of the most effective scribes, in the widest and fullest sense of the term, that the PCF had at its disposal. The recognition and success from both within and outside the Party that status brought were considerable; to run the risk of losing them and of incurring disapproval was, if only subconsciously, more than Courtade could contemplate.

Notes

1. *France-Observateur*.

2. Vailland, *Ecrits Intimes*, Gallimard, Paris, 1968, pp. 270–1.

3. Ibid., p. 269.

4. Roy, *Nous*, p. 409

5. Ibid., p. 417.

6. *Paris–Montpellier*: PC–PSU, 1945–1963, Gallimard, Paris, 1982, p. 55.

7. A. Spire, *Profession: permanent*, Seuil, Paris, 1980, p. 243.

8. Roy, *Nous*, p. 417.

9. Vailland, *Ecrits Intimes*, pp. 677–8. See above, pp. 199–200.

10. 'Pourquoi je suis communiste', Editions du PCF, [1947], p. 15.

11. 'Entretien avec Pierre Courtade', *L'Ecole et la Nation*, October 1956, 27.

12. The following entry in his diary (24 November [1955]) is typical: 'Fouiller dans les souvenirs de mon enfance, de mon adolescence et construire un plan de roman à partir de ça.'

13. *L'Ecole et la Nation*, October 1956, p. 27.

14. One area where Soviet policy began to disturb Courtade deeply was that of culture, and of art in particular. Despite a token attitude of liberalism opposition to many forms of Western art remained. In *Pravda* on 4 January 1963, for example, an article by Laktionov voiced the official position and attacked artistic forms – in the main of French origin – that he claimed were representative of self-indulgent bourgeois ideology. Courtade was indignant, and wrote to *Pravda*:

    L'académicien Laktionov a certes le droit de ne pas aimer les Impressionnistes (par exemple), mais il devrait au moins

> comprendre que, pour nous Français, l'art de Manet, de Cézanne, de Renoir et de tant d'autres est un art national à travers lequel nous aimons notre pays, ses paysages et ses gens.
>
> J'ajoute que, comme communiste, je ne peux rester insensible au fait que j'appartiens au Parti de Picasso, de Léger, à un Parti qui est entouré de l'amitié de milliers d'artistes et d'écrivains qu'on ne saurait confondre avec les champions de 'l'art pour l'art'.

In spite of (or perhaps because of) his official position Courtade's letter was never published. See Nicole Chatel, Carnets russes, Julliard, Paris, 1971, pp. 50–2.

15. Karl in Elseneur and Janse in *Le Jeu de paume* both turn at one point to prostitutes, but are unable to bring themselves to have sex with them.

16. Images based on water obviously reflect this. In some forms water can represent purity, the achievement of an ideal; in others it signifies contamination or corruption. A psychocritical analysis of such images as well as those of barriers would almost certainly lead us back to Courtade's relationship with his parents.

17. In *Les Lettres françaises* (25–31 July 1957) Courtade published a letter to André Wurmser, who had savaged Vailland's novel. He reminds Wurmser that Vailland is still a Party member, and moreover that 'il est impossible de trouver, dans *La Loi*, un mot, une ligne qu'un anti-communiste pourrait citer contre le Parti dont Vailland est membre. Cela compte et pouvait, à mon avis, inspirer au critique une compréhension fraternelle.' When, later in 1957, *La Loi* won the Prix Goncourt Wurmser congratulated its author 'de grande valeur, parvenu à une si belle maîtrise de sa langue et de son art' (*Les Lettres françaises*, 5–11 December 1957).

Bibliography

(Places of publication Paris or London unless otherwise indicated.)

1. ***Works by Courtade***

(a) **Fiction**

Les Circonstances, La Bibliothèque française, 1946; with illustrations by Edouard Pignon, Editeurs Français réunis, 1954; with an introduction by J. E. Flower, Le Temps des Cérises, Paris, 1995.

Elseneur, La Bibliothèque française, 1949

Jimmy, Les Editeurs Français réunis, 1951

La Rivière noire, Les Editeurs Français réunis, 1953

Les Animaux supérieurs, Julliard, 1956

La Place rouge, Julliard, 1961

Two unpublished typescripts of novels:

Eric et Irène
Le Jeu de paume

A number of short stories in *L'Humanité, L'Humanité-Dimanche, Les Lettres françaises,* and *Marie-Claire* which have not been published in volume form. Where necessary details are included in the notes.

(b) **Essays**

Pour connaître la pensée de Darwin, Editions Françaises nouvelles, Grenoble [1945]

Essai sur l'anti-soviétisme, Editions Raison d'être, 1946

L'Affaire Rajk, Editeurs Français réunis, 1949

L'Albanie, Editions sociales, 1951

La Nouvelle Chine est à nous, Editions PCF, 1953

Khrouchtchev inédit, Editions sociales, 1960

L'Arabe sans maître, an essay on the Algerian war, remains unpublished.

(c)   **Journalism**

Courtade's output was immense and ran to thousands of articles. He contributed principally to: *Action, Les Cahiers du Communisme, Compagnons, La Démocratie nouvelle, L'Humanité, L'Humanité-Dimanche, Les Lettres françaises, Marie-Claire, La Nouvelle Critique, Parallèle 50, Le Progrès de Lyon.*

Where necessary details of individual articles are included either in the text or in the notes.

2.   *Selected Secondary Material*

Books and articles containing substantial comment on Courtade are indicated by *. Roger,

ADERETH, Max *The French Communist Party*, Manchester University Press, Manchester, 1984

ADLER, Alexandre (ed.), *L'URSS et nous*, Editions sociales, 1978

AMORETTI, Henri, *Lyon capital 1940–4*, Editions France Empire, 1964

ARAGON, Louis, *L'Homme communiste* (2 vols), Gallimard, 1946 and 1953

BLACKMER, D. L. M. and TARROW, S. (eds), *Communism in Italy and France*, Princeton University Press, Princeton, 1975

BOURDIN, Janine, 'Des intellectuels à la recherche d'un style de vie: l'Ecole nationale des cadres à Uriage', *Revue Française de science politique*, Vol. IX, No. 4, December 1959

CASANOVA, Laurent, *Le Communisme, la Pensée et l'Art*, Editions du PCF, 1947

———— *Le Parti communiste, les intellectuels et la nation*, Editions de la Nouvelle Critique, 1949

* CAUTE, David, *Communism and the French Intellectuals*, André Deutsch, 1964

* CHATEL, Nicole, *Carnets russes*, Julliard, 1971

* *Chorus*, 'Pierre Courtade, intellectuel communiste', Autumn 1965

* COURRIERE, Yves, *Roger Vailland, ou un libertin au regard froid*, Plon, 1991

DAIX, Pierre, *J'ai cru au matin*, Lafont, 1976

———— *La Crise du PCF*, Seuil, 1978

* DESANTI, Dominique, *Les Staliniens*, Fayard, 1975

ELLENSTEIN, Jean, *Histoire du phénomène stalinien*, Grasset, 1975

* ETIEMBLE, *Littérature dégagée (1942–1953)*, Gallimard, 1955

* FARDEAU, Patrice et POIRSON, Alain, 'Nizan, Vailland, Courtade: même combat', *La Nouvelle Critique*, No. 105 (2e série), 1977

FAUVET, Jacques, *Histoire du PCF*, Fayard, 1977

FIGUERES, Léo, *Le parti communiste français, la culture et les intellectuels*, Editions sociales, 1962

† FLOWER, J. E., *Literature and the Left in France*, Macmillan, 1983; Methuen, 1985

† ———— 'A forgotten novel of the Resistance: Pierre Courtade's *Elseneur*', *Journal of European Studies* (Special issue on the 'Invasion and Occupation of France 1940–44: intellectual and cultural responses', edited by Christopher Flood and Richard Golsan), Vol. 23, 1993

GARAUDY, Roger, *D'un réalisme sans rivages*, Plon, 1963

GIRODIAS, Maurice, *Une Journée sur la terre*, Editions de la Différence, 1990

† GISSELBRECHT, André, *'La Place rouge'*, *La Nouvelle Critique*, July–August 1962.

† ———— 'Pierre Courtade: un intellectuel communiste', *La Nouvelle Critique*, June 1963

HALLS, W. D., *The Youth of France*, Clarendon Press, Oxford, 1981

HERVE, Pierre, *La Libération trahie*, Grasset, 1945

———— *Dieu et César sont-ils communistes?* La Table ronde, 1956

———— *Lettre à Sartre et à quelques autres par la même occasion*, La Table ronde, 1956

———— *La Révolution et les fétiches*, La Table ronde, 1956

HERVET, Robert, *Les Compagnons de Franc*, Editions France-Empire, 1965

HUDSON, Robert, 'Et Bourreaux et Victimes'. Eye-witness accounts of the French war of decolonization in Indo-China, *Les Temps modernes* 1946–1950', *Journal of European Studies*, Vol. 19, September 1989

JOHNSON, R. W., *The Long March of the French Left*, St Martins Press, New York, 1981

JUDT, Tony, *Marxism and the French Left*, Oxford University Press, 1986

———— *Un passé imparfait: les intellectuels en France, 1944–1956*, Fayard, 1992

KANAPA, Jean, *Situation de l'intellectuel*, Editions sociales, 1957

KEDWARD, R. and AUSTIN, R. (eds), *Vichy France and the Resistance*, Croom Helm, 1985

KELLY, Michael, *Modern French Marxism*, Blackwell, Oxford, 1982

KRIEGEL, Annie, *Les communistes français*, Seuil, 1970

———— *Communisme au miroir français*, Gallimard, 1974

LECOEUR, Auguste, *Le PCF. Continuité dans le changement*, Lafont, 1977

† LEDUC, Victor, *Les Tribulations d'un idéologue*, Syros, 1985

LEGENDRE, Bernard, *Le Stalinisme français. Qui à dit quoi? (1944–1956)*, Seuil, 1980

MER, Jacqueline, *Le Parti de Maurice Thorez ou le bonheur communiste français*, Payot, 1963

* MORIN, Edgar, *Le vif du sujet*, Seuil, 1969

* —— *Autocritique*, Seuil, 1970

NAVILLE, Pierre. *La Révolution et les intellectuels*, Gallimard, 1975

* POIRSON, Alain, 'Pierre Courtade, écrivain et communiste', *Découvrir*, 22 May 1978

* RECANATI, Jean, *Un gentil stalinien*, Mazarine, 1980

RICE MAXIMIN, Edward 'The French Communist Party and the first Indochinese War', *Contemporary French Civilization*, Spring, 1978

ROBIN, Régine, *Le Realisme socialiste*, Payot, 1986

ROBRIEUX, Philippe, *Histoire intérieure du Parti Communiste* (4 vols), Fayard, 1980–1984

* ROLLAND, Jacques-Francis, *Un dimanche inoubliable près des casernes*, Grasset, 1988

ROSS, Georges, *Workers and Communists in France*, Berkeley University Press, Berkeley, 1982

ROY, Claude, *Moi je*, Gallimard, 1969

* —— *Nous*, Gallimard, 1972

—— 'Les Séquestrés de la croyance', *Nouvelle Revue de Psychanalyse*, No. 18, 1978

RUSCIO, Alain, *Les Communistes français et la guerre d'Indochine, 1944–1959*, Harmattan, 1985

* F.S., 'New Writing in France', *The Modern Quarterly*, Spring 1953, Vol. 8, No. 2

SPIRE, Antoine, *Profession: permanent*, Seuil, 1980

TIERSKY, Ronald, *French Communism, 1920–1972*, Columbia University Press, New York and London, 1974

TISSIER, Jean, ' Le Parti Communiste Français et les intellectuels', *Revue Française de science politique*, Vol. XVII, No. 3, June 1967

TUCKER, Robert C., 'The Theory of charismatic leadership', *Daedalus*, Vol. 3, Summer 1968

* VAILLAND, Roger, *Ecrits intimes*, Gallimard, 1968

WALL, Irwin, *French Communism in the Era of Stalin*, Greenwood, New York, 1983

ZHDANOV, André, *Sur la littérature, la philosophie et la musique*, Editions de la Nouvelle Critique, 1948

Details of any work not listed here are included in the notes.

Index